Exemplary Science in Informal Education Settings

Exemplary Science in Informal Education Settings

Standards-Based Success Stories

Robert E. Yager
and
John H. Falk, Editors

NATIONAL SCIENCE TEACHERS ASSOCIATION

Arlington, Virginia

NATIONAL SCIENCE TEACHERS ASSOCIATION

Claire Reinburg, Director
Judy Cusick, Senior Editor
J. Andrew Cocke, Associate Editor
Betty Smith, Associate Editor
Robin Allan, Book Acquisitions Manager

ART AND DESIGN, Will Thomas, Jr., Director

PRINTING AND PRODUCTION, Catherine Lorrain, Director
  Nguyet Tran, Assistant Production Manager
  Jack Parker, Electronic Prepress Technician

NATIONAL SCIENCE TEACHERS ASSOCIATION
Gerald F. Wheeler, Executive Director
David Beacom, Publisher

Library of Congress Cataloging-in-Publication Data
Exemplary science in informal education settings : standards-based success stories / edited by Robert Yager and
John Falk.
    p. cm.
  Includes index.
  ISBN 978-1-933531-09-0
  1. Science--Study and teaching--United States--Case studies. 2. Science--Study and teaching--United States--
Standards. 3. Science--Study and teaching--United States--Methodology. 4. Science teachers--Training of. I.
Yager, Robert Eugene, 1930- II. Falk, John H. (John Howard), 1948-
  Q181.E855 2005
  507.1'073--dc22
                        2007032048

Contents

Using the National Science Education Standards for Improving Science Education in Nonschool Settings

Robert E. Yager, Editor
University of Iowa

The Exemplary Science Program (ESP) series has become a featured activity in terms of publications and conference features for the National Science Teachers Association. This fifth volume is the first that has departed from a focus on formal education with specific ties to teaching levels in schools and the professional development of classroom teachers and the visions for them included in the National Science Education Standards (NSES). Although attention to professional development was undertaken almost as a last-minute addition to the 262-page first draft of the NSES, it was the topic of the first ESP monograph that was completed and the one attracting the most interest in terms of chapter authors and use of the changes envisioned. This, no doubt, is the result of college and university faculty being more familiar with publications and their requirement for promotion and tenure. The Professional Development monograph's popularity may also relate to the importance of staff development for teachers and others vitally concerned that our teaching efforts be more related to real learning, i.e., learning with understanding—learning that results in something other than remembering what one is told, instructed to do, or asked to repeat as evidence of learning (none of which indicate real learning let alone its being "exemplary!")

This work in the Informal Science Education arena has been possible because of the interest and support of the Association of Science-Technology Centers (ASTC). It expands the opportunities for real learning because it is not restricted to a place and building called "school"—a 180-day exposure each year, six-hour days, where science is a focus for a single class period.

The excitement is that the NSES focus upon nine ways teaching must change if more learning on the part of students is to be achieved. Many now argue that the nine *More Emphasis* conditions outlined in the NSES represent the primary needs for educators (including parents) if learning is to be enhanced. Further, the 14 ways that staff-development efforts must change (teaching teachers) provide further indications of what is needed in terms of experiences for teachers (both in formal and informal settings), if real learning is to occur. This means learning that relates to the science enterprise itself, affecting daily lives, enabling persons to make informed citizenship decisions, and improving economic productivity by using the information and skills in related careers. These are all important goals that frame the NSES (p. 13).

The National Advisory Board (NAB) for the ESP, whose efforts resulted in the first four monographs, recommended to NSTA Press and the Executive Committee that the ESP efforts be continued—with varying NAB membership to coincide with given foci for nominating exemplars. Although several areas were proposed for the 2007 effort, the one that emerged as top choice was Informal Science Education. It resulted in this new publication that has been nurtured and directed by the 2007 NAB, which includes several ASTC leaders to supplement the NSTA leadership. This new group of 21 NAB members who worked diligently on this fifth ESP Monograph are acknowledged and listed (see p. xvii).

In addition to the NSES, the NSTA official Position Statement on Informal Science Education guided the work, as did the involvement and advice provided by the NSTA Committee on Informal Science. The NSTA leadership also urged the involvement of ASTC in interpreting and elaborating the criteria, attracting needed nominations, and assisting with analyzing the extensive information included in the nominations. But the visions for improved science education were all included in the NSES, where lists of *Less* and *More Emphases* conclude each chapter. These were distributed widely as "the" criteria for ESP. As with the other ESP Monographs, these *Less/More Emphasis* summaries are included in Appendix 1 (p. 252).

History of the National Science Education Standards

Before discussing the content of this book at greater length, a brief history is offered of how the National Science Education Standards came to be. Most educators credit the National Council of Teachers of Mathematics (NCTM) with initiating the many efforts to produce national standards for programs in American schools. In 1986 (10 years before the publication of the NSES), the board of directors of NCTM established a Commission on Standards for School Mathematics, with the aim of improving the quality of school mathematics. An initial draft of these standards was released in the summer of 1987, revised during the summer of 1988 after much discussion among NCTM members, and finally published as the *Curriculum and Evaluation Standards for School Mathematics* in 1989.

The NCTM standards did much for mathematics education by providing a consensus for what mathematics should be. The National Science Foundation (NSF) and other funding groups had not been involved in developing the math standards, but these groups quickly funded research and training to move schools and teachers in the direction outlined in those standards. Having such a "national" statement regarding needed reforms resulted in funding from private and government foundations to produce school standards in other disciplines, including science.

NSF encouraged the science education community to develop standards modeled after the NCTM document (1989). Interestingly, both the American Association for the Advancement of Science (AAAS) and the National Science Teachers Association (NSTA) expressed interest in preparing science standards. Both organizations indicated that they each had made a significant start on such national standards—AAAS with its *Project 2061* (1989) and NSTA with its *Scope, Sequence, and Coordination* project (1992). Both of these national projects had support from NSF, private foundations, and industries. The compromise on this "competition" between AAAS and NSTA leaders led to the recommendation that the National Research Council (NRC) of the National Academy of Science be funded to develop the National Science Education Standards. With NSF funding provided in 1992, both NSTA and AAAS helped to select the science leaders who would prepare the NSES. Several early drafts were circulated among hundreds of people with invitations to comment, suggest, debate, and assist with a consensus document. A full-time director of consensus provided leadership and assistance as final drafts were assembled. Eventually, it took \$7 million and four years of debate to produce the 262-page NSES publication in 1996.

There was never any intention that the Standards would indicate minimum competencies that would be required of all. Instead, the focus was on visions of how teaching, assessment, and content should be changed. Early on, programs and systems were added as follow-ups to teaching, assessment, and content. And, as mentioned earlier, Staff Development Programs were added just prior to final publication.

The NSES goals were meant to frame the teaching, staff development, assessment, content, program, and system efforts as visions for change and reform. These goals represented a step beyond those central to Harms' earlier Project Synthesis in 1978. The major difference was with the first goal. For Project Synthesis it was science for preparing for further study of science. (Unfortunately, that was the goal used by over 95% of the teachers and schools for justifying school science.) Instead of academic preparation, the NSES included a goal that focused upon the actual practice of science. It was considered the most important goal of all and one on which the most time and energy would be spent! The four goals (justifications) for K–12 science listed in the NSES encompass preparing students who:

(1) experience the richness and excitement of knowing about and understanding the natural world;
(2) use appropriate scientific processes and principles in making personal decisions;
(3) engage intelligently in public discourse and debate about matters of scientific and technological concern; and
(4) increase their economic productivity through the use of the knowledge, understanding, and skills of the scientifically literate person in their careers (NRC 1996, p. 13).

Basically, the goals do not suggest any content or any glamorized process skills that must be transmitted or experienced for their own sake. Paul Brandwein (1983) frequently called for teachers and schools to ensure that each high school graduate would have one full experience with science. He suggested that this would create a revolution in science education—something we still badly need. Some NSES enthusiasts suggest that one such experience each year would be a better goal during the K–12 years—a 13-year continuum of science in school—and perhaps one each 9-week grading period would be an even better goal!

The NSES volume begins with standards for improved teaching. This is followed by chapters on professional development, assessment, science content, and science education program and systems. Content was placed in the document after the other three for fear that placing it first would invite a focus only on what should be taught—almost relegating teaching, staff development, and assessment to "add-on" roles. Nonetheless, the major debates in the development of the Standards centered on what should appear in the three discipline-oriented content chapters.

NSES "Content"

A major direction in the NSES with respect to content was the identification of eight facets of content. These facets change the focus from a traditional discipline focus with a list of major concepts under each discipline, to a much broader listing that is more indicative of the goals (justifications) for science in schools. These eight facets of content elaborated in NSES are (1) Unifying Concepts and Processes in Practice; (2) Science as Inquiry; (3) Physical Science; (4) Life Science; (5) Earth and Space Science; (6) Science and Technology; (7) Science in Personal and Social Perspectives; and (8) History and Nature of Science. Just as the first NSES goal is considered the most important one, the first facet of content (Unifying Concepts and Processes in Practice) is similarly considered the most important. It was envisioned as being so basic that it was first thought to be included as the preamble for each content section of NSES. However, many felt that too many would simply move to a new listing of basic discipline-bound concepts and ignore the preamble. Although life, physical, and Earth/space science still appear, some lists combine them into a listing of basic science concepts as a single content focus—thereby suggesting a more integrated approach to the major concepts comprising modern science. Major debates occurred in identifying these eight content constructs and the specific content included in each of the "discipline-bound" content areas.

Important current reforms must focus on the four less familiar content facets, namely: (a) science for meeting personal and societal challenges (referring to goals 2 and 3); (b) technology—which now enjoys a whole set of standards produced by International Technology Education Association (ITEA 2000); (c) the history and philosophy of science; and (d) science as inquiry.

The *More Emphasis* conditions for inquiry represent what the current reforms are all about and indicate why the use of social issues is considered essential. The *More Emphasis* conditions for inquiry are meant to reverse the failures in 1981 in finding examples of teaching science by inquiry in American schools. After the Project Synthesis report, Paul DeHart Hurd (1978) reported:

"The development of inquiry skills as a major goal of instruction in science appears to have had only a minimal effect on secondary school teaching. The rhetoric about inquiry and process teaching greatly exceeds both the research on the subject and the classroom practice. The validity of the inquiry goal itself could provide from more scholarly interchange and confrontation even if it is simply to recognize that science is not totally confined to logical processes and data-gathering" (p. 62).

Issues related to student lives, their schools, and their communities can provide the contexts that invariably require the knowledge of skills related to the concepts and skills that appear in science programs in typical schools. The Informal Science Education community can (and should) take the lead in changing the focus for science learning and the introduction of new contexts for ensuring learning with understanding.

Features of Real Science

Most science courses in school are devoid of any of the features that characterize real science. These include the following features, each important and in a fixed order: (1) curiosity abut the objects and events encountered in the natural world; (2) offering possible explanations for them; (3) collecting evidence to establish the validity of the personally advanced explanations; (4) communicating the explanations for which evidence has been collected; (5) responding to criticisms and counter-explanations from others, including scientists.

Most science courses in K–12 schools no longer focus on technology since the 1960 reforms, which boldly proclaimed that science for schools should exemplify pure science (i.e., information concerning what is known by scientists about the natural world) and not the human-made world. Reform efforts now openly include the design-world and further see it to be a way of studying the natural world in terms of better instrumentation as well as a meaningful way of using the same processes to gain new standards constructed for human betterment. The techniques characterizing technology are like those of science. The major difference is that the answers to real questions about the natural world have no initial answers (scientists start with the unknown!). In the case of technology, the persons involved know from the start what answers they hope and plan to attain. Current efforts in science education often give equal (or even primary) emphasis to the design world over the natural world. This is a real strength for the science encountered in informal settings—for it is not bound to textbooks, state curricula, or a focus on mastery of basic concepts.

Questions are basic to science. They provide the focus for all science efforts. But, it is rare for science in formal settings to focus on questions. Similarly, in schools, student questions rarely serve as starting points in classrooms. Ideally, learning is enhanced if student questions are "higher-level ones." Questions offered by learners and/or educators in informal settings should focus on the following types of questions:

(1) Questions that ask others for information such as: What did you do? What happened? What did you observe?

(2) Questions that ask: What will you do next? What will happen if you…? What could you do to prevent that?

(3) Questions that relate to situations with others: How does that compare to…? What did other people find?

(4) Questions that seek explanations: How would you explain that? What caused it to happen?

(5) Questions that ask for advice: What evidence do you have for that? What leads you to believe that?

Attracting Nominations

After publicizing the plans for this ESP monograph among members of the NSTA Informal Committee and the total ASTC membership, and encouragement from the NAB team formulated for this new monograph, over 60 nominations emerged. All received word of the nomination and information regarding the plan for the monograph and a general structure for what would comprise a chapter. All were asked to submit a content outline that would include:

    (1) nature of the informal organization;

    (2) an indication of importance of the NSES visions on their programs;

    (3) outline of a proposed chapter;

    (4) indication of program features; and

    (5) information concerning assessments of program impact.

All of the plans and initial information concerning programs were read and evaluated by five members of the NAB. These evaluations were forwarded to each proposed author team. Semifinal drafts were then requested. A total of 36 were received and again evaluated by members of the NAB. Summaries of comments from the NAB reviewers were forwarded to all authors; all were encouraged to consider the recommendations and to prepare final drafts for final decisions about which would be included as monograph chapters. The 17 chapters comprising this volume represent those judged best to illustrate successful features of the NSES that resulted in most learning on the part of those who were targeted groups, i.e., participants in the informal settings.

Conclusions

The 17 chapters that follow provide the cooperative endeavors of the authors indicated as well as the involvement of at least four members of our NAB. Certainly the expertise of my coeditor John Falk was of utmost importance in assembling the exciting program described. Informal science education has been his focus for his entire professional life. I am in his debt for being continually involved. Of most significance is the assessment data that are included in each chapter, especially the goal that real evidence of learning would comprise at least a third of each chapter. This was certainly the most difficult aspect for many authors. Many pleaded for the opportunity to provide assessment data on a continuing basis. Several initially offered only a plan for assessing impact.

It has been our intent to make science education more of a science—where all the ingredients that define science are involved. This means starting with not knowing, but moving to and modeling "how to know." We offer the evidence for success included in each chapter as evidence that our efforts in the informal arena are like science itself—starting with a question, having ideas as possible answers, collecting evidence from as many sources as possible to validate the answers suggested, and communicating the results (something we hope this volume illustrates) for others to use, possibly to formulate new questions.

We feel that our successes with the visions that guide the NSES will be greater with the union of the formal and informal providers for the learning of all people. We feel that science literacy for all will be a reality when there is a seamless connection between formal and informal education and life. These are facts one emphasized with a quote from Stephanie Pace Marshall (IMSA):

"To educate our children wisely requires that we create generative learning communities, by design. Such learning communities have their roots in meaning, not memory; engagement, not transmission; inquiry, not compliance; exploration, not acquisition; personalization, not uniformity; interdependence, not individualism; collaboration, not competition; and trust, not fear."

References

American Association for the Advancement of Science (AAAS). 1989. *Science for all Americans: Summary—Project 2061.* Washington, DC: Author.

Brandwein, P. 1983. *Horizon committee report.* Washington, DC: National Science Teachers Association.

Harms, N. 1977. *Project synthesis: An interpretative consolidation of research identifying needs in natural science education.* (Proposal prepared for the National Science Foundation.) Boulder, CO: University of Colorado.

Hurd, P. DeH. 1978. The golden age of biological education 1960–1975. In *BSCS biology teacher's handbook.* 3rd ed., ed W. V. Mayer, 28–96. New York: John Wiley and Sons.

International Technology Education Association (ITEA). 2000. *Standards for technological literacy.* Reston, VA: Author.

National Council of Teachers of Mathematics (NCTM). 1989. *Curriculum and evaluation standards for school mathematics.* Reston, VA: Author.

National Research Council (NRC). 1996. *National science education standards.* Washington, DC: National Academy Press.

National Science Teachers Association (NSTA). 1992. *Scope, sequence, and coordination of secondary school science: Volume I, the content core. A guide for curriculum designers.* Arlington, VA: Author.

Acknowledgments

Members of the National Advisory Board for the Exemplary Science Series

Hans O. Andersen
Past President of NSTA
Professor, Science Education
Indiana University–Bloomington
Bloomington, IN 47405-1006

Bonnie Brunkhorst
Past President of NSTA
Professor
California State University-
San Bernardino
San Bernardino, CA 92506

Rodger Bybee
Executive Director
Biological Sciences Curriculum
Study
5415 Mark Dabling Blvd.
Colorado Springs, CO 80918

Roger T. Johnson
University of Minnesota
Dept. of Curriculum and
Instruction
60 Peik Hill
Minneapolis, MN 55455

Mozell P. Lang
Science Consultant
3700 Colchester Road
Lansing, MI 48906

LeRoy R. Lee
Executive Director
Wisconsin Science Network
4420 Gray Road
De Forest, WI 53532-2506

Shelley A. Lee
Science Education Consultant
WI Dept. of Public Instruction
PO Box 7841
Madison, WI 53707-7841

Edward P. Ortleb
Science Consultant/Author
5663 Pernod Avenue
St. Louis, MO 63139

Gerald Skoog
Texas Tech University
College of Education
15th and Boston
Lubbock, TX 79409-1071

Sandra West
Texas State University–San Marcos
Department of Biology
San Marcos, TX 78666

Karen Worth
Senior Scientist
Education Development Center
55 Chapel Street
Newton, MA 02458

Bonnie VanDorn
Executive Director
Association of Science-
Technology Centers
1025 Vermont Avenue, NW
Suite 500
Washington, DC 20005-6310

Wendy Pollock
Director, Research, Publications,
and Exhibitions
Association of Science-
Technology Centers
1025 Vermont Avenue, NW
Suite 500
Washington, DC 20005-6310

Joe E. Heimlich
Senior Researcher
Institute for Learning Innovation
3168 Braverton Street, Suite 280
Edgewater, MD 21037

Elsa Bailey
NSTA Division Director,
Informal Science '06-09
Director/Principal
Elsa Bailey Consulting
1050 Noriega Street
San Francisco, CA 94122

Vanessa Westbrook
Director, District XIII
Senior Science Specialist
Charles A. Dana Center
Univ. of Texas at Austin
2901 IH-35, Suite 2200
Austin, TX 78722

Alan McCormack
Professor of Science Education
San Diego State University
College of Education
5500 Campanile Drive
San Diego, CA 92128

Jon Schwartz
General Manager
Wyoming Public Radio
Knight Hall/Basement 76
1000 E. University Avenue
Laramie, WY 82071

Dale McCreedy
Director, Gender and Family Learning
Programs
The Franklin Institute Science
Museum
222 North 20th Street
Philadelphia, PA 19103

Cynthia Vernon
Vice President of Education,
Guest, and Research Programs
Monterey Bay Aquarium
886 Cannery Row
Monterey, CA 93940

Mary Ann Mullinnix
Assistant Editor
University of Iowa
Iowa City, Iowa 52242

About the Editors

Robert E. Yager—an active contributor to the development of the National Science Education Standards—has devoted his life to teaching, writing, and advocating on behalf of science education worldwide. Having started his career as a high school science teacher, he has been a professor of science education at the University of Iowa since 1956. He has also served as president of seven national organizations, including NSTA, and has been involved in teacher education in Japan, Korea, Taiwan, and Europe. Among his many publications are several NSTA books, including *Focus on Excellence* and *What Research Says to the Science Teacher.* Yager earned a bachelor's degree in biology from the University of Northern Iowa and master's and doctoral degrees in plant physiology from the University of Iowa.

John H. Falk has spent more than 30 years investigating and supporting free-choice learning. He is considered one of the world's leading authorities on learning in informal settings such as museums, science centers, zoos, and aquariums. He is currently Sea Grant Professor of Free-Choice Learning at Oregon State University; he is also founder and President Emeritus of the Institute for Learning Innovation, a world-renowned free-choice learning research and development center located in Annapolis, Maryland. Falk has published more than 100 scholarly articles and 17 books in this area. He earned bachelor's and master's degrees in zoology, and a joint doctorate in ecology and science education; all from the University of California, Berkeley.

A Burger, a Beer...
and a Side of Science

Nancy Linde
WGBH Boston

Monday nights in Somerville, Massachusetts, are usually quiet. Frigid Monday nights in November in Somerville are exceptionally quiet. But in late November 2006, scores of people braved the cold and headed to the Thirsty Scholar Pub. What lured them out? The surprising answer is science, or more precisely a Science Café, an informal public event in which people from all walks of life gather to discuss science. Organized by WGBH, Boston's public television station, Science Cafés are part of a unique national informal education outreach initiative for NOVA ScienceNOW, a new magazine-format science series that premiered on PBS in January 2005.

The Thirsty Scholar Pub is not easy to find. It's nestled among tightly packed triple-deckers and two-family homes in a blue-collar neighborhood in Somerville, Massachusetts. The interior is simple but welcoming with low lighting and comfortable tables and chairs. As in most Irish pubs in the Boston area, televisions are scattered around the room for the ever-present sports fans that make up most of the pub's clientele.

Thirsty Scholar is a misnomer. Perhaps it's so-named because of its proximity to Tufts University to the west and Harvard and MIT to the east, but this is not a place professors tend to frequent. The patrons generally reflect the neighborhood—a mix of hourly wage earners and young professionals attracted by the moderately priced apartments in the area.

A group of four former Marines was sitting at the center table when Ben Wiehe, WGBH outreach coordinator, walked in at around 5:30 p.m. carrying a DVD with a program clip from *NOVA scienceNOW* and a thick folder of papers. Ben was dismayed to see the table he had planned as the focal point of the evening's activity occupied by a group that had clearly not come for the Science Café. He thought about asking them to move, but decided against it. After handing the DVD to the tavern owner and making preparations for the evening, Ben ambled over to the group.

"I hope you don't mind," he said, "but we've planned an event tonight." Ben explained how the night would go. He'd show a short video, a scientist would talk for about 10 minutes, and the audience would then participate in a conversation about global warming and mass extinctions.

"Sure, no problem," said the group amiably but without much interest. As the waitress brought another round of beers to the table, Ben told them that he hoped they'd stick around.

At six o'clock the pub began to fill up. Within 15 minutes, all 80 seats were occupied. The atmosphere was festive with plenty of food and drink. Thirsty Scholar regulars who knew nothing about the Science Café night composed about 20% of the crowd. The rest, a mix of students, young professionals, and working people, had heard about the Science Café from fliers posted in the area, e-mail alerts, word of mouth, and community newspaper calendar announcements.

Fighting the din of restaurant activity and loud conversation, Ben tried to explain to the crowd what the evening was all about. But when the program clip rolled, the room quieted down, and

NOVA program on mass extinction.

all eyes focused on the television screens. It was a serious subject: the cause of a mass extinction 250 million years ago that ended the Permian era. But the treatment was light and humorous with playful animation. The crowd laughed at the right places and when it was over, they all shared the same background knowledge needed for the rest of the discussion.

Next up, Charles Marshall, Harvard professor and Curator of the Museum of Comparative Zoology. In his 40s, tall, thin, and bearded, Marshall looks the part of a Harvard professor. In his brief presentation, lasting less than seven minutes, he connected mass extinctions to global climate change and pondered the perils to come. When Marshall was done, he opened the floor to the pub patrons. And a surprising thing occurred.

The first to speak up were the ex-Marines. Skeptical about global warming, they peppered Marshall with questions—both scientific and philosophical. "How do we know that humans are causing this problem?" "Are there any beneficial aspects to global warming?" they asked. And later, they even challenged what Marshall had described as a moral imperative on behalf of future generations, "So what if humans go extinct? Extinctions have happened before. Maybe it's our fate?" The ex-Marines, holding tickets to a concert that night they would never attend, set the tone for a stimulating and thought-provoking discussion.

After 90 minutes, Ben closed the Science Café with a request that everybody fill out a brief evaluation survey. As an incentive, he announced that all completed surveys would be entered into a prize drawing. Some people finished their dinners and left. But others stayed on until after nine o'clock, debating global warming and mass extinctions. The owner of the Thirsty Scholar was thrilled to see all the new faces in his pub and immediately started planning the next event.

The next day, Professor Marshall called Ben. He asked to see the completed evaluations and he wanted to thank WGBH for a wonderful experience and express his eagerness to do more Science Cafés. The Café had provided a refreshing opportunity for Marshall to explain his deeply held beliefs about his work and research to a new, and bluntly questioning audience.

It was a successful Science Café—informing scores of citizens about a critically important scientific issue, providing a forum for public debate and discussion, and, at least for one night, tearing down a barrier that often separates scientists and the larger community.

This event marked one year of Science Cafés staged throughout the country by the *NOVA scienceNOW* team and partners—43 events in all, signaling the beginning of an emerging movement to enhance public engagement in and understanding of science and to make science a more integral part of our national culture.

Background and Project Overview

The *NOVA scienceNOW* project was created to increase and improve coverage of science on television and to produce a lasting impact on Americans' appreciation and understanding of current scientific research, including its ethical, social, and economic implications. Produced by WGBH, a leading producer of national prime-time and children's programming for public television, the series exposes its audience to the rich and varied scientific work underway today while reaffirming the importance of science and technology in our national life. The project's special focus is to reach new audiences—especially those younger than traditional PBS watchers and those not usually drawn to science programming—both on-air and off.

The series features diverse content, lively style, fast-paced editing, dynamic graphics and music, and humor, all designed to appeal to younger viewers without sacrificing the rigorous approach to content that traditional PBS audiences expect. Analysis of the first season's viewing audience verifies that the program goals are being met. The total audience ranged from 4.7 million to 5.3 million viewers per week. Nearly 10% of the viewers for the first four episodes were young men (ages 18–34), as compared to the PBS primetime average of 6%. Moreover, the audience of young women (ages 18–34) also grew, particularly by the third and fourth episodes. The summative evaluation underscored this data, determining that 25- to 35-year-old viewers were the demographic "most satisfied" with the tone of the programs.

But *NOVA scienceNOW* is much more than a television program. It is a multidisciplinary, multimedia project that reaches its audience through an integrated set of components that include (in addition to the nationally broadcast series) a high-profile pbs.org website with new media platforms; educator resources; and the Science Cafés, a groundbreaking informal education outreach initiative with multiple partnerships. Each component of *NOVA scienceNOW* has been subject to comprehensive formative and summative evaluation studies, conducted by independent professionals, to help guide the direction of the ongoing project and ensure that its goals are met.

The *NOVA scienceNOW* website (*www.pbs.org/nova/sciencenow*) is a key element in maintaining awareness of the series between broadcasts and is its main vehicle for providing continued

audience engagement and interaction. It is designed to be fully integrated with the series, offering a broad range of content- and visually rich features including slide shows, graphic timelines, a discussion board, educator resources, and an "Ask the Expert" feature that enables visitors to interact directly with scientists. In order to reach out more fully to the tech-savvy younger audience, the website team streams every episode of the series and, in August 2005, introduced podcasts. The first podcast, on alien encounters and antimatter, climbed from #35 to the #1 position on iTunes within a month and remained at the top of the list for almost two weeks. Overall first season analysis of the *NOVA scienceNOW* website reveals a steady increase in visitor traffic over the broadcast

NOVA scienceNOW web page

season with a remarkable year-end total of nearly 3.5 million visitors.

One of the more exciting aspects of the *NOVA scienceNOW* project, and the focus of this report, is the Science Café initiative led by WGBH's Educational Outreach team. Electronic media, like television and the internet, are powerful platforms that can reach millions of individual learners. But the impact of more personal, face-to-face engagement between the public and the scientific community may, in the end, prove even more profound and lasting.

Embracing NSES's *More Emphasis* Conditions in Informal Settings

At first glance, it seems contradictory to discuss education standards as part of a project that goes out of its way to not seem like a classroom. Science Cafés are generally held in pubs, restaurants, coffee houses, and other casual public venues. The scientists who participate are encouraged to converse with their audience, not lecture to them. Presentations are kept short to allow for more public debate and discussion. And traditional teaching tools, such as slides, are discouraged. Although the audience may not be in school, the National Science Education Standards (NSES) still apply, and there is substantial synergy between those standards, which emphasize inquiry-based learning and the acquisition of a scientific mindset, and the key goals of the Science Cafés.

Specific NSES-recommended *More Emphasis* conditions reflected by this initiative include:
- Providing opportunities for scientific discussion and debate
- Supporting cooperation, shared responsibility, and respect
- Assessing what is most valued

- Assessing achievement and opportunity to learn
- Investigating and analyzing science questions
- Managing ideas and information
- Public communication of ideas

All of these values underlie two key goals that the Science Cafés share with NSES, both in spirit and in practice: that participants experience the richness and excitement of knowing about and understanding the natural world and that they engage intelligently in public discourse and debate about scientific and technological ideas.

Science Cafés provide rare opportunities for people from all walks of life to learn about, reflect on, and engage in discussions about scientific research and topics, helping to create an informed and active public. *NOVA scienceNOW* Science Cafés have explored topics such as sustainability and public policy, STEM cell research, and scientific ethics. Café participants have commented that they learned: "emergent behavior exists in many places in nature," "the importance of continuing [STEM cell] research," and that "political and policy considerations drive the development, or neglect, of new [alternative fuel] technologies."

Science Cafés: History and Overview

Science Cafés were not invented by WGBH. They are modeled on the Café Scientifique (*www. cafescientifique.org*) movement that began in Leeds, England, in 1998 and was itself inspired by the Café Philosophique, started in France a couple of decades earlier. Café Scientifique quickly blossomed and by 2005 there were more than 30 in the United Kingdom and 17 more throughout Europe. But when WGBH first learned of the idea in the early 2000s, (from Nobel Prize winner and *NOVA scienceNOW* advisor Roald Hoffmann) there were only a handful of Cafés in the United States—mostly unconnected to one another. As a producer of a new national science series, WGBH realized that Science Cafés could be an ideal way to accomplish several goals: to promote *NOVA scienceNOW* and extend its impact, to attract the elusive 18- to 34-year-old demographic, to foster scientific debate and discussion between scientists and the public, and to enhance the public understanding of science. And WGBH could play two important roles: as an organizer of Science Cafés in the Boston area (home base for WGBH), and as a central clearinghouse to foster the growth of new and existing Science Cafés across the country. Funding for the *NOVA scienceNOW* project is provided by the Corporation for Public Broadcasting (CPB) and public television viewers, the National Science Foundation (NSF), the Howard Hughes Medical Institute (HHMI), and the Alfred P. Sloan Foundation.

Science Cafés are a simple, but powerful idea. They are grassroots events that anyone with interest and energy can organize. They are flexible and adaptable to the resources found in most any community (see how different communities have adapted them in the Cafés Sampler section). In their ideal form, Science Cafés are held outside traditional learning environments such as schools, universities, museums, or libraries, and in comfortable and casual public venues including pubs, restaurants, coffee houses, and galleries. (It is important to note that each community should determine for itself the best venue for a local Science Café and that in some communities more traditional venues might be the best option.) These venues provide an opportunity to engage members of the public who are neither students nor workers in the science field, and who might not attend a formal lecture. They also push the scientist/presenter out of his or her usual academic or research environment to meet the public on its own turf. Ideally, the scientists/presenters do not lecture and their presentations are short to avoid creating a hierarchical teacher/students dynamic that might stifle the discussion. Starting the evening with a brief video clip from the *NOVA scienceNOW* series is uniquely advantageous. In addition to being entertaining, it focuses the crowd's attention on the event and the subject to be discussed. The video gives the entire audience the same knowledge base for the upcoming discussion, allowing the scientist/presenter to assume a certain level of understanding in the participants, and providing the scientist/presenter a natural springboard to discuss his or her individual work in the field.

Sample Trivia Questions

1. Name the device that allows you to turn appliances and lights on and off without having to touch a button or switch.
THE CLAPPER

2. What movie, based on a famous Isaac Asimov short story, stars Will Smith?
I ROBOT

3. Enjoying the blizzard of 2005? Every snowflake is unique, yet the ice crystals that form them grow in a pattern rooted in the same geometric shape. What shape?
HEXAGON

Science Cafés sometimes have an added feature of Trivia Nights. In this format, the Q & A is abbreviated to allow time for the audience to participate in a trivia game. Teams are organized (a great way for strangers to get acquainted), then rounds of trivia—including a mix of popular culture, science, and audiovisual clues—are played. (Trivia questions are available from WGBH or organizers can create their own.) After playing for approximately 30–40 minutes, the winning team receives a small prize (WGBH gave $50). Trivia Nights bring people in right off the street by just posting a large sign outside the venue or having a person hand out information and invite the public in.

To encourage Café participants to learn more about the topic discussed or to pursue self-directed research or action around other science topics, "Get Involved!" handouts are distributed at the end of each event. This handout lists resources and suggests ways that participants can stay involved, including watching the *NOVA scienceNOW* series for information on other science topics, participating in an actual computer-based research project that uses the idle time on their computer, and signing up for the *NOVA scienceNOW* electronic newsletter. Participants are encouraged to visit the website to keep abreast of the latest science news and to explore topics of interest in an interactive environment.

```
┌─────────────────────────────────────────────────────────────┐
│                    NOVA ScienceNOW                            │
│                                                               │
│                     Get Involved!                             │
│                                                               │
│  ❑ Watch NOVA ScienceNOW, Tuesdays at 8pm (check your local listings) │
│    NOVA's new science magazine mini-series explores today's amazing scientific │
│    breakthroughs                                              │
│  ❑ Join a Real Research Project                               │
│    Put your computer's idle time to work solving complex science problems. │
│    Learn more: http://www.pbs.org/nova/sciencenow/involved/   │
│  ❑ Read Science in the News                                   │
│    Keep current with today's top science headlines from around the world. Go │
│    to http://www.pbs.org/nova/sciencenow/news/                │
│  ❑ Visit the NOVA ScienceNOW Web Site                         │
│    From streaming video to online polls to Web-exclusive extras, go to │
│    http://www.pbs.org/nova/sciencenow/ for the latest on cutting-edge science │
└─────────────────────────────────────────────────────────────┘
```

The Power of Partnerships

Strategic collaborations have been key to the success of the Science Café initiative. The WGBH outreach team began by contacting the organizers of existing Cafés, learning from their experiences, and offering *NOVA scienceNOW* resources for collaborative events. They reached out to national organizations with stated commitments to the public understanding of science including, most notably, Sigma Xi, a scientific research society. With nearly 65,000 members across the United States, Sigma Xi is able to tap into networks of scientists who might be interested in hosting and/or participating in Café events. Public television stations, science centers, museums, libraries, and other informal education organizations were also tapped as organizers and supporters. These new partners were guided through the process of launching a Café. Some even received small grants to defray start-up costs for the new Cafés. Science Cafés already in existence were provided with speakers, video clips, and "Get Involved!" handouts.

Building Community: The Science Café Conference

As Science Cafés generated more and more excitement and interest, organizers expressed the need to come together as a community. A conference of all stakeholders was organized at the Sigma Xi's headquarters in North Carolina. WGBH organized the one-day conference, funding travel and living expenses for 35 attendees from across the country. The American Association for the Advancement of Science (AAAS), American Institute of Physics (AIP), American Chemical Society (ACS), the American Society of Civil Engineers (ASCE), and the National Center for Outreach were also invited. This first-ever American conference for Science Cafés provided a much needed forum for organizers to share stories, talk about how to shape the future of this emerging movement, and discuss every aspect of Science Cafés—from selecting venues and promoting Cafés to choosing topics and presenters and deciding whether to charge a small fee to cover expenses.

This one-day conference not only cemented the bond among conference organizers but it inspired new activity. The American Chemical Society (ACS) became a new partner and avid supporter of Science Cafés, holding their first one (which attracted almost 100 attendees) a few months later in San Francisco. They also created a fund to provide up to twenty $500 grants to

ACS chapters that want to start a Science Café in their communities. The American Society of Civil Engineers is considering hosting trainings on Science Cafés at all its regional meetings. WGBH also decided to collaborate with Sigma Xi to create a Science Café–designated website, which will serve as a one-stop shop for Café organizers and the public (see more information below).

A second Science Café conference, planned for 2008, will be expanded to two days and, hopefully, twice the number of participants.

Virtual Headquarters: A Science Café Website

To enhance communication and continue building community among Science Café organizers, scientists, and those interested in establishing new Cafés, as well as to provide the general public with information on Cafés, WGBH and Sigma Xi are creating a dedicated website, scheduled to launch in summer 2007. Essentially a virtual headquarters for Science Cafés in the United States, the website will serve as a central clearinghouse for Cafés nationally, offering tips and resources, contact information, coordination with local public television stations, help in finding scientist/ presenters, downloadable video clips from *NOVA scienceNOW*, customizable press materials, evaluation surveys, links to local Science Cafés, and more.

A Science Café Sampler

This chapter opened with a detailed description of a Science Café in Somerville, Massachusetts. What follows is a brief description of three other Cafés with which the *NOVA scienceNOW* outreach team was involved.

> **Organizer:** Bell Museum of Natural History, Minneapolis, Minnesota
> **Venues:** Kitty Kat Klub, Varsity Theater (cabaret-style club), and Bryant-Lake Bowl

Organizers at the Bell Museum learned about Science Cafés in 2003 through Britain's Dana Centre, a space for experimental dialogues to provoke discussion about science and real engagement with the key issues of the day. The Bell Museum's first event was at the über-hip Kitty Cat Klub near the University of Minnesota, Minneapolis campus. Later, they moved to the Varsity Theater and Café. And, because of space constraints, they added a second venue in mid-2006—the Bryant-Lake Bowl, a combination restaurant, bowling alley, and theater.

Twice a month on Tuesday nights, an average of 65 people pour into the Bryant-Lake Bowl to discuss subjects such as the complexities of collecting comet stardust, the science of the ethics of using "professional" experimental guinea pigs, the architecture of ant nests, and, of course, the physics of bowling.

In 2005, the Bell Museum hosted a Café on mirror neurons, special circuitry in the brain that helps humans feel empathy for others. They used the *NOVA scienceNOW* video clip on the topic and WGBH paid for Lindsay Shenk, a young scientist featured in the program segment, to travel to Minneapolis to present her work. Approximately 100 people attended and, of those who filled out surveys, almost 60% were women, more than a third were under 30, and almost half were nonscientists.

The Bell Museum is now in the process of expanding Science Cafés to other parts of Minnesota by helping groups start their own Cafés. They are also sharing ideas and expertise with the Minnesota Sea Grant, which plans to start Cafés focusing on topics of local importance such as invasive species, fishing, and environmental topics.

In addition to contributing to the public understanding of science, the Bell Museum reports that the Cafés have built new audiences and garnered a significant amount of press (print, online, and local radio) for the museum.

Organizer: KNME, Albuquerque, New Mexico
Venues: New Mexico Museum of Natural History and Science;
National Atomic Museum; Explora Science Center;
Warehouse 21 (teen center), and others

KNME is the PBS television station serving northern and central New Mexico and licensed in Albuquerque/Santa Fe. The station received a small grant from WGBH to launch Science Cafés. KNME has been so successful with the Cafés that they have increased the number to run 6–8 times a year.

KNME Cafés are driven by local interests, talent, and resources. Topics have included "Tyrannosaurus Rex and his New Mexico Cousins," "The Avian Flu: In the United States and New Mexico," and "Lightning and Thunderstorms: New Mexico and the United States" Their first Café featured Dr. Neal Shin from the Center for Integrated Nanotechnology (CINT) located in Albuquerque—one of five such centers under the Department of Energy. After showing the  *NOVA scienceNOW* video clip on nanotechnology, Dr. Shin engaged more than 70 participants at the National Atomic Museum in a discussion about these microscopic marvels.

In November 2006, KNME hosted its first Science Café for Young Thinkers (ages 13 to 19) at Warehouse 21, a Santa Fe teen community center. This Café, "Predicting Natural Disasters," drew 47 students, some receiving extra credit for their participation, and helped excite them about science. As one student noted, the Café showed them that "science is not just about talking heads."

KNME's Science Café on "Ben Franklin, The Glass Armonica, and Sound Waves" was presented in conjunction with the 300th Anniversary of Franklin's birth. It featured the glass armonica, a musical instrument invented by Franklin, and included a performance by Mayling Garcia, one of only 13 glass armonica players in the world. Ms. Garcia spoke about the unique qualities of this rare instrument and the audience participated in a hands-on discussion with an acoustic scientist about sound waves and glass and water. The Café was so popular that KNME hosted two sessions, with 107 participants at one and 69 at the other.

KNME credits the Science Cafés with helping solidify existing partnerships and build new ones. New Café partnerships planned for the upcoming year include a program with the Albuquerque Aquarium on fish surgery, one with the Rio Grande Botanic Garden on genetic diversity in plants, and another with the Rio Grande Zoo called "Climate Change and Polar Bears on Earth Day," which utilized the *NOVA scienceNOW* video clip "Fastest Glacier."

Organizer: Science on Tap
Venue: Ravenna Third Place Books, Seattle, Washington

Inspired by Britain's Café Scientifique, Science on Tap in Seattle is one of the earliest Science Cafés in the United States. Organized in 2003 by a group of scientists from the Fred Hutchinson Cancer Research Center, Boeing, the University of Washington, and the Swedish Meditation Center, along with a couple of freelance science writers, Science on Tap's goals are to make science a more significant part of the national culture, to reach out to families, and to remove the shroud of mystery that all too often surrounds scientific endeavors. Science on Tap is located in a unique neighborhood venue called the Ravenna Third Place Bookshop that also houses a Café and an "all ages" pub.

Cafés are held on the last Monday of each month. Recent topics have included women and science, alien life, string theory, and appropriately, the science of brewing beer. Other topics have included hurricanes and the threat to New Orleans (held several months prior to Hurricane Katrina) and fuel cells, which was coupled with a very successful science trivia game designed by WGBH. Sigma Xi sponsored prizes for the winning team of an exciting and tightly contested game that was won by a single point.

Science on Tap has averaged between 30 and 40 attendees, including high school students. A recent feature article in the *Seattle Times,* however, has resulted in a spike in attendance. The last few Cafés have averaged 100 audience members and the pub managers have had to add staff to handle the crowd. The organizers are looking for a second venue and are considering trying outdoor events and raising funds to enhance their website, promotion, and marketing efforts.

Evaluation Findings

The success of Science Cafés can be measured by the number and diversity of venues that are picking up the idea and bringing new audiences to science and to their doors. These establishments have reached thousands of ordinary people, and the numbers are increasing (see Looking to the Future for more details). In 2006, a summative evaluation of the *NOVA scienceNOW* series, website, and Science Cafés was conducted by Goodman Research Group of Cambridge, Massachusetts, a firm specializing in the evaluation of educational programs, materials, and services. The overarching objective of the evaluation was to determine the extent to which the project was meeting its goals of increasing public awareness and understanding of science content and increasing public engagement in science-related activities.

The goals of the summative evaluation of the Science Cafés were to:

- Gather data on the demographics of attendees
- Solicit feedback on the Cafés
- Assess learning (that is, the extent to which the Science Café experience and content were new to attendees)
- Assess the extent to which the Science Café motivated attendees to engage in science-related activities after the Café

Working in three locations around the country (Cambridge, Massachusetts; San Diego, California; and Seattle, Washington), Goodman Group administered a post survey to 131 Science Café attendees at the end of their Café event. Two to three months later, 71 of those attendees (the ones who provided contact information) were invited to complete a follow-up survey; 31 (44%) completed the survey.

The key findings of the summative evaluation, based on more than 30 Science Cafés held across the country, were extraordinary.

- NOVA scienceNOW **Science Cafés are an effective way to reach participants who traditionally do not attend science events.**

  The summative evaluation confirmed that Science Cafés are an effective way to engage audiences who do not typically have the opportunity to interact directly with scientists and presentations of their work. Specifically, the evaluation demonstrated that the *NOVA scienceNOW* Science Cafés served a diverse audience including those aged 35 and under, women, and nonscientists. Half the attendees were in the target age range of 35 or younger and 42% were women.

- **Nontraditional settings and the topics covered are appealing to attendees.**

  Attendees appreciated the casual setting of the Cafés, with approximately one in five stating that this aspect was what they liked most about the event, followed by the presentation (60%). Their comments ranged from enjoying "the ability to interact with people actively at work in scientific research" to "[the demonstration, by the lecturer, of] robot singing," to "meeting people and seeing who shows up." They also indicated that the topics covered were of high interest, with the majority (79%) reporting that the content was *very* to *extremely interesting*.

  Seventy-seven percent of the attendees reported that this was their first Science Café experience. In addition, the Science Café was either the first time most attendees (33%) had learned about the topic being presented or had heard a scientist speak about the topic, and a full 97% stated they were likely to attend future Science Cafés.

- *NOVA scienceNOW* **Science Cafés are effective at providing attendees with new science-related experiences.**

  In the follow-up survey completed three months later, almost all of attendees had retained information they had learned at Cafés. Below are some of their sample summaries.

"Very complex patterns can arise from large groups of seemingly unintelligent entities." (Robots/Emergent Behavior)

"When a person watches somebody else performing an action, the brain of the observer activates in the same areas as needed to perform the task. This has been proposed to account for human empathy and understanding." (Mirror Neurons)

"Climate change can be abrupt: A tipping point can usher in an era of very different climate." (Climate)

- **The Science Cafés are effective at encouraging attendees to continue engaging in science-related activities.**
  Sixty-one percent of the attendees reported they had completed 1 to 4 activities from the Get Involved! handout and just over one-third had plans to complete activities. They attended another Science Café, watched *NOVA* on TV, signed up for a science newsletter, or joined the distributed computing research project, where people can donate idle time on their computer to crunch scientific data. Another 35% reported they intended to complete one of these activities. Over one-third (39%) reported that they had shared what they learned or experienced at the Science Café with friends, family, and colleagues. Sixteen percent indicated that they took more notice of the science topics that had been covered at the Café in other media. One person attended a seminar on emergent patterns, architecture, and biology, another read an online story about mirror neurons on the BBC Web site, and still others listened to and read reports about hurricanes on public radio, the NOAA listserv, and in journals.

  An astounding 97% of Science Café participants surveyed were interested in attending future Cafés. As one survey participant stated, "I think it is a great service for nonscientists in the community to speak with professionals about what they are reading and hearing, and to have it put into some sort context that is often not available in news stories in the paper or on 20-second clips on TV."

Looking to the Future

At this writing, *NOVA scienceNOW* and the Science Café initiative are in their second season. By any measure, these are early days, but the pace of growth in Science Cafés during this short time is remarkable. The WGBH outreach team has been involved in 51 Science Cafés from Sacramento, California, to Rochester, New York, from Brownville, Nebraska, to Carbondale, Illinois. Another 28 Cafés were held by the end of spring 2007. Some locations include Greenbelt, Maryland; Kalamazoo, Michigan; Cleveland, Ohio; and Melbourne, Florida.

Partnerships with public television stations, Sigma Xi, and the American Chemical Society are flourishing; the American Science-Technology Centers' member organizations are consolidating and expanding their work with the project; and new partners, such as the American Library Association (ALA), American Society of Civil Engineers, and the Astronomical Society of the Pacific are joining the initiative.

Science Café outreach goals have been expanded to include establishing new partnerships to reach additional segments of the target audience, reaching out to a broader spectrum of scientists, and growing and strengthening the network of Science Cafés around the country to establish a lasting, self-sustaining legacy of public outreach. To achieve these goals, new resources and materials will be generated, including the following items:

- Training and information materials developed by and for the scientists/presenters to help other scientists/presenters understand the informal nature of Science Cafés and increase their comfort in these types of settings
- An annotated "top 10" list of why people come to Science Cafés to help coordinators better organize and tailor their events to meet audience expectations
- Reproducible handouts for Science Café participants that offer expanded ways individuals can continue to engage in learning about science and technology

Plans are also underway to continue to share information and resources through the new dedicated website, at the second Science Café conference, and at annual meetings of organizations including the American Association for the Advancement of Science (AAAS), the Association of Science-Technology Centers, and others. WGBH will also continue to promote the Science Cafés through published articles, such as the one in the November/December 2005 issue of *The Informal Learning Review* (see Reference).

Science Cafés seem to be catching on not only because they are entertaining (which they are) but because they respond to a deep-seated need for all of us to understand a world that is being changed by science and technology on a daily basis. Science Cafés provide nonthreatening venues for ordinary citizens to confront, converse, and have a voice in the direction of scientific progress and the values we embrace.

In a world of genetically modified foods, artificial intelligence, biological warfare, nuclear technology, cloning, global climate change, and uncertain environmental sustainability, it is clear that choices about how science is applied and prioritized should be made only after the widest possible discussion by an informed and engaged public. The Science Café initiative is creating an enduring network of people and organizations dedicated to enhancing the public understanding of science. This movement will live on in communities across the country, fostering scientific debate and helping strengthen the ties between scientists and the people that support, benefit from, and are affected by their work.

Reference
Desai, B. 2005. Building new audiences: Science cafés. *The Informal Learning Review* 75 (Nov/Dec): 12–16.

Youth Leadership at the Franklin Institute:

What Happened When the Grant Ran Out

Carol A. Parssinen
The Franklin Institute

The Franklin Institute, founded in 1824 and housed in its current building in central Philadelphia since 1934, is organized into three Centers of Excellence. The Science Center is the public museum space that welcomes visitors of all ages to explore science in interactive exhibits and public programs. The Center for Innovation in Science Learning develops model programs in science learning for the K–12 education community, both inside and outside the museum walls. The Benjamin Franklin Center is the link to the community of science researchers and university scholars and curates the Institute's unique collections in the history of science. The Institute fulfills its mission to "inspire a passion for science and technology learning" through the integrated programs of these three centers.

Founded in 1995, the Center for Innovation in Science Learning has sustained grant-funded science learning research and the development of model programs in four areas of national focus in science education: teacher development, educational technology, gender and family learning, and youth leadership. In keeping with the mission of the Franklin Institute, the core philosophy of all Center for Innovation programs is the commitment to inquiry learning in science.

In Philadelphia, Center for Innovation programs strengthen relationships with the Institute's major constituencies—teachers, students, and families—and bring in new community populations of diverse young people and their families. Nationally, the progress and results of grant research are widely disseminated to the broader educational community via presentations, publications, and media recognition (Williams 2006). In 2006, the Center for Innovation conducted science learning programs for 12,000 teachers, students, and family participants through grant-based programs in Philadelphia, eastern Pennsylvania, and 48 states across North America. Through the Institute website at *www.fi.edu*, the Center for Innovation has created a leading destination worldwide for online science content resources, with a 2006 year-end total of nearly 20 million individual visitors.

This chapter will profile PACTS (Partnerships for Achieving Careers in Technology and Science), the Institute's youth leadership program for African American middle school and high school students, the majority of whom attend Philadelphia public schools. PACTS began as a three-year NSF-funded initiative in 1993, with a core offering of Saturday morning hands-on basic science activities in several Philadelphia community center sites, led by staff, students, and African American professionals; a summer recruitment program; and career development, including field trips to local universities. When the grant ran out in 1996, the Institute and the Center for Innovation were faced with the thorny issue of how to sustain funding for a valuable, but expensive community service initiative, largely removed from the annual operations of the Science Center and the Franklin Center.

In keeping with the Institute's mission of free-choice, inquiry-based learning, and spurred by an ongoing commitment to diverse young people as emerging scientists and youth leaders, Institute President Dennis Wint and PACTS Director Michael Burch plotted a new course for PACTS, incorporating the strengths of the original program. The key design features of the new PACTS have become its strong foundation over the past decade. They are:

- the Franklin Institute as the primary program locale, with activities throughout the school year on Saturday and after school and a month long recruitment program for new students in July/August;
- limited enrollment of about 100 diverse students per year, roughly half of whom are female, primarily from the School District of Philadelphia;
- environmental science and (since 2000) robotics as the identified science and technology learning strands;
- inquiry-based workshops and research activities, both in field locations and in the Institute;
- formation of a leadership cadre of high school junior and senior students, called "Explainers," who work as unscheduled part-time employees in departments throughout the Institute;
- college and career counseling, including targeted field trips, supported by adult mentors;
- ongoing integration of PACTS-hosted events into the annual programmatic calendar of the Institute; and
- participation in community service events outside the Institute.

Since 1996, when the original NSF funding ended, PACTS has been sustained almost entirely by multiyear and annual grants. The Institute has received two major grants for PACTS student environmental action research in Philadelphia's Fairmount Park: Student Leadership in Science, funded by the Howard Hughes Medical Institute, 1997–2001; and PEERS (PACTS Environmental Education, Research, and Service), funded by NSF from 2002–2005. In addition, the Institute has made PACTS a priority for annual grant funding, and a substantial roster of Philadelphia corporations and foundations has provided annual support for PACTS.

PACTS recruits students, ages 10–18, who primarily attend Philadelphia city schools, although the program has also enrolled students from parochial, suburban, and independent schools. There are no explicit academic criteria for enrollment in PACTS, but applicants are interviewed and screened for program interest, motivation to participate, and age-appropriate maturity. Parents/caregivers must sign each student's application. Since 1996, PACTS has enrolled more than 1,300 students, offered 239 Explainers employment as junior staff in the museum, and had 125 students remain enrolled through high school graduation, 97% of whom have gone on to higher education and 42 of whom have returned as college interns to work in the program. Year after year, PACTS has sustained an almost even mix of young men and women. On an annual basis, PACTS reaches thousands of additional students through outreach programs and events, such as "Careers in Science Day" for high school students throughout the region.

PACTS and the NSES

There are three essential features of the PACTS program that most directly embody the areas of *More Emphasis* in the Content and Inquiry Standards and the Goals for School Science: Environmental Action Research, PACTS Explainers as Junior Staff, and PACTS Leadership of Institute Annual Events. The discussion of each of these features will also draw on the major evaluation studies of PACTS that have been completed since 2000. They are:

- Simon, E. 2000. *PACTS as a learning environment: The view from participants*. Philadelphia, PA: Department of Urban Studies, University of Pennsylvania.
- Kessler, C. 2005. *PEERS (PACTS environmental education research and service): Year 3 summative evaluation report*. Edgewater, MD: Institute for Learning Innovation.
- Kessler, C., and J. Luke. 2005. *Partnerships for achieving careers in technology and science (PACTS): Retrospective evaluation study*. Edgewater, MD: Institute for Learning Innovation.

PACTS as a learning environment (Simon 2000) uses the literature on community youth programs as the analytic frame for the study and cites, in particular, the work of Shirley Brice Heath and Milbrey McLaughlin on voluntary youth organizations (1993). Simon interviewed 10 former PACTS students who were then in college, in order to document the benefits of long-term participation and link those benefits to particular program elements of PACTS. The reports concludes that for "sustained participants" who continued with PACTS through high school graduation, there are program benefits in communication skills, career awareness and experience, academic performance, social and personal growth, and sense of community responsibility. These benefits were linked to science workshops and exploration activities, being an Explainer and leading Institute public events, field trips, and sustained relationships with the PACTS staff and adult mentors.

The *PEERS Year 3 Summative Report* (Kessler 2005) also cites McLaughlin and her research concerned with the characteristics of successful programs for urban youth (youth-centered, knowledge-centered, assessment-centered, and community-centered) as the guiding framework for the study (2000). The study was both the summary of findings from year 3 of the NSF PEERS grant and a summative assessment of the program's implementation and progress over the full grant period. Kessler and her colleagues from the Institute for Learning Innovation (ILI) used a mixed methods evaluation design of pre- and post questionnaires, focused observations at the Centennial Lake research site, and semi-structured telephone interviews. Nine of twelve students interviewed in years 1 and 2 were interviewed again in year 3 to determine the program impact on their ideas and attitudes as young adults toward the natural environment and science. Kessler concluded that:

> The PEERS program has proved to be extremely successful in engaging Philadelphia youth in environmental education and research. Beyond understanding and caring for their own community, PEERS students demonstrate an appreciation and an awareness of environmental issues that affect humans and the world around them. Overall, most students show an increased understanding of scientific concepts, the skills and knowledge necessary for pursuing a career in science, and the importance of science in their lives…. Situated within McLaughlin's community-based learning framework, PEERS clearly has proved to be a youth-centered and knowledge-centered program. Students are encouraged to follow their interests, use their talents and skills, and build on their strengths. (2005, p. 19).

The *PACTS Retrospective Study* (Kessler and Luke 2005) expands and deepens the earlier studies, in order to evaluate the role that the program has played in participants' lives over time. Kessler and Luke focused on three key questions:

- How has PACTS contributed to youth's academic and career pursuits?
- How has PACTS shaped youth's social development and sense of identity?
- How has PACTS enhanced youth's interest in and perceptions of science?

The evaluation design methods were a literature review on youth free-choice learning, an online survey, and semistructured telephone interviews. The survey included informational questions to determine demographics and the nature of participation in PACTS, Likert-scaled questions to assess participants' perceptions of program impact, and open-ended questions. There were 91 participants in the survey (47 female, 42 male), which included both PACTS graduates (52) and students still in the program (39). A total of 23 survey participants, who were generally representative of the survey sample, were interviewed by ILI researchers.

Kessler and Luke extensively document the responses to the study, including many verbatim student comments that indicate the age and gender of the respondent. The study concludes:

> Data clearly suggest that the program has positively impacted youth's academic and career choices, social development and sense of self, and science interest and knowledge. This was especially true for those who participated in the program for 3 years or more; such sustained participation led to significantly more positive perceptions of the program's impact in all areas. With few exceptions, the PACTS experience is considered by

participants to have influenced and supported many of the important decisions they made during their teen and young adult years. (2005, p.22).

Environmental Action Research

NSES Content and Inquiry Standards—*More Emphasis* on:

- Understanding scientific concepts and developing abilities of inquiry
- Activities that investigate and analyze science questions
- Investigations over extended periods of time
- Process skills in context
- Applying the results of experiments to scientific explanations
- Communicating science explanations

NSES Goals for School Science:

- Experience the richness and excitement of knowing about and understanding the natural world
- Engage intelligently in public discourse and debate about matters of scientific and technological concern

PACTS environmental study and action research takes place at Centennial Lake in Philadelphia's Fairmount Park, a natural urban environment of more than 8,900 acres and one of the largest city parks in the world. Centennial Lake, one of the largest lakes in the West Fairmount Park watershed, reflects the stress of an urban environment. It supports a diverse plant and animal population, but has been colonized by a wide variety of invasive plants, which threaten native species.

On an ongoing basis, PACTS students pursue environmental research and monitoring at the lake site, conducting periodic water and soil testing, and surveying plants, animals, and insects. They then bring the collected specimens and data from the lake to the Institute's PACTS Laboratory for further investigation, using water monitoring chemical test kits and bacteria test kits. Students have also assisted Fairmount Park in ongoing preservation efforts, including the removal of invasive plants and replenishment of native plants, and the safeguarding of native animal, insect, and plant habitats.

Specimen collecting at Centennial Lake.

In connection with the NSF-funded PEERS (PACTS Environmental Education, Research and Service) initiative (2002-05), students pursued the long-term research goal of determining whether or not the lake ecosystem could support the re-introduction of aquatic life. A memorable feature of the project were three "fish assessments," the first two conducted in collaboration with the Philadelphia Water Department, during which fish were given a mild shock so they would rise to the lake surface where they could be classified, weighed, and measured, before being returned to the lake. The leadership of older students was an important factor in the fish assessments. Kessler (2005) writes about her site visit to the third assessment:

> The general atmosphere was relaxed as students focused on the tasks at hand. Students who had previously participated in the fish assessment activity conducted their work with confidence, sharing their knowledge and experience with younger students. There was a strong sense of camaraderie and friendly teasing as students pulled on and off the waders

Fish assessment.

and ventured cautiously into the lake…. As the activity came to a close, students were reluctant to stop their work…. Students continued to talk on the bus ride back to the Franklin Institute about the fish and other wildlife that they observed. (Kessler 2005, pp. 9–10).

Back at the PACTS Lab, students used hatcheries to breed fish that would be suitable for restocking the lake. At the conclusion of the PEERS project, having determined that Centennial Lake has low oxygen levels and so cannot support any new aquatic populations, students presented their full research results to the Environmental Education department of Fairmount Park.

Students involved in the PEERS project expressed strong satisfaction in doing authentic work in science that had a positive environmental impact:

- Being able to do more than see sciences in a textbook or on some [TV] special… to actually do science. (Kessler 2005, p. 14).

PACTS Lab.

PACTS group in the field.

- I never went to any of the parks. I've helped out before but never cleaned up. I helped do something, accomplished something. I liked doing that. (Kessler 2005, p. 16).
- The bird watching—it was really fun seeing how they interacted in the environment and learning about their anatomy—and using the binoculars. (Kessler 2005, p. 14).
- Using the equipment because if I want to be a doctor I need to know what to expect; using chemicals for testing the lake. (Kessler 2005, p. 15).
- Working in the pond with the waders on… getting dirty… how big of an impact PEERS had—not just picking up bottles, but when you look at all we've done as a group. (Kessler 2005, p. 14).
- That we were dealing with a project of that magnitude. We were researching a lake. Learn the history of the lake and we were the ones who researched the lake. (Kessler and Luke 2005, p. 15).
- [PEERS] helped me to see how the things we do everyday can mess up our world. Just dropping one piece of trash on the floor can harm us. It can get washed out to the ocean and can harm the animals that live in the ocean. I knew that littering wasn't good, but I didn't think about it that way—how it can get washed out to the ocean and stuff (13-year-old girl) (Kessler and Luke 2005, p. 21).
- The PEERS water testing really enhanced my knowledge. Before [PEERS] I didn't know water had all these components to help fish and animals down there breathe. [I didn't know that] if the pH level wasn't right, or was too hard, or the nitrate level too low or too high…everything has to be balanced out. PACTS gave me the perfect opportunity to help clean up the environment. PACTS opened up my eyes to a lot of information I never knew existed…. (19-year-old male) (Kessler and Luke 2005, p. 21).

Public engagement was another key feature of PEERS and challenged students to articulate their experiences and discoveries at the lake to a variety of audiences. Staff and students visited Philadelphia middle schools to present their research findings and raise awareness about environmental issues and the opportunities that young people have to make a positive contribution to the health of the environment in their own city. Students spoke about their personal growth:

- The social part, being a leader and role model. Most of the kids in the program were younger than me, so it helped me to fill those shoes, like being a big brother. Also preparing and giving presentations helped me with public speaking, gave me respect and confidence in my everyday life. (Kessler 2005, p. 15).
- To be a self-initiator. From doing a job to putting my name on that job and doing a good job…. I have the ability to take and give directions and the ability to lead. (Kessler 2005, p. 15).

Staff and students also created a new annual program for Institute visitors to commemorate Earth Day, held on the Saturday closest to April 22 and hosted by PACTS students for public visitors—primarily family groups—to the Institute. Students demonstrate what they have learned at the lake and in the lab and seek to engage visiting families in water testing and other nonthreatening activities. In June, PACTS staff and students also shared their year's work, including their work at the lake and in robotics, to an audience of parents, Institute staff from other departments, funders, and community supporters in a program called, "Students Making a Difference."

PACTS Explainers as Junior Staff

NSES Content and Inquiry Standards, *More Emphasis* on:

- Learning subject matter disciplines in the context of inquiry, technology, science in personal and social perspectives, and history and nature of science
- Integrating all aspects of science content
- Communicating science explanations
- Management of ideas and information
- Public communication of student ideas and work

NSES Goals for School Science:

- Use appropriate scientific processes and principles in making personal decisions
- Engage intelligently in public discourse and debate about matters of scientific and technological concern
- Increase students' economic productivity through the use of the knowledge, understanding, and skills of the scientifically literate person in their careers.

Manning the "Brain Bar."

In 1996, PACTS Explainers began as unscheduled part-time (hourly wage) employees in the Institute's Interpretive Services department, under the collaborative direction of Interpretive Services and PACTS staff. As frontline staff for weekend visitors to the museum, now as then, Explainers are trained in the science content and physical operation of the Institute's exhibit areas and current/ongoing programs, as well as in the techniques of public engagement. Their goal is to facilitate the experience of visitors of all ages, usually in family or other social groupings, and enhance their opportunities for learning science. In the weekly sessions that PACTS staff has developed as a support structure for Explainers, the importance of communication and interpersonal skills, especially in a public setting, is an ongoing topic of discussion, as is the public visibility of being an Explainer. The formulation is this: For visitors who come in contact with you, you *are* the Franklin Institute.

PACTS Explainer guides children through an activity.

Explainers reflect on the responsibility of being an Explainer and communicating with the public:

- That was my first job. That was one of the things that really helped me to become more outgoing, because....I'd have to learn something, then I'd have to explain it to people. And it wasn't just people who were my own age, there were adults, there were children that were younger, there were people that probably didn't understand English too well. Being an Explainer was one of the things that helped me decide I wanted to pursue a career in engineering. (Simon 2000, p. 14).

- While I was at the Franklin Institute, I had to deal with visitors and staff with many different personalities. I wasn't exposed to that before PACTS. My elementary school and middle school were primarily African American so it really helped me having been in PACTS when I got to high school and college, which were mixed. (26-year-old female) (Kessler and Luke 2005, p. 13).

- PACTS put me in the position to say what we did, outlining it for the audience, showing how proud we were of what we'd done. Having confidence, doing well, and being willing to embrace the things I've accomplished [are things that PACTS has instilled in me]. (21-year-old male) (Kessler and Luke 2005, p. 14).

- PACTS has given me the confidence that a minority like myself can pursue a science career, and do it so well. (20-year-old female) (Kessler and Luke 2005, p. 16).

Over time, the positive reputation of the Explainers has grown, both throughout the Institute and within the PACTS program. The term "Explainer" has come to mean a junior staff member with maturity, high motivation and reliability, and strong communication and interpersonal skills. Middle-grades students who enter PACTS often indicate on their application form that they "want to be an Explainer," and current Explainer classes make it clear to younger students that being an Explainer is a serious responsibility and expectations for performance are high. The Explainers are also an elite group, limited by the annual total of approximately 25 students per year and the total number of funded hours for Explainer labor.

Today, Explainers are the recognized junior leadership cadre of the PACTS program. They work in departments and programs throughout the Institute, including Visitor Services, Exhibit Design, Camp-In, Theatres, and Information Technology Services, and engage in substantive projects or services that develop their talents and preprofessional abilities. As such, they are a continuing visible commitment of the Institute to the science-related career development of diverse young people. Explainers are also regularly called upon as staff for Science Center events, such as the twice-annual Educators' Night Out for teachers throughout the region; the annual "Fun Fest" fundraiser for families; and the recently developed monthly "Community Nights," which are free to the public and are drawing an average of 2,000 diverse visitors to the museum.

PACTS staff has also created a differentiated leadership structure within the Explainer program. One student each year is named the "Explainer Supervisor," and has the overall responsibility for Explainer activities and performance, including the solicitation of students to work Institute events. In addition, individual Explainers are given leadership responsibility for the PACTS lab, the PACTS newsletter, and PACTS student support for community outreach activities.

- I was trusted with the role of supervisor, which proved to me that I could achieve self-esteem. I was the first Explainer Supervisor. The average employee [Explainer] was responsible for workshops and had to learn about exhibits, do museum tours. As the Explainer Supervisor, I was responsible for making sure that PACTS students were on the schedule, making sure they got there on time or calling them to find out where they were, making sure time cards were filled out properly, reprimanding them if they were late, and writing incident reports. In my everyday life, it helps me stay organized. (26-year-old female) (Kessler and Luke 2005, p. 17).
- As a direct result of PACTS, and the leadership experiences I gained, especially through the Explainer program, I have become a more direct and confident leader, especially in direct management experiences. From being a shy young man to see myself as a confident and effective leader, I don't think there's any way you can teach that in a classroom. When any kid spends a lot of time in a youth program, especially at a place like the Franklin Institute, you automatically become a leader… because you're involved in something positive. You're picking up new skills every day that influence other kids who are in or out of the program. (26-year-old male) (Kessler and Luke 2005, p. 17).

PACTS Explainers also have an ongoing opportunity to serve as mentors to younger students in the program and to be mentored by former Explainers. Each summer, Explainers are a prominent junior staff presence for the monthlong recruitment program for new students. They also provide vital one-to-one support for students participating in the year-round activities of the junior Robotics Team, which extends through ninth grade. At the same time, former Explainers serving as paid college interns during the summer or as volunteers during the winter and spring breaks, return to work in PACTS programs and create a powerful mentorship ladder of older and younger Explainers. Currently, two former Explainers are providing daily role models, as they work in the Institute Visitor Services department, while they are completing their college degree.

- Part of [PACTS] was working with other students [which] helped my social skills through cooperative working in teams. It helped my confidence in understanding science. Once I felt more confident that I understood concepts, I felt like science was obtainable and I participated more. (23-year-old female) (Kessler and Luke 2005, p. 13).
- The team work of building the robot [was influential] because I kept sharing my ideas with other people. Then, I would test those ideas and sometimes combine them with other people's ideas. (12-year-old male) (Kessler and Luke 2005, p. 13).
- One of the things that came out of the PACTS program was the feeling [of being] service oriented. We have to take time to help. It wasn't just the water quality of the lake; we would see that it had been polluted. We did a program on Radon to educate the public… for people who live in areas of high radon and might be in danger. The service part of the program stayed with me for sure. A lot of the work that I did with students was volunteer work. (21-year-old male) (Kessler and Luke 2005, p. 14).
- My volunteer work is at more of an elevated level now, so I can mentor other students since I've done the things they have. Right now I am mentoring my nephew who just started the PACTS program. (22-year-old male) (Kessler and Luke 2005, p. 14).

PACTS Leadership of Institute Annual Events

NSES Content and Inquiry Standards, *More Emphasis* on:

- Learning subject matter disciplines in the context of inquiry, technology, science in personal and social perspectives, and history and nature of science
- Integrating all aspects of science content
- Communicating science explanations
- Management of ideas and information
- Public communication of student ideas and work

NSES Goals for School Science:

- Use appropriate scientific processes and principles in making personal decisions
- Engage intelligently in public discourse and debate about matters of scientific and technological concern
- Increase students' economic productivity through the use of the knowledge, understanding, and skills of the scientifically literate person in their careers.

Leadership of Institute annual events is a special feature of the Explainer program; and for many Explainers, hosting these events is a capstone of their PACTS experience. The most prestigious event is the Meet the Scientists forum, held in conjunction with the annual Franklin Awards Convocation, a program of the Institute's Benjamin Franklin Center. Each April, the Franklin Institute Awards honor a group of eminent international men and women for their contributions in science, engineering, and technology. The Awards, begun in 1824, identify individuals whose great innovation has benefited humanity, advanced science, launched new fields of inquiry, and deepened our understanding of the universe. The list of awardees is a "who's who" of the greatest names in science and engineering, including Edison, Einstein, Marie Curie, and the Wright Brothers. The Meet the Scientists forum brings the Franklin laureates together as a panel for a question-and-answer session with selected junior- and senior-level high school students from the Philadelphia region. The schools represented are an eclectic mix of urban and suburban, public, charter, independent, and parochial schools; the students are in upper level or AP science classes.

Hosting Meet the Scientists can be a daunting prospect. The Explainers who are selected as hosts must prepare themselves to be knowledgeable about the laureates and their awards and to create an introductory statement for each of the 7–10 members of the panel. They must also prepare some initial questions to get the panel started and then field questions from the audience, facilitated by other PACTS students with handheld microphones. There are a number of possible complications, including students whose questions are not entirely clear, laureates whose English is not easy to understand, and laureates who pique the audience's interest and so receive repeated questions, while others are neglected. The Explainer hosts must manage these and other issues while moving the program forward.

I had to speak in front of crowds of my peers and the public, which increased my ability to communicate as an adult. We did it for the Franklin Awards. We had to write speeches and talk in front of 500 people in the gallery. (26-year-old female) (Kessler and Luke 2005, p. 12).

Two Explainers host the Meet the Scientists forum.

When the panel is over, Explainers and any other audience members who wish to stay are invited to spend another informal hour with the laureates, having refreshments and continuing the conversation. This is an unparalleled opportunity for young people to meet and interact one-on-one with distinguished men and women of science and technology. Each year, a group of Explainers—including the hosts of Meet the Scientists—is invited to attend the Franklin Awards Ceremony, a black-tie event attended by some 800 people, during which the laureates receive their awards. During the reception prior to the event, Explainers have presented their work to the ceremony attendees at the lake and in robotics.

Careers in Science Day, another major event hosted by PACTS Explainers, grew out of Meet the Scientists. Every year, students attending Meet the Scientists were keenly interested in the backgrounds of the laureates and the decisions that had led them to pursue a life in science. PACTS staff and Explainers picked up on this interest and have created the annual Careers in Science program that features panels of science and medical practitioners across a broad profes-

Explainers meet with scientists before the ceremony.

In 2001, former Explainer Sabryia Scott, about to enter medical school, spoke during the Franklin Awards ceremony about the impact of PACTS on her life and her aspiration to return one day as a laureate herself. Ms. Scott graduated from Drexel University College of Medicine in 2006.

sional range, including medicine, academia, business, government, and the cultural community. Many of the panelists are in the early stages of their careers, unlike the Franklin laureates, and each year, the panel includes graduates of PACTS. The program, which is intended to give the audience a firsthand grasp of the multiple professional options in science and medicine, is open on a first-come basis to approximately 250 high school students from the Philadelphia region.

Explainer hosts for Careers in Science Day introduce the panelists, who give a brief statement about why they chose their profession, what its educational requirements are, and what they actually do. Then the hosts must field the audience questions, which range from the admiring to the impertinent, and manage the program flow, so that all the panelists get an opportunity to respond. Audience responses to this program, both from teachers and students, are strongly positive. Following the program, the Explainers and other PACTS students have the opportunity to pursue one-on-one interactions with the panelists over lunch.

PACTS students reflect on how the program has influenced their academic development and helped to shape their college and career aspirations:

- I definitely would not have gone to college if it weren't for PACTS. I took the SAT in 11th grade and had good scores but I had no motivation to go to college until I was in the [PACTS] program and [was exposed to] the positive peer pressure. I saw that it wasn't out of my reach. In South Philly, in my neighborhood, we didn't do that; it wasn't part of our plan. (26-year-old male) (Kessler and Luke 2005, p. 6).
- At first I wanted to be lawyer. There was a lady who was an environmental lawyer who came to talk to us at one of the "Careers in Science" talks. It was a connection to science in everyday life. I'd always wanted to do law but didn't know what to do law for. I saw an opportunity to do environmental science law. (17-year-old female) (Kessler and Luke 2005, p. 8).
- I wanted to be a game designer. I always know there was some science in it, but I see it (science) as a really big part of being a game designer. You have to code the game, you have to experiment with it, you need to test and test and test again, just like in the experiments [we did in PACTS]). (15-year-old male) (Kessler and Luke 2005, p. 8).
- I will be going to the University of Pennsylvania School of Nursing as a junior in September. [In PACTS I learned to] just exhaust all possibilities. People around here are surprised when they learn I'll be going to UPenn. They say 'How did you get into Penn?' I guess people are kind of scared of the University of Pennsylvania. I just tell them you have to try everything and not give up. (20-year-old female) (Kessler and Luke 2005, p. 7).

PACTS and the Science Leadership Academy

In the past four years, the Franklin Institute's recognition of PACTS as a visible and highly valued youth leadership resource has led to a dramatic new partnership with the School District of Philadelphia. In September 2006, the District, in partnership with the Institute, opened the Science Leadership Academy (SLA), a progressive magnet public high school, with a focus on science, mathematics, technology, and entrepreneurship. Located within easy walking distance of the Institute, the SLA has begun with a class of 115 freshman students from across the city and will grow into a four-year school with 400–500 students by 2010. SLA students learn in a project-based environment—both in school and in the Institute—which emphasizes the core values of inquiry, research, collaboration, presentation, and reflection.

The Institute was integrally involved with the School District in the planning and development of the SLA, including two "curriculum summits" with national participation, space planning, selection of faculty, hosting of informational events for parents and students, and hosting of summer institutes for inaugural faculty and the class of 2010. In addition to providing all students and their parents with a Family Membership, the Institute has also initiated two ongoing programs in support of the SLA-Wednesdays@The Franklin and the SLA Ambassadors. The

At the SLA "ribbon-cutting" ceremony, students dressed in their lab coat school uniforms demonstrated their creation of a guillotine triggered by a chemical reaction. Institute President Dennis Wint and SLA principal Chris Lehmann set the process in motion.

Wednesdays program brings students to the Institute on a weekly basis to learn about its exhibits, programs, and unique resources in the history of science and to draw on their perspective as young adults in developing innovative projects. The SLA Ambassadors are a group of university, business, government, and community leaders who have agreed to open doors to institutional and professional resources for the school and to serve as public advocates for the SLA in the Greater Philadelphia area.

Under the leadership of the Center for Innovation and PACTS, the Franklin Institute anticipates that the relationship with the SLA will become one of growing mutual benefit, founded on the mutual commitment to inquiry as the basis for learning. Increasingly, SLA faculty and students will incorporate the Institute's learning opportunities and external relationships into the ongoing life of the school and its community; and the Institute will incorporate the perspective and talents of SLA faculty and students into its exhibits and programs. The foundation for this promising partnership, with national implications for the collaborative relationship of formal and informal learning and their joint support of the NSES, is the PACTS program, developed by the Franklin Institute after the grant ran out.

References

Heath, S. B., and M. McLaughlin. 1993. *Identity and inner-city youth: Beyond ethnicity and gender.* Palo Alto: Stanford University Press.

Kessler, C. 2005. *PEERS (PACTS environmental education research and service): Year 3 summative evaluation report.* Institute for Learning Innovation.

Kessler, C., and J. Luke. 2005. *Partnerships for achieving careers in technology and science (PACTS): Retrospective evaluation study.* Institute for Learning Innovation.

McLaughlin, M. 2000. *Community counts: How youth organizations matter for youth development.* Public Education Network.

Simon, E. 2000. *PACTS as a learning environment: The view from participants.* Department of Urban Studies, University of Pennsylvania.

Media recognition in 2006 includes:

Johnson, G. 2006. Franklin institute program highlights science jobs. *The Philadelphia Tribune Learning Key* (September 26): 6–7.

Williams, D. C. 2006. A program that would make Ben Franklin proud. *Philadelphia Daily News* (April 28): 1A.

From 1996–2008, the following corporations and foundations have provided or pledged grant support for PACTS for three years or more: ARAMARK, Comcast Foundation, GlaxoSmithKline, Janus Foundation, William M. King Charitable Foundation, Christian R. and Mary F. Lindback Foundation, Rohm and Haas Company, SAP America, Inc., and Unisys Corporation.

Inquiry Is Taking Flight Through Project Butterfly WINGS

Betty A. Dunckel, Kathy C. Malone, and Nikole K. Kadel
Florida Museum of Natural History

L ike the amazing changes that take place during the metamorphosis of a butterfly from a small egg to an adult, 4-H youth in Project Butterfly WINGS (Winning Investigative Network for Great Science) become young scientists as they take flight on the wings of discovery. WINGS is a collaborative project of the University of Florida's Florida Museum of Natural History (FLMNH), Department of Wildlife Ecology and Conservation, and 4-H, Florida Cooperative Extension Service. It is designed to foster adolescent interest, understanding, and long-term involvement in science, as well as promote positive youth development. WINGS is funded in part by a three-year grant from the National Science Foundation (ESI-0406173).

A youth *Project Guide, Leader and Helper Guide*, and an interactive website engage fourth through eighth graders in butterfly-related explorations. The 83-page *Project Guide*, designed for 4-H youth to use individually with facilitation by a volunteer 4-H leader/helper (hereinafter referred to as "leader"), introduces participants to the outdoors and butterfly behavior, identification and monitoring. Cumulative activities build skills and knowledge, culminating in a youth-centered inquiry investigation. The 64-page *Leader and Helper Guide* offers a collection of group activities that reinforces discoveries children make through the project guide. Most of the activities in both guides are completed outdoors.

Through WINGS, students form a network of butterfly observers, or citizen scientists. Citizen scientist projects engage nonscientists in scientific investigations that involve the collection of large datasets, usually over broad geographic areas (Bonney 2004; Evans et al. 2001; Krasny and Bonney 2005; Trumbull et al. 2000). In the case of WINGS, FLMNH scientists are interested in the distribution and population trends of common butterfly species in urban, suburban, and natural areas. A network of observers can gather data on an ongoing basis over a large area. Over time, these data provide critical information about the responses of species to human and natural factors.

Armed with close-focusing binoculars, data sheets and a field guide, 4-H youth monitor the abundance of butterflies.

WINGS extends the research potential of the Florida Museum of Natural History through the ongoing monitoring network. Initially developed in Florida, it now encompasses the 4-H Southern Region, which includes 13 states and Puerto Rico, and extends north to Virginia and west to Texas. The 4-H southern region states are: Alabama, Arkansas, Florida, Georgia, Kentucky, Louisiana, Mississippi, North Carolina, Oklahoma, South Carolina, Tennessee, Texas, and Virginia. The FLMNH has a strong research mission that builds on its extensive collection of specimens and artifacts. The FLMNH is the largest collections-based natural history museum in the southeast and the collections rank among the top 10 natural history collections in the nation. Of particular importance for WINGS, the museum's McGuire Center for Lepidoptera and Biodiversity has the largest collection of butterfly and moth specimens in the world. Scientists use these invaluable research materials to answer fundamental questions in biology, evolutionary change, genetics, ecology, and biodiversity.

For a natural history museum with both research and education mandates, WINGS promotes understanding of science inquiry through direct engagement in science (Bonney 2004; Farmelo 2004). As children participate in WINGS, they progress from beginners to engaged citizen scientists.

WINGS is accomplished in the informal education setting through 4-H, described as the largest out-of-school youth organization in the United States (*www.4husa.org*). 4-H is a part of the Cooperative Extension System, a nonprofit program operated through each state's land grant university. Most 4-H programs center around three areas: leadership, citizenship, and life skills.

The life skills, which fall into various categories, are developed through subject matter experiences. The categories have detailed indicators, or outcomes, associated with them. Among the categories are: communication skills; decision-making, problem-solving, and critical-thinking skills; goal-setting, planning, and organizing; positive relationship skills with others; leadership skills; citizenship and civic engagement; self-esteem and self-confidence; workforce preparation skills; self-responsibility; personal ethics/character; and positive social skills.

4-H also has categories of "subject matter outcomes." WINGS fits within the categories of environmental knowledge/skills and science and technology skills. WINGS activities include 4-H life skills, along with science inquiry skills that dovetail with the National Science Education Standards (see Table 1).

Table 1: WINGS 4-H Life Skills and Science Inquiry Skills

Life Skills	Science Inquiry Skills
Self-confidence	Observing
Learning to learn	Comparing
Communication	Communicating
Problem solving	Classifying
Decision making	Recording and mapping observations
Personal ethics and character	Gathering and recording data
Critical thinking	Using the scientific method
Goal-setting	Researching
Planning and organizing	
Positive relationship skills	

The WINGS curriculum can be tailored to the varying levels of skills, resources, and interests of youth from ages 9 to 13 years. It also is adaptable to different 4-H delivery systems including clubs, summer camps, after-school programs, and individual participants. Leaders are trained volunteers who guide children through the program and their project books. Children self-select WINGS from a wide array of 4-H offerings, such as "Eco-Adventures," "Bicycle Adventures," "Keeping Fit and Healthy," "Afterschool Agriculture," "Consumer Savvy," and "Woodworking Wonders."

The following example shows how a WINGS participant acquires life skills and develops the abilities of scientific inquiry through exploration, investigation, asking questions, and making decisions:

A busy insect catches Bella's eye. She moves closer, as the directions prompt her, to examine the small creature while it is self-absorbed gathering pollen. Bella touches the leaves of the plant and makes a note of the sandpaper like feel in her Project Butterfly WINGS Project Guide. She reflects on the experience...what surprises her, what she wonders, and what she learns about herself.

A few days later, Bella returns to look for butterflies. She sees one flit by, but wonders why she does not see more on such a warm and lovely day. She then reads about the things that attract butterflies. Later, she goes to a different place where she thinks there may be more. Now she sees a lot of butterflies. She analyzes the two places and explains why one place had fewer, and the other more.

Meanwhile, Bella attends weekly meetings of her 4-H club. This week they sort butterfly photos into categories. The spokesperson for each group describes the reasons they sort them in a particular way. Then the 4-H leader asks the group a series of questions about their experience. The 4-H youth are accustomed to this since their leader always asks questions after each activity.

Bella continues to look for butterflies as she learns more about how to identify them. Bella becomes an expert on hairstreak butterflies and she teaches other children about them. A custom identification sheet she made with butterfly photos on the Project Butterfly WINGS website helps her identify butterflies. She spots a Cloudless Sulphur, marks it on her data sheet, and enters this information into the WINGS website database. She loves participating in Project Butterfly WINGS, because she knows she is part of a larger citizen science effort. Other kids also enter data that butterfly scientists will use to study trends in butterfly populations.

Bella always looks forward to seeing what she can find outside—it's like a treasure hunt. The more she goes outside, the more she discovers, and the more questions she has. Bella is sorting things out and making sense of the patterns she sees, while also framing new questions. For example, she wonders how butterflies survive during winter.

So Bella designs her own investigation on this topic that personally interests her. Pieces begin to come together and it's as though Bella emerges as a butterfly, spreading her wings and sharing her discoveries.

Bella certainly knows this is not the end of her curiosity. She will keep exploring and thinking of new questions—a cycle that will repeat itself, just like the life cycle of a butterfly.

WINGS Exemplifies the Metamorphosis of the National Science Education Standards

Just as WINGS transforms young participants analogous to the life cycle of the butterfly, WINGS reflects the changing emphasis suggested throughout the teaching, assessment, content and inquiry, and staff development standards of the National Science Education Standards (NSES). With these standards (NRC 1996) providing a framework, "best practices" for free-choice science learning and 4-H youth development are the foundation for WINGS. This chapter primarily addresses the WINGS components that illustrate the *More Emphasis* conditions in the content and inquiry standards as shown in Table 2.

Table 2: A comparison of the inquiry content emphasis in the science standards and Project Butterfly WINGS.	
Content for Science Education*	**Project Butterfly WINGS**
Emphasizing how we know what we know from a scientific point of view	Science inquiry activities like Question Quest
Presenting knowledge about what scientists do	Scientist biographies and stories
Understanding that science is a community discourse about knowledge	Citizen science data entry and discussions

Developing explanations based on empirical evidence	Participants conceptualize, create, and conduct an investigation of their choice to share with their community
Understanding how science is done	Holistic nature of project with emphasis on science inquiry

*Adapted from Bybee, R. W. 2001. Achieving scientific literacy: Strategies for insuring that free-choice science education complements national formal science education efforts. In *Free-choice science education: How we learn science outside of school*, p.57.

With a focus on inquiry, WINGS helps develop the science skills and understandings recommended by the NSES, "Students need to learn the principles and concepts of science, acquire the reasoning and procedural skills of scientists, and understand the nature of science as a particular form of human endeavor" (NRC 1996, p. xiii).

WINGS weaves these connections throughout the program. During the introductory activities, Bella moves through inquiry skills while she acquires science knowledge and practices critical thinking and reasoning. She assimilates WINGS experiences to create a richer understanding of science. Bybee (1997) describes this as, "The national standards challenge educators to move beyond 'science as a process,' in which students learn skills (observing, inferring, and hypothesizing) and to combine these skills with scientific knowledge, scientific reasoning and critical thinking to construct a richer understanding of science" (p. 111).

In particular, WINGS achieves this rich intimacy with science through each individual activity, as well as the cumulative progression of the activities. Well-rounded discovery components contribute to the depth of the experience. The activity components are:

- A science inquiry connection that complements the activity content
- A daily life skill youths can apply to other areas of their lives
- A stewardship solution that is a "call to action" for children, and encourages them to think about how their actions affect the "big picture"
- A series of "Reflect and Connect" questions that stimulate children to share, process, generalize, and apply both the inquiry and life skills
- A journaling exercise with prompts that weaves together the inquiry and life skills
- One or more "Explore More" projects that children may select to further enhance their WINGS experience

WINGS uses content not as an end, but as a means to develop inquiry abilities. Bella learns how to identify butterflies, and uses this information to formulate questions about them. She learns how to do science and learns about science through her butterfly investigations and monitoring.

WINGS features not only knowledge about butterflies, but emphasizes a deeper understanding of how studying them fits into the broader framework of science. Mestre and Cocking (2002) describe the importance of this focus as, "The emphasis should be on in-depth understanding in a few major topics rather than in the memorization of facts about many topics; the former has lasting value, the latter is quickly forgotten" (p. 19). In doing so, WINGS gives science a context and relevance that, in turn, reinforces inquiry skill acquisition. "An alternative to simply progressing through a series of exercises that derive from a scope and sequence chart is to expose students to the major features of a subject domain as they arise naturally in problem situations" (Bransford, Brown, and Cocking 2000, p. 139).

Life Skills

The way in which WINGS integrates skill acquisition relates in part to the interaction among the inquiry skills and the 4-H life skills in each activity. Life skills are frequently goals of middle school science education (Hurd 2000). Self-confidence and decision-making are two examples of life skills WINGS fosters. Bella's foray outdoors may have been the first time she explored in unfamiliar territory. Her discoveries may have boosted her self-confidence in her ability to make observations and try new things.

When it is time to develop an investigation toward the end of WINGS, Bella has to determine what to study. Among the goals of the NSES for middle school science are to "experience the richness and excitement of knowing about and understanding the natural world" and to "use appropriate scientific processes and principles in making personal decisions" (NRC 1996, p. 13). In WINGS, these life-skill-related goals work with the science inquiry goals, and culminate in Bella having the abilities to choose, create, and conduct her own investigation.

Free-Choice Science Learning

Because WINGS is a free-choice science education program, the nature of WINGS as free-choice fosters inquiry ability. Participants choose WINGS from a menu of 4-H offerings; they self-select for the program. Choosing a program voluntarily is a characteristic of free-choice learning, and participants are probably driven by their unique intrinsic needs and interest in the subject (Falk 2001; Falk and Dierking 2000). Bybee describes this as, "free choice experiences allow the learner opportunities to stop at will, repeat at will, spend more time or less time, and share the learning process with friends or family members" (2001, p. 47). This flexibility likely adds to learner motivation, and possibly results in a more focused individual who is primed for inquiry.

Learning Science, Learning to Do Science, and Learning About Science

Finally, WINGS, as a free-choice science education program, reinforces some of the goals of the NSES (Bybee 2001). Bybee envisions the standards as a replacement for today's thinking about inquiry. WINGS dovetails with the NSES standards that connect learning science, learning to do science, and learning about science:

- *Learning science*—When Bella uses her senses in the guided exploration activity, she forms new knowledge as a foundation upon which to draw throughout WINGS. Learners build on existing knowledge to discover new things (Bransford, Brown, and Cocking 2000; Bybee 2002; Mestre and Cocking 2002). Bella enhances her ability to learn science when she becomes an expert on hairstreaks. By teaching other children about them, she further constructs her own science knowledge (Bransford, Brown, and Cocking 2000; Mestre and Cocking 2002).

- *Learning to do science*—The BSCS 5E Instructional Model (Bybee 1997; Bybee 2002) aligns closely with the experiential model (Pfiffer and Jones 1979) used in 4-H programs, including WINGS. In the experiential model, children experience an activity, share the results, process their experience and generalize the experience to real-world examples, and finally, apply what is learned to similar situations. Bella participates in these steps during each WINGS activity. The experiential model guides youths through each activity, as well as through the entire project guide.

  The following illustrates how this works across the entire WINGS program: In the 5E model, the first step is for youth to "engage." Bella's initial observations outdoors, especially when she compares the two sites, encourage her to ask, "How do I explain this situation?"

  When Bella later monitors butterflies, she "explores," the second step in the 5E model. This is where WINGS participants gather data and compare their findings for different areas. This step challenges kids to ask, "How do my exploration and explanation of experiences compare with others?"

  The remaining steps, "explain," "elaborate," and "evaluate," occur via rich experiences with real-world scientists through the sharing of their butterfly surveys. The steps also may take place during the children's culminating investigations, which can be based on butterfly surveys if kids choose to explore these.

- *Learning about science*—The citizen science component of WINGS facilitates learning about science within the context of authentic, real-world research over an extended period of time. This replaces the traditional "one-time investigation in the classroom" with a project that integrates many aspects of science content as it implements inquiry as a strategy.

In a nutshell, WINGS emphasizes learning through understanding, rather than memorization of facts. This deep understanding, in which an individual possesses a rich body of knowledge about a subject matter, enhances an individual's ability to think and solve problems (Bransford, Brown, and Cocking 2000). This level of understanding and depth comes only with continued practice and exposure to an array of aspects about a subject. "We reflect on the world around us by observing, gathering, assembling, and synthesizing information. We develop and use tools to measure and observe as well as to analyze information and create models. We check and recheck what we think will happen and compare results to what we already know. We change our ideas based on what we learn." (NRC 2000, p. 5).

Using the butterfly life cycle as an analogy to the depth of learning in WINGS, what begins as an egg eventually becomes a butterfly, but only after experiencing different stages and changes. WINGS participants shape their knowledge and inquiry ability along a continuum of situations until they take flight on the WINGS of inquiry as butterflies!

Program Description

Nature of the Program

WINGS reaches youths on several different levels. WINGS ushers each participant through a discovery process that supports individual exploration and takes the youth from novice to expert butterfly watcher. On a parallel track, the individual is part of a community of learners who enrich each other's experiences and contribute to citizen science.

A series of cumulative activities, each with an umbrella life skill and science-inquiry skill, culminate in a final activity in which students create a custom research project or investigation on a topic that interests them. Finally, each activity is designed to foster deeper reflection, meaning, and impact. While content is important in WINGS, it primarily is a tool for science inquiry and life skills. The skills combine in a dynamic interplay to equip each participant with rich, life-enhancing experiences they can apply to other areas.

Sample Activities

Explore Your World

The WINGS journey begins with "Explore Your World," an outdoor sensory extravaganza, during which kids experience familiar things in nature in a new way through their senses. The activity encourages curiosity, setting the tone for WINGS. Through guided inquiry, the activity provides a shared experience in the outdoors for all participants that in turn enriches future learning with past knowledge of the encounter.

Here is how it works: An inviting, artistic nature trail illustrated in the project guide prompts participants as they navigate their way through "Explore Your World" outdoors. For example, participants are asked to "First, use your eyes. What do you see?" and list what they see. Then they are asked to "zoom in" to look at detail. The next prompt says, "Pick one thing (you see). Get your eyes close to it to see as much detail as possible." and "Describe what you see." These and additional prompts that include the other senses develop the youths' inquiry abilities through an "open your eyes" approach.

Simple but thoughtful "Reflect and Connect" questions related to the observation-inquiry skill and the self-confidence life skill enhance and deepen the experience. Discussion and journal questions encourage children to reflect inward: "How did you feel about exploring outside? Why is it important to try new things? How do scientists use their senses to help them understand the world around them? What was the most important thing you learned about yourself?" The premise is that increased self-confidence may make kids more willing to try new things. Trying new things strengthens our experience, and thus what we notice and discover about the world around us.

Immediately following "Explore Your World," another outdoor exploration activity takes inquiry further. In "Step Into the World of Butterflies," participants are asked to draw upon past experiences by thinking about places they have seen butterflies. They then visit a site where they think they might find butterflies. They take notes about the site and list three things they predict attract butterflies. After the site visit, children are given guidelines on where to find butterflies in preparation for a visit to a different place. The information aids their decision on where to go next. At the second site, they compare the two sites as part of the science inquiry skill, "comparing."

In the journal, two questions—"How did having butterfly habitat information help you choose the second site?" and "What other times have you researched information to make a better decision?"—manifest the "learning to learn" life skill.

Sort It Out

In addition to outdoor exploration, WINGS provides group activities in the *Leader and Helper Guide* that also combine skills. In "Sort It Out," children work in groups to organize pictures of butterflies into categories, and then defend their categories through a spokesperson. While an uncomplicated and simple activity on its face, multiple layers of skill-building enrich the sorting process.

In particular, "positive relationship skills" is the life skill and "comparing" is the science skill. Participants select a leader from within their group. The leader's job is to make sure everyone contributes and the group comes to a consensus on the categories. The "Reflect and Connect" questions examine the role of the leader as facilitator, "If some of the team members could not agree, how was a decision reached? What was the leader's role in this?" The children also reflect on what makes the decision process difficult in groups. "Sort It Out" is an example of the national science standard that encourages discussion and debate among scientists.

Citizen Science and the WINGS Website

Another group activity in the *Leader and Helper Guide* is the citizen science component of WINGS, in which participants contribute to the ongoing, long-term investigation of butterfly trends through the WINGS website. The tools and skills developed throughout WINGS prepare youths for this effort. The website provides opportunities for data entry and viewing, sharing WINGS experiences through a photo gallery, help with butterfly identification, and learning about butterfly species.

Collectively, the citizen science effort represents a long-term investigation of trends in populations and distribution of common butterflies. Participants learn to identify the most common butterflies in their area using ID sheets they create through the WINGS website (*www.flmnh.ufl. edu/wings*) and through other activities such as "Butterfly Detective," in which youths learn to recognize the six butterfly families. Kids create "Date Lists" of the targeted butterfly species and enter this information in the WINGS database. In addition, 4-H clubs adopt sites for monitoring the abundance of the targeted butterfly species along set pathways or "transects" that the 4-H youths create.

In addition to its importance for data comparisons at the group level, the monitoring exercise is valuable for each individual. The monitoring protocol involves a pair of youths who regularly walk the established transects. With one child the spotter and the other the recorder, they collaborate to record accurate data. Each participant learns about the significance of a scientific protocol and its role in obtaining valid data, and the importance of ethics in science. All of the concepts and skills youths acquire through WINGS present themselves holistically while monitoring transects and entering data. Concurrently the students use a scientific protocol, an important part of the scientific method; their cognitive skills to identify butterflies; their sense of ethics and responsibility with data collection and reporting; and they learn the importance of teamwork as they work together monitoring the sites.

Question Quest

The "Question Quest" research and investigation activity is the culminating WINGS activity. While the stated skills are the scientific method, critical thinking, and communication, Question Quest brings together all of the skills addressed in WINGS.

Introductory text reminds youths that "the questions they choose [to investigate] lead to an exciting adventure." By allowing children to choose their investigation, the leader shares responsibility for learning with the children and the kids exercise critical thinking skills as they decide what to study. Finally, the flexible nature of Question Quest is a design feature that permits accommodations to match the youth's ability, time, and resources.

A WINGS youth records butterflies to make a "Date List" of the species she sees.

The activity begins as the children are asked to "notice things about the world" as the first step in the science-inquiry process. Specifically they are asked to "think about the many observations" they have made and to list what they want to know more about. The project guide provides advice on narrowing a topic and also gives a sample quest.

The example investigation asks the question, "What is the black swallowtail's favorite host plant?" Planters are set up with plants in the family the butterfly uses as its host. Daily observations reveal an answer. Or do they? The black swallowtail laid eggs on dill first, but does that mean dill is the favorite host plant? This example helps children think about reducing variables, replicating investigations, and obtaining defensible data. It also gives youths a reference point from which to conduct their investigation, but does not prescribe the project.

Children also may gain ideas for their Question Quest from the description of a study a master's-level student completed. The study, which involved observation and modification of variables to investigate whether longwing butterflies use sight or smell to find a place to roost, is the subject of a biography in the WINGS Project Guide. The example demonstrates how cognitive, procedural, and manipulation inquiry skills work together concurrently.

At the end of Question Quest, students share the story of their Question Quest with others. Because 4-H emphasizes community service and sharing results through presentations at the club and community level, children are not simply relaying their project to their "teacher" or leader. Students are asked how they can tell the story in a way that's easy for others to understand, and they are given ideas about using drawings, pictures, and graphs. In this way, they are asked to defend their conclusions and explain their findings in clear, interesting, and "user-friendly" ways. Finally, kids are asked to "celebrate their success" by telling friends, teach-

A national, award-winning speech competitor researched butterfly gardening for her Question Quest project.

ers, and even the community via the newspaper. A final "call to action" statement at the very end encourages them to keep exploring: "Remember…The adventure doesn't end here. There's always more to discover about butterflies and all the fascinating creatures that share the Earth."

I've Got Butterflies: Youth Participation in WINGS

A sign of effectiveness for a science education program may be when children are engaged in science, but do not realize they are gaining science-inquiry skills. When asked at a Florida 4-H camp whether he likes the subject of science at school, a youth woefully shook his head "no." But when asked if he likes to observe butterflies, he enthusiastically replied "yes!"

Students begin making observations as they explore their surroundings with their senses in "Explore Your World." Here are some of their observations: "Mulch smells sour," "I was surprised by how stinky the mushroom was," "I was surprised by all the butterflies after that cold night," "I discovered it [observing outdoors] is cool and full of interesting animals and insects." One youth displayed a degree of empathy when he or she commented, "I wonder how the fish feel being in a small pond and not free." Another made good use of adjectives when he or she described a plant: "tan and brown, fluffy, big, soft on end and spiky in the middle."

Other youths share the enthusiasm of discovery as they have completed a range of Question Quest projects, including simple research projects on rare butterflies and butterfly gardening. In particular, one child researched butterfly gardening and shared her newly constructed knowledge with her local 4-H club through speaking competitions. Her winning record culminated in a fourth-place award in a national competition with children older than she.

Assessment

The WINGS program underwent a rigorous formative evaluation and materials refinement process as it developed. The Institute for Learning Innovation (ILI), an Annapolis, Maryland–based nonprofit learning research and development organization, conducted the formative evaluation of the project. ILI conducted focus groups and interviews with 4-H youths, leaders, and agents regarding specific activities and the overall program. In addition, the WINGS authors made

Examing a chrysalis raised from a caterpillar.

in-the-field observations of children and leaders using the program materials and butterfly monitoring methods. Finally, the WINGS national advisory committee conducted a critical appraisal of the WINGS materials and butterfly monitoring methods. Committee members have expertise in citizen science, informal science education, butterfly science and monitoring, and 4-H youth program development. Based on the evaluation findings, participant observations, and advice from program advisors, the authors revised the activities, website, monitoring process, program organization, and reflection questions.

A variety of methods assess participant understanding in WINGS. Throughout the project, the 4-H youth participant has frequent interactions with their project leader. These interactions are opportunities for the leader to monitor the child's progress, and the leader uses multiple methods to evaluate the participant's understanding and skills.

Harlen (1999) describes four main ways to gather assessment information in inquiry settings: observing students engaged in inquiry, asking questions designed to probe reason and understanding, looking closely at the evidence from class work, and setting special tasks or assignments. WINGS includes all of these assessment methods.

Observing

Observing participants while they conduct program activities is an effective way for WINGS leaders to assess progress. The leader monitors how well students understand the program instructions and keeps track of their questions as they do the activity. The leader can observe the extent youths are engaged in the inquiry process and how much guidance they seek from the adult leader. The leader also may observe how the children perform specific skills, such as using a field guide, recording data, and using the WINGS website.

Asking Questions

The "Reflect and Connect" questions at the end of each activity are tools to guide the leader and student discussions. These questions prompt the kids to talk about what they learn as well as their reflections. Some questions are specific to content in the activity, while others include questions prompting kids to think about the broader applications of what they learn or skills they practice. A specific question is, "Why is it important to record a butterfly as unidentified when you don't know what it is?" A broader application question is, "In what other ways can you use problem-solving skills?" (Kessler 2005b).

The Reflect and Connect discussions are examples of "embedded assessment tools," an assessment that occurs within the flow of the activity, to guide the leader (Hein and Price 1994). The leader also can ask impromptu questions at this time to probe other aspects of the youth's experience. The end-of-activity discussions encourage both youth and leader to share their thoughts, thus reinforcing learning. Simply asking children what they learned after an activity can elicit an enthusiastic response. After learning the parts of a butterfly, one youth expressed, "I didn't know that butterflies tasted with their legs... I didn't know that the tip of a wing is an apex... I didn't know that the dots were called margins" (Kessler 2005b). Another youth remarked that Reflect and Connect questions help remind her of what she learned. In response to one of the questions, she said, "Well, like if you saw a certain butterfly and you saw it again, you could like, 'oh, well I just saw that and I know what it is,' and it makes you feel good that you could actually identify it right off the bat" (Kessler 2005a).

Evidence of Work

The WINGS Project Guide is a portfolio of the participant's completed work that can be reviewed at the end of the project, in lieu of a final test. However, there also are other embedded and informal assessment opportunities throughout the project. There are things the children can show to illustrate their progress along the way. The leader may ask to see the youth's website data entries, site descriptions and maps, butterfly monitoring data sheets, journal entries, and notes.

Using scientific terminology to guide the youth, one of the activities in the WINGS Project Guide directs children to color butterflies to reinforce identification of the butterfly. One youth remarked the activity helped her with butterfly identification: "...I colored this in because it was my favorite, the monarch. But the coloring helps me, I'm visual. I think it helps by identifying it. I get the picture stuck in my head" (Kessler 2005a).

Special Tasks and Assignments

There are many ways a leader may assign a special task or assignment in order to assess their students' progress in WINGS. These tasks can be simple and quick, or more challenging and involved. The leader may simply check the youth's butterfly identification skills by asking the child to identify a butterfly and then verify they identified it correctly. Leaders can devise other games or tasks to "spot-test" the youth. One child explained the process of identifying butterflies for the WINGS BINGO game and said, "You had to look carefully at the butterflies, and really know what you were looking at, but everything was right there for you, so you could do it without any problem...It was cool...You actually got to learn something while you were having fun" (Kessler 2005b).

A more involved way to assess understanding is to ask children to share what they learn with others. At the end of the final chapter, the students must figure out how to bring what they have learned into the broader community. To share what was learned, the participant must feel confident in their learning and comfortable with the information to communicate it in a meaningful way. To assist with assessment, the leader may provide other outreach opportunities for the kids.

Future Plans for WINGS

WINGS began its third year in fall 2006, with program implementation throughout the 4-H Southern Region. ILI is conducting the summation evaluation of the project. They are working with 4-H youth and leaders in Florida, North Carolina, Alabama, and Oklahoma to determine program effectiveness in fostering the science inquiry and life skill goals. Of particular interest is the preliminary development of an instrument for use across 4-H science programs to examine and compare effectiveness. The current evaluation is the pilot phase for the instrument development, and it is hoped that future phases of this project will allow further development and testing of the instrument across a variety of 4-H science content programs.

Because of interest in WINGS shown by 4-H agents and leaders in states outside the 4-H Southern Region, a nationwide expansion is planned, pending additional funding. This expansion will include reaching 4-H youth and leaders in new states and adding to the website to make the resources even more comprehensive.

Through a rigorous review process, WINGS has been conditionally accepted as a national 4-H curriculum. Once the minor program modifications suggested by the review committee have been completed and the summative evaluation findings submitted, we anticipate that WINGS will be accepted as a national 4-H curriculum, taking WINGS to new heights!

References

Bonney, R. 2004. Understanding the process of research. In *Creating connections: Museums and the public understanding of current research*, eds. D. Chittenden, G. Farmelo, and B. V. Lewenstein, 199–210. Walnut Creek, CA: AltaMira Press.

Bransford, J., A. Brown, and R. Cocking, eds. 2000. *How people learn: Brain, mind, experience, and school.* Washington, DC: National Academy Press.

Bybee, R. W. 1997. *Achieving science literacy: From purposes to practices.* Portsmouth, NH: Heinemann.

Bybee, R. W. 2001. Achieving scientific literacy: Strategies for insuring that free-choice science education complements national formal science education efforts. In *Free-choice science education: How we learn science outside of school*, ed. J. Falk, 44–63. New York: Teachers College Press.

Bybee, R. W. 2002. Scientific inquiry, student learning, and the science curriculum. In *Learning science and the science of learning*, ed. R. W. Bybee, 25–35. Arlington, VA: NSTA Press.

Evans, C. A., E. D. Abrams, N. R. Barrett, and S. L. Spencer. 2001. Student/scientist partnerships: A teachers' guide to evaluating the critical components. *The American Biology Teacher* 63 (5): 318–323.

Falk, J. H. 2001. Free-choice science learning: Framing the discussion. In *Free-choice science education: How we learn science outside of school*, ed. J. Falk, 3–20. New York: Teachers College Press.

Falk, J. H., and L. D. Dierking. 2000. *Learning from museums: Visitor experiences and the making of meaning.* Walnut Creek, CA: AltaMira Press.

Farmelo, G. 2004. Only connect: Linking the public with current scientific research. In *Creating Connections: Museums and the Public Understanding of Current Research*, eds. D. Chittenden, G. Farmelo, and B. V. Lewenstein, 1–26. Walnut Creek, CA: AltaMira Press.

Harlen, W. 1999. Assessment in the inquiry classroom. In *Inquiry: Thoughts, views, and strategies for the K–5 classroom*, 87–97. Arlington, VA: National Science Foundation.

Hein, G. E., and S. Price. 1994. *Active assessment for active science: A guide for elementary school teachers.* Portsmouth, NH: Heinemann.

Hurd, P. D. 2000. *Transforming middle school science education.* New York: Teachers College Press.

Kessler, C. 2005a. *Project Butterfly WINGS focus group interview transcripts.* Annapolis, MD: Institute for Learning Innovation.

Kessler, C. 2005b. *Project Butterfly WINGS: Winning investigative network for great science: Year 2 final report.* Annapolis, MD: Institute for Learning Innovation.

Krasny, M. E. and R. Bonney. 2005. Environmental education through citizen science and participatory action research. In *Environmental education and advocacy: Changing perspectives of ecology and education,* eds. E. Johnson and M. Mappin, 292–319. Cambridge, UK: Cambridge University Press.

Mestre, J. P., and R. R. Cocking. 2002. Applying the science of learning to the education of prospective science teachers. In *Learning science and the science of learning,* ed. R. W. Bybee, 13–22. Arlington, VA: NSTA Press.

National Research Council (NRC). 1996. *National science education standards.* Washington, DC: National Academy Press.

National Research Council (NRC). 2000. *Inquiry and the national science education standards: A guide for teaching and learning.* Washington, DC: National Academy Press.

Pfiffer, J. W., and J. E. Jones. 1979. An experiential model. In *The reference guide to handbooks annuals, Vol I–VII, 1972–1979,* 3–4. San Diego, CA: University Associates and Consultants.

Trumbull, D. J., R. Bonney, D. Bascom, and A. Cabral. 2000. Thinking scientifically during participation in a Citizen-Science project. *Science Education* 84 (2): 265–275.

Knowledge and Wonder:

Engagements With Light and Color
in the Hands-On Optics Project

Stephen M. Pompea, Constance E. Walker, and Robert T. Sparks
National Optical Astronomy Observatory

This chapter describes how the *More Emphasis* conditions of the National Science Education Standards (NRC 1996) have influenced our informal optics education project for middle school–aged children. At first glance, it may seem odd that the changing emphases, which were largely motivated by the conditions of the formal education system, should be so strongly applicable to an informal education program such as ours. However, it should not be surprising since the exploratory nature of high-quality informal education programs are in many ways parallel, congruent, and even extensions of the changing emphases. Informal and formal science education also have the common starting point of developing an understanding of the best educational research on a concept of interest to facilitate the development of instructional materials. Similarly, they share a commitment to and reliance upon high-quality professional development. Thus the effect of changing emphases on middle school science projects (Yager 2006) has many parallels to our informal project seeks to expose middle school–aged children to optics and optical technology.

The project's instructional materials and its professional development programs were designed for a number of primary settings. One is the after-school setting of achievement programs often offered in school buildings and run by teachers, but occurring apart from the school day and school requirements. Examples of this setting are MESA (Math Engineering Science Achievement) after-school programs ubiquitous in most of the western states. A second setting is in science centers of all sizes, with our program offered in a variety of ways. Science center programs range from optics camps, to enrichment programs, to programs done in conjunction with schools. The professional development program we have designed for science center educators is different from that for MESA science and math teacher educators. We have also established the program in two Boys and Girls clubs for the past year, and are planning to expand to other sites in Arizona.

Table 1. Summary of Hands-On Optics Settings

MESA After-School Math and Science Programs	Boys and Girls Clubs	Larger Science Centers	Small Science & Nature Centers (selected)
California, Washington, Oregon, Colorado, New Mexico, Arizona, and Maryland [after-school "classes," statewide competitions, career activities]	Cities of South Tucson and Sells Arizona on the Tohono O'odham Nation [A year-round program using all six modules plus additional activities for younger kids on optical illusions, cameras, stereo vision, magnifiers]	Orlando Science Center, New York Hall of Science, Chabot Space and Science Center, 'Imiloa Astronomy Center of Hawai`i, Adventure Science Center, California Science Center [optics camps, special programs, festivals, competitions]	Padre Island National Seashore (Corpus Christi), Nature Discovery Center (Bellaire, Texas), Mountains Recreation & Conservation Authority (Pacific Palisades, California), Santa Barbara Museum of Natural History, Explorit Science Center (Davis, California) [nature camps, outdoor activities, optics camps, special programs, festivals, competitions]

Summary of Key Standards Addressed

An area of particular interest to our project is how to create "active, prolonged engagement" (Humphrey and Gutwill 2005), a term often applied to museum exhibits. We believe the same can be achieved in an informal program setting through the proper mix of activities and explorations. Indeed, the emphases are particularly relevant for achieving active, prolonged engagement. This chapter will explore how the emphases work in four general areas—the development of high-quality instructional materials for prolonged engagement, teaching for prolonged inquiry, professional development for prolonged engagement, and the role of authentic assessment in informal programs designed for active, prolonged engagement.

Free-choice science education often consists of learning activities performed in small groups that are voluntary and that encourage exploration and curiosity. If these activities are successful, an experiential basis (and motivation) for further learning in this topic area will occur. *Hands-On*

Optics: Making an Impact With Light, funded by NSF Informal Science Education, is designed to reach middle school–aged children in after-school settings and in science centers. It blends science, mathematics, and technology with the goals of not only helping these children achieve a better understanding of basic optics concepts, science process, and knowledge of optics career opportunities, but also to encourage a sense of wonder that can stimulate additional exploration.

The value of this combination of knowledge and wonder that lies at the heart of our project was perhaps best expressed by Francis Bacon: "…for all knowledge and wonder (which is the seed of knowledge) is an impression of pleasure in itself …."

The Hands-On Optics (HOO) project has three interesting, though not unique, programmatic aspects. HOO represents a working model (with many lessons learned) of how two professional optics societies focused on graduate and undergraduate education can work cooperatively with a research observatory experienced in K–12 science education. HOO also provides a model of an after-school program that is used extensively by the same teachers in their formal education classrooms. Finally, HOO provides a well-organized, flexible plan of professional development and ongoing support for the HOO modules as well as for special high-visibility public events (e.g. festivals).

The Hands-On Optics project particularly values and applies the following areas of *More Emphasis* from the National Science Education Standards.

The Key Teaching Standards:
- More emphasis on guiding students in active and extended scientific inquiry

Key Professional Development Standards:
- More emphasis on learning science through investigation and inquiry
- More emphasis on collegial and collaborative learning

Key Assessment Standards:
- More emphasis on students engaged in ongoing assessment of their work and that of others

Key Content and Inquiry Standards:
- More emphasis on investigations over extended periods of time
- More emphasis on process skills in context
- More emphasis on using multiple process skills-manipulation, cognitive, procedural
- More emphasis on studying a few fundamental science concepts

Key Program Standards:
- More emphasis on connecting science to other school subjects such as mathematics and social studies

These *More Emphasis* areas will be described later in this chapter in the context of how we try to achieve our general goal of active prolonged engagement by the children with optical phenomena and tools.

The specific National Science Education Standards (NRC 1996), grades 5–8, supported by our modules include:

- Evidence consists of observations and data on which to base scientific explanations. Using evidence to understand interactions allows individuals to predict changes in natural and designed systems (Unifying Concepts and Processes, p. 117).
- Use appropriate tools and techniques to gather, analyze, and interpret data (Standard A—Inquiry, p. 145).
- Develop descriptions, explanations, predictions, and models using evidence (Standard A—Inquiry, p. 145).
- Think critically and logically to make the relationships between evidence and explanations (Standard A—Inquiry, p. 145).
- Communicate scientific procedures and explanations (Standard A—Inquiry, p. 148).
- Use mathematics in all aspects of scientific inquiry (Standard A—Inquiry, p. 148).
- Light interacts with matter by transmission (including refraction), absorption, or scattering (including reflection). To see an object, light from that object— emitted by or scattered from it— must enter the eye (Standard B—Physical Science, p. 155).
- Design a solution or product (Standard E—Science and Technology, p. 165).
- Implement a proposed design (Standard E—Science and Technology, p. 165).

The specific mathematics and technology standards supported by our modules are given in this chapter's appendix.

Project Motivation and Programmatic Structure

The field of optics crosscuts many areas of science and engineering. Optics and optical technology are keys to many technical areas and fuel innovations in many fields such as astronomy, biology, materials science, and electrical engineering. However, these innovations are largely hidden in these larger fields. Optics education also cuts across many of the large themes and subject matter areas in science education. Similarly, optics education rarely appears in the curriculum in an obvious manner (such as a course named "Optics") until junior- or senior-level physics or perhaps even graduate school. The examination of light and color is enormously appealing to kids of all ages, making it a valuable entry path into science for kids, and the study of optical phenomena provides very solid ground for further studies in physical science.

To address this need for greater and more direct exposure of students to optical phenomena, the National Optical Astronomy Observatory (NOAO) and the two major optics professional societies—The International Society for Optical Engineering (SPIE) and The Optical Society of America (OSA) teamed together to create an optics education program for middle-school aged students. OSA and SPIE each have over 15,000 members worldwide and recognized the need for professional societies to "feed the pipeline" by encouraging an interest in optics by children as well as to support their members' needs for graduate and professional education. A careful study under an NSF planning grant of how such a program might be delivered to a nationwide audience led us to design a program for an informal audience to be delivered through science center and after-school programs. NOAO has designed the materials and kits and is providing the professional development for the informal science educators. The optics professional societies have concentrated on providing a cadre of volunteers from their societies who can work with these informal educators. The project has created an integrated professional development program that works with both educators and optics industry volunteers (which we call Optics Resource volunteers) together to effectively use the six kits we have developed.

The Hands-On Optics project is a four-year informal science program designed to bring the excitement of light, color, and optics technology to tens of thousands of underserved middle school–aged students nationwide. One part of our audience is reached through the Math Engineering Science Achievement (MESA) after-school program, which is in eight western states and Maryland. HOO is also being delivered to a different informal audience via science center nationwide and other after-school programs such as the Boys and Girls Clubs. The program provides exemplary, national standards–based materials coupled with high-quality professional development and support, in order to create a long-term enrichment program for students. The MESA-oriented component of the program has focused on reaching underserved groups—primarily Latino students in the western states. The science center partners in the program are spread across the country.

Now entering its fourth year, the HOO project (Pompea et al. 2005) has developed six hands-on activity modules intended to engage and enrich the math/science learning experience for students in the middle grades. Each module offers six to seven hours of exploratory science activities that can be grouped into 30- to 90-minute sessions. Thus the collection of the six HOO modules can be used for a full week of camp programs. Additional components of the program extend this experience to greater depth through telescope building competitions and other extended activities. When all components of the program are used, children are engaged in the discovery and use of optical phenomena and equipment for upwards of 70 hours, providing an extended engagement with optics.

Context of the Project Development

To produce such an extended engagement program, the National Optical Astronomy Observatory (NOAO) has relied on its experience in creating shorter programs. NOAO, headquartered in Tucson, Arizona, was founded in 1958 under the sponsorship of the National Science Foundation to provide state-of-the-art astronomical telescopes and instruments to astronomers. A key element of NOAO's mission is to provide national leadership in astronomy (and related physical science) education for all educational audiences. NOAO is a developer of informal science education programs and exhibits, innovative programs for teacher professional development, programs promoting authentic research by teachers and students, and in particular of high-quality, nationally tested instructional materials in different media.

The Kitt Peak Visitor Center, a small science center and ASTC member, has an extremely active night observing program for the public and for amateur astronomers from all over the world. NOAO also supports a small astronomical education center in La Serena, Chile, near its southern hemisphere telescopes: The Centro de Apoyo a la Didáctica de la Astronomía (CADIAS), which has vigorous education programs in observational astronomy, light pollution education, and

The Visitor Center at Kitt Peak National Observatory near Tucson: one venue for the Hands-On Optics program.

trains many of the educators and guides at public observatories in northern Chile. NOAO is also active in finding, evaluating, and distributing Spanish language physical science education materials. The NOAO science education staff members in Tucson are particularly qualified at creating programs teaching the technology of astronomy such as optics because all of its core education staff members have advanced degrees in astronomy or physics and a mix of teaching experience in formal and informal settings at pre-K to university level.

The Kitt Peak Visitor center represents a typical small science center site for Hands-On Optics. All of the activities can be done using any floor (concrete, linoleum, carpet) as an optical "bench" or cafeteria tables. A typical setup space for 30 kids needs to be about the size of a regular classroom or can be a hallway of the same area.

Hands-On Optics Program Goals

The HOO program has, and has achieved, the following programmatic general goals established by the three partners:

- **Goal 1**: To create links between the professional optics community and the informal science education community.

  Approach: The project partners have established strong linkages with Association of Science Technology Centers, other informal programs and institutions, and after-school programs such as MESA and Boys and Girls Clubs. Objective measures such as meetings attended, workshops given and attended, and presentations and talks given show strong involvement of the partners with the informal science community.

- **Goal 2**: To reach underrepresented middle school–age students with informal material about optical science and technology.

  Approach: Through careful partnering, the project is reaching our target audience. Evaluation shows that our target audience is being reached in the numbers desired to make a national impact.

- **Goal 3**: To provide opportunities for the underrepresented youth to succeed in collaborative learning and problem solving through inquiry-based, hands-on applications of optical and engineering skills and knowledge.

  Approach: Design materials and activities that emphasize problem-solving and collaborative learning. Measurement of our level of success in teaching and implementing problem-solving tasks are not yet available, but are being measured in our program year four.

- **Goal 4**: To increase science and technology knowledge for students, and to increase awareness of optics as a discipline and career that crosscuts numerous fields.
  Approach: Provide an extended learning opportunity for a large number of students and create and distribute career education materials. Provide optics industry volunteers to work with educators. Our evaluations show success in these volunteer and career areas. Evaluation of student content knowledge shows very significant gains but these date are interview-based. There are no projectwide pretest/posttest score results available yet.

Goal 4 is related to our professional development program for the project. The project has placed an emphasis on high-quality professional development of all educators using the Hands-On Optics materials. This translates to a minimum of two days for the professional development of the educator with the optics industry volunteer, with the training utilizing a variety of approaches to build pedagogical content knowledge and facility with the kit activities and investigations.

High-quality professional development serves to build the knowledge base and confidence of the educators delivering the program. The higher the knowledge base and confidence of the educators, the richer the experience is for the student, and the greater chance of sensible gains in the student's content knowledge. An evaluation of knowledge gains by educators from the training is given later. Educators have been extremely pleased with the two-day professional development experience in their evaluation sheets submitted after the training and in follow-up interview with the evaluator.

Changing the Emphasis in Science Education

Overview

The *More Emphasis* areas most applicable to the program can be examined in the light of the whole program in this section. Of particular emphasis is how the program supports guiding students in active and extended scientific inquiry, which will be one theme that carries through the program description. Another key theme is how the use of the Optics Resource volunteers reinforces the key professional development standard of more emphasis on collegial and collaborative learning. The program supports students engaged in ongoing assessment of their work and that of other students. In the area of content and inquiry standards, the program emphasizes an array of process skills, placed in the context of experimentation. The six modules in our program cover relatively few science concepts. The science of optics is also connected to basic mathematics areas useful in optics, such as measuring angles, and even simple explanations of Fermat's principle are used to illustrate the paths of light rays.

Program Description

The Hands-On Optics program consists of six modules, each dealing with a different area of light and color phenomena or optics technology. Each optics area has been chosen for its inherent interest to students at this age, its relevance to key science concepts, and its significance to core areas of optics or optical engineering.

The HOO core program is built around six learning modules. Each module features a series of fun and challenging activities designed to get students interested in science, math, and technology through optics and photonics. The program is targeted to middle school and younger students. We want to reach students when they are forming their attitudes about science and technical careers. However, program elements are adaptable and can be used successfully with students as early as fourth grade and even throughout high school.

An important feature of Hands-On Optics is that it pairs educators with optics resource volunteers from the academic and corporate communities. Educators receive a complete set of materials—all the equipment and supplies they need to run the program for 20 to 30 students. The first cohort of HOO educators reached more than 7,000 students and a larger number have been reached through the second cohort.

Each module write-up has been tied to science content standards, has a strong inquiry-based approach, and has open-ended components for student investigations. Small-group work is emphasized in each module. The modules are flexible in the ways they can be used with different groups or in different settings. For example, the modules have recently been adapted by the NOAO group to serve a younger audience at Boys and Girls Clubs in the city of South Tucson and in Sells, on the Tohono O'odham Nation, an hour-and-a-half drive from Tucson.

The HOO program most strongly addresses the need for changing emphasis in science education programs through its efforts to create a set of long-term investigations in optics that provide depth in an informal atmosphere. This effort to create a prolonged engagement with optics phenomena builds on all of the changing emphases listed earlier. The teacher and Optics Resource volunteer work together to achieve a comfort level in using the modules. The volunteer is a valuable resource for educators with a weaker physical science background and he or she also serves as a role model and career counselor. In the professional development workshops the volunteer is trained on how to be successful in the educational settings, and each volunteer receives a "how to" guide built on the highly successful Project ASTRO program partnership guide created by the Astronomical Society of the Pacific. The HOO program builds on this previous work on best practices in professional development work for educator/volunteer partnerships.

A key issue for the program was how to strengthen knowledge of key optics concepts in an informal setting. We wanted the sequence of the modules to build on knowledge of and the educational research on how kids view the nature and behavior of light. If the material in the modules did not reflect this understanding, it would be likely that this informal experience might reinforce naïve theories or misconceptions in a way that would be difficult to alter in a later formal education setting. Thus great care went into understanding what research and practice say about children's ideas on light and color.

Building on Studies of Concept Development

In the area of instructional materials, the HOO materials are based on previous efforts at creating inquiry-based materials that explore the electromagnetic spectrum (Pompea and Gould 2003; Pompea and Gek 2002), and on a survey of topics appropriate for formal optics education (Pompea and Stepp 1995) and for informal education programs (Pompea and Hawkins 2002). The program works to instill a sensible conceptual foundation for a limited number of optics concepts. The professional development work for the volunteers was based on previous work by Hall-Wallace, Regens, and Pompea (2002) on how optics professionals could work more effectively in multi-cultural settings—an area with great applicability to industry volunteers working in the very different culture of science centers or after-school programs.

The activities have been built with an understanding of the naïve concepts many children (and adults) have about light, color, or optical phenomena. Our own experience is that the concepts that children and adults have of light are often not that different. For example, most

Experiments with reflection from multiple mirrors and an understanding of symmetry are an important part of Module 2 and a preparation for construction of kaleidoscopes.

people understand the concept of a light source, that it may be an effect, but do not understand that light is an entity (like a wave) (Guesne 1985). Indeed there is some confusion of "light," the physical entity that scientist talk about, with "light," the fixture and source. Light paths and rays are also not well understood (Ramadas and Driver 1989). Many people view seeing as an active process, as if the eye is the source as well as a detector of light. There is a basic misunderstanding of shadows and even where they appear. The formation of images by plane mirrors and their location is only poorly understood (Goldberg and McDermott 1986). There is also a very poor understanding of how filters work in blocking or transmitting specific colors of light (Zylbersztajn and Watts 1982; Watts 1985). Finally, materials such as mirrors are considered reflective, while more diffusely reflecting materials are not. Other related studies on perceptions of optics were done by Anderson and Smith (1986) and Andersson and Karrqvist (1983). These studies led us to focus first in the first two modules on reflection from plane mirrors (but not image formation) and in the third module on image formation and position, as formed by lens and curved mirrors. Then we experiment with the applications of polarization, phenomena related to ultraviolet and infrared light, and with how light can be used in communication. Our testing indicates that this sequence and level is appropriate. We also include as a reference book for the educator *Light: Stop Faking It!* from NSTA Press (Robertson 2003).

Inquiry Activities

The Hands-On Optics program is designed to provide an in-depth approach through the use of numerous discrete activities organized into six larger modules. Each module provides an average of 6.5 hours of activities and instruction, with additional time that can be devoted to "going further" activities. Additionally, each module can lead to open-ended activities and long-term investigations, since the optical equipment and materials in each module are quite extensive and of high quality.

The modules are investigational in nature. We try to provoke discussion and disagreement. Learning groups do experience "creative abrasion." In Module 5, on ultraviolet and infrared light, students can pursue many different investigations using a passive infrared thermometer, which can measure the temperature of an object without touching it. For example, the temperature of different animals and different kinds of lights (incandescent and fluorescent) can be accurately measured at a short distance, and safely.

We include the fascinating Leslie's Cube in the kit for Module 5. It is a hollow cube that can be filled with hot water. Each side of the cube has a different finish such as bare metal, diffuse black, specular black, or diffuse white. These surfaces all register different temperatures even though they are at the same temperature, allowing an exploration of the emissivity properties of the materials: how efficiently a surface radiates infrared radiation. This provokes discussion, and even optics professionals aren't able to predict which surfaces will appear hotter or colder. In module 3, the different lenses and mirrors provided allow an investigation of image formation in a wide variety of telescopic and microscopic optical system arrangements.

The materials in the kits are durable. To choose red lasers for the modules we conducted repeated drop tests on concrete floors from chest height to identify the survivors. The kits contain everything needed to conduct the activities, down to the level of rubber bands. The kits have few expendables to keep kit refurbishment costs to a minimum. In most cases, there are redundant pieces of equipment, to account for some level of failure or breakage after many uses. Batteries *are* included.

Table 2 below gives a short description of the HOO modules, key concepts, and authentic assessment activities.

Table 2. Summary of Hands-On Optics Modules and Authentic Assessments

Module Title Key Science/Engineering Concepts	Sample Activities	Primary (Culminating) Authentic Assessment Activities
(1) *Laser Challenges* • Laser safety • Law of reflection: angle of incidence equals angle of reflection • Reflection off of a plane mirror • Specular and diffuse reflection-similarities and differences • Reflection from a micro-rough diffusely reflecting surface as simple reflection from multifaceted surfaces	• Measuring angles using protractors • Tracing rays using string. Viewing reflection in milky water to trace angles • Ray tracing from source to detector and vice-versa • Focal point of a flat mirrors place on a curve • Focal point and rays tracing for curved mirror surface using Mylar	• "Hit the Target" challenge. Challenge is to position two mirrors and a laser using protractors, string, and other tools available to hit a small stationary target, without turning on the laser

Module Title Key Science/Engineering Concepts	Sample Activities	Primary (Culminating) Authentic Assessment Activities
(2) *Kaleidoscope Adventures* • Reflection off of multiple plane surfaces • Symmetry of objects • Principles behind the simple kaleidoscope • Principles behind the periscope	• "Titanium Dioxide symmetry paradox • Ray tracing • Symmetry and the alphabet • Experiments with nearly parallel mirrors • Hinged mirror experiments • Building a kaleidoscope • Periscopes and mirror rotation	• Construction, use, and understanding of kaleidoscopes • Using teleidoscopes, which have an open view of the world (no beads)
(3) *Magnificent Magnifications* • Formation of images using lenses and curved mirrors • Focal length of lenses • Focal length of curved mirrors • Concepts of magnification and resolution • Concave versus convex mirrors	• Lasers and light as seen through acrylic blocks • Finding the focal length of a lens • Magnification of different lenses • Forming images with lenses • Arranging lenses to build a refracting telescope • Three lens systems for upright image • Measuring telescope resolution • Using Fresnel lenses • Forming images with mirrors	• Construction of a simple refracting telescope similar to Galileo's and measurement of its resolution and magnification • Proper use of this telescope
(4) *Peculiar Polarizations* • Waves and linearly polarized light • Polarization by reflection • Polarized sunglasses and how they work • Polarized light and corn syrup • Polarization and stress testing of plastic forms • Polarization of skylight • 3-D images using filters and using polarization	• Using springs and waves to demonstrate polarization • Polarization through low-angle reflection • Producing colors through optically active materials such as corn syrup • Using polarizing materials and polarizers to construct artwork of different colors • Using polarizers to observe stress in plastic materials • Viewing 3-D images	• Construction of a colored window using layers of birefringent material • Testing for stress in common materials using polarization

Module Title Key Science/Engineering Concepts	Sample Activities	Primary (Culminating) Authentic Assessment Activities
(5) *Ultraviolet and Infrared Light* • Understanding waves, wavelength, and amplitude • Electromagnetic spectrum • Effects of ultraviolet light • Detection of infrared light • Differences among luminescence, fluorescence, and phosphorescence	• Large number of experiments using phosphorescent, luminescent, and fluorescent materials • Experiments with ultraviolet-sensitive beads • Using a passive infrared thermometer • Use of infrared thermometer and Leslie's Cube	• Numerous embedded assessments • Experiments with Leslie's Cube • Identification of minerals using its fluorescent signature
(6) *Communicating Over a Beam of Light* • Encoding of information • Laser light and the concept of coherence • Coding of information, Morse code • Laser transmission of information • Fiber optics	• Construction of a laser transmission system for voice communication • Use of fiber optics for information transmission	• Students are challenged to communicate by laser over the largest distance using combination of lenses and mirrors • Students can apply all previous modules and equipment in all previous modules. Culminating module

Many of the modules have open-ended challenges that are used as a form of authentic assessment as well as an opportunity for further investigations. In Module 6, *Communicating Over a Beam of Light*, students investigate ways to extend the distance at which they can send their voice over a laser communication system. The use of mirrors, lens, and optical fibers all support more extended investigations. The students can also investigate how well the system works with room lights on, outside in sunlight, and with filters. This module provides an opportunity to experiment with all of the previous equipment (e.g., polarizers and filters) and principles.

Thus the design of the modules serves to extend the engagement

Some of the polarization demonstration and experimental materials used in Module 4. Corn syrup is used for experiments on producing colors from the optical activity of the syrup.

period for the students. The 40 hours of the six modules makes an ideal one- or two-week optics camp. We are also committed to extending the engagement period through several other activities. The students can try to solve the monthly optics puzzler, a web-based puzzle based on some area of optics that is on our website. Students can submit their answers and win a prize. Often, experimentation is necessary to find the answers. Another successful strategy we have used to extend the program is the use of optics competitions.

South Tucson Boys and Girls Club kids exploring reflections from mirrors.

Optics Competitions

Informal education activities can benefit through the application of strategies to extend the engagement time. A number of strategies that are used for creating active prolonged engagement exhibits are applicable to programs (Humphrey and Gutwill 2005; Pompea et al. 2005). These activities also provide a capstone to the modules.

The use of optics competitions is another element in prolonging the engagement period with the optics materials. In Arizona, the project has sponsored a statewide MESA program–based competition for four years. In the first three years teams from southern Arizona built simple Newtonian-design reflecting telescopes using a piece of 2 × 4 wood, a long focal-length spherical mirror, and a simple plane mirror. The judging was based on how well one could see through the telescope when looking at a resolution target across the room. In order to construct the telescope, students had to determine the focal length of the mirror and of the eyepiece and position the parts at the appropriate locations. How well the image appeared was determined by the quality of the students' measurements of focal length. The judges were judging the end-to-end optical system performance as well as assessing the core knowledge of the team of 3–4 students. This assessment of end result was in contrast to many such competitions where models are judged more by their looks rather than by their functionality.

In spring 2006, 27 MESA program schools participated (16 middle schools and 11 high schools). During check-in, the students filled out short questionnaires about their preparation for the event. From this questionnaire we found that an average of 3–4 students and 1–2 teachers worked on each telescope. They spent an average of 16 hours each on the telescopes, with one school working an estimated 50 hours. The purpose of this event is to give students a goal that encourages long-term experimentation in optics. In addition to the assessment of the performance of the student teams, student outcome data is also gathered informally by the judges and in postcompetition interviews with teachers and students.

The HOO program also sponsors Tucson citywide events. A citywide Optics Fest had students from 25 fourth- and fifth-grade teams from various schools compete in a "Hit the Target" competition where students attempted to apply the law of reflection to hit a target by reflecting the laser off of mirrors. While the students were waiting for their turn to compete, they participated in optics activities that illustrated concepts such as polarization, multiple reflections and kaleidoscopes, ultraviolet light, communicating over a light beam, and optical illusions in stations spread over the whole gymnasium. The event is held every year. No formal student assessment is done for the station activities but the attainment of the skills needed for the competition are recorded.

Short-Term Engagements and Festivals

The Hands-On Optics program is also used in larger informal settings to create interest in optics that can be translated later into longer-term programs. FunFest is an event that occurs in conjunction with the Southern Arizona Regional Science and Engineering Fair and is attended by many Tucson families. During the March 2006 FunFest, NOAO sponsored four sessions, each on a different Hands-On Optics (HOO) theme. Between

Experiments with lenses and image formation on a vellum target.

the four sessions ("Essence of Luminescence," "Hit the Target," "Kaleidoscopes," and "Telescopes"), we had 1,700 students and 400 adults participating over the three days of just this one event. This type of program builds visibility and interest in our much longer-term program. HOO has also sponsored similar activities at science and research centers at nearly all of the HOO sites. The effectiveness of these activities in this setting on children's learning has not been evaluated. We are attempting to remedy this through a greater emphasis in the project's last year on evaluating student learning and activity effectiveness.

Evidence for Success: Assessment and Program Effectiveness

A number of cases where success is evident have been previously described. In this section, we will concentrate on a few areas: professional development, the use of the modules as a series of extended investigations, the role of the volunteers, and the modes of use of the program by science centers.

Effectiveness of Professional Development

One goal of HOO is to give teachers an effective professional development experience in optics education, in conjunction with the optics volunteers. The Hands-On Optics project has prepared 83 teachers in its first cohort and is in the process this year of training many of these teachers on the second set of modules. The project has also prepared educators at our seven science center sites. Over 25 professional development workshops have been organized by the project in the last two years. Most of these were two days in duration.

The program is also sponsoring shorter-term professional development on Module 3 (image formation and constructing telescopes) to an additional 80 educators per year at small science and nature centers through the NSF-sponsored *Astronomy from the Ground Up* professional development project for science center educators.

HOO is being used by after-school teachers in Math Engineering Science Achievement (MESA) programs in the states of California, Washington, Oregon, Colorado, New Mexico, Arizona, and Maryland. Professional development workshops are held over two days and each after-school MESA program teacher is trained in unison with an optics industry volunteer serving as the teacher's partner. The optics industry volunteers are geographically co-located with the teachers through matches created by the Optical Society of America (Washington DC) or by SPIE—the International Society for Optical Engineers (Bellingham, Washington). Teachers are assisted by a team consisting of two or more NOAO science education staff members. The professional development leaders have experience both as classroom teachers and in informal science settings.

For our initial instruction of cadre, the use of the modules after training has been adequate. The educators receive each module only after completing the previous one. This provides an impetus to use the modules, but it also helps to reduce the number of kits residing in locations where they cannot or will not be used. Table 3 below indicates the attrition rate from instruction to the use of Module 3 over a one-year period where educators were trained in the late summer and their module use was evaluated in May. Some of the educators will be using the kits after this reporting period but ran out of time to use them in their after-school program during this school year.

Table 3. Use of modules by after school educators in Cohort 1, showing attrition between workshop and use of first three modules.

State	Educators Trained	Number of After-School Groups With Completed Modules		
		Module 1	Module 2	Module 3
Arizona	21	18	17	16
California	30	26	24	22
Colorado	17	16	15	14
Maryland	8	5	4	4
Oregon	3	3	2	2
Washington	4	4	4	4
Total	**83**	**72**	**66**	**62**

Our NSF project evaluator has measured educator concept and knowledge development as a result of our two-day workshop, where educators used the kits, explored the concepts, and worked with their volunteers. The educators have made very significant gains in optics knowledge as exhibited by pretest and posttest results related to our professional development workshop, using instruments devised by our evaluator (Table 4, p. 62).

Table 4. Assessment of participant knowledge before and after professional development for Modules 4, 5, and 6 at five sites.

Site (Number of Educators)	Pretest Mean*	Posttest Mean*	Percent gain
Cal Science Center (11)	62	81	31
Lawrence Livermore (12)	59	75	27
Tucson (18)	62	75	21
Longmont (15)	71	88	24
Maryland (15)	61	80	28
Overall (71)	63	80	26

* Percent correct

Student Outcomes

Student outcomes were originally evaluated by level of engagement, time spent on the modules, attendance percentages (for free-choice programs) in extended program covering all of the modules, and completion rate. Of particular value was an assessment of the completion of specific assessment tasks associated with each module, and performance on authentic assessment tasks used as culminating activities for each module or section of each module. Reported outcomes were high in each area, but there was no normative comparison done with regard to other programs. Quantitative assessment of student content knowledge before and after using the materials was not a key part of the original NSF project assessment plan. To acquire more content knowledge assessment data, a science education PhD candidate was hired to evaluate the ongoing HOO programs at the Boys and Girls Clubs in Tucson and in Sells, Arizona. This evaluation is still in progress. A similar effort to quantify knowledge and skill attainment using a more detailed analysis of the authentic assessment activities is also underway by our NSF evaluator.

The use of objective student outcome assessment has not generally been used at NOAO in our education programs. For example, in our program on student astronomical research, student outcomes are reported as number of science papers published in our student research journal, in peer-reviewed professional journals, as telescope time awarded by peer-review committees, and by science fair success. There has been little effort to assess science concept knowledge across the target student audience since this was not funded as part of the original program proposal. Instead we rely on higher-level indicators of success correlated with successful acquisition of content knowledge, science process knowledge, and performance of productive small group research work. Similarly in the HOO project we have relied more on these "meta-indicators" of success and only more recently have we attempted to measure specifically more individual impacts sampled across the target population. In future projects there will be a greater emphasis on collecting student outcome data, as it has proven to be invaluable in demonstrating program success and in specific formative evaluation–driven project decisions.

The Optics Modules and Their Use

The program set a target goal of having our audience consist of 75% underserved students. So far the program is serving an audience of which 72% are from underserved groups. We expect to reach our target as several of our sites that have come online recently have a large percentage of kids who match our target audience.

The usage of the six modules has averaged about 6.5 hours per module, though some teachers have created more extensive programs around the modules. The distribution of usage is given below. Not all of the activities in each module are done in each program. Although the modules are designed for middle school, a significant number of educators are using them at lower- or higher-grade levels.

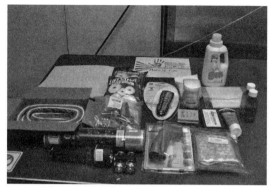

Some of the materials for glow-in-the-dark experiments in Module 4. Chemiluminescence, phosphorescence, triboluminescence and fluorescence are explored.

The learning goals for each module reflect a few fundamental concepts in optics. Each goal is achieved through investigations and experimentation conducted through small group work. Each module has an authentic assessment built in as culminating activity or set of activities. These three points make the HOO modules highly congruent with the *More Emphasis* conditions discussed earlier. Each module has the following general format:

- Module Overview, Summary of Module Activities, Safety Information if Needed
- Learning Goals, Standards, and Assessment
- Activities
- Materials Master List, Handout, Signs, Stations Directions, Completion Certificates
- More Background for the Interested Educator, Common Misconceptions About Light, Glossary
- Reproducible Materials, Templates

Table 5. Average number of hours devoted per student to Modules 1, 2, and 3 in programs delivered by MESA after-school educators. Not all activities of each module are used, but each module is used an average of about 6.5 hours.

State	Module 1		Module 2		Module 3		Overall Hours/ Student
	Students	Hrs*	Students	Hrs*	Students	Hrs*	
Arizona	903	5.3	704	7.6	614	4.0	13.9
California	1032	6.9	765	5.9	692	6.0	15.3
Colorado	600	5.3	508	4.6	332	6.6	12.8
Maryland	215	5.3	93	4.7	46	4.8	8.4
Oregon	71	2.2	125	5.0	120	4.5	10.7
Washington	158	15.9	155	14.3	125	23.6	48.6
Total	2979	6.3	2,350	6.6	1,929	6.7	15.0

* Average hours per student

Table 6. MESA Distribution of Implementation Grade Level for Cohort 2, Modules 1 and 3, by State

State	Elementary		Middle School		High School		Total	
	Mod 1	Mod 3	Mod 1	Mod 3	Mod 1	Mod 3	Mod 1	Mod 3
Arizona	0	0	5	8	6	4	11	12
California	4	3	19	15	0	0	23	18
Colorado	2	2	11	8	2	2	15	12
Maryland	2		3	0	0	0	5	0
Oregon	0	0	3	1	0	0	3	1
Washington	0		4	3	0	0	4	3
Total	8	5	45	35	8	6	61	46

Role of the Volunteers

The value of the partnership of the educators with volunteers has been validated through evaluator interviews with both educators and volunteers. The volunteers range from graduate level students, young optics professionals, faculty members, to retired optics industry personnel. The evaluation describes how the volunteer/after-school teacher partnerships have been utilized in the MESA after-school programs, shown in Table 7 below. A similar evaluation effort for science center programs is underway but no data are available yet.

Table 7. Activities of Optics Resource volunteers working with MESA after-school classes

	State						
	AZ	CA	CO	MD	OR	WA	Total
Number of Volunteer/Teacher Partnerships	11	12	10	3	2	2	40
Volunteer assisted in the following ways:							
Made a presentation to the students	7	8	5	2	2	2	26
Answered my questions about the subject matter of the module	9	12	7	3	2	2	35
Answered my questions about the equipment provided in the module	6	10	8	3	1	2	21
Provided additional educational material for the module	5	5	6	3	2	1	22
Provided additional equipment or demonstrations for the module	5	5	5	2	1	1	19
Assisted the students with the activities in the module	10	10	6	3	2	1	32
I rate* the helpfulness of the volunteer	4.4	4.8	4.8	5.0	5.0	5.0	4.7
Visited the students __ times	2.3	2.6	1.9	3.0	4.0	4.5	2.5
Emailed/phoned __ times	5.7	5.2	4.6	11.5	4.0	13.0	6.0

*Scale 1–5, 5 = highest

Mode of Use in Science Centers

The program in the science centers takes on a more flexible format than the after-school programs. The activities are used in stations, in moderate-length programs and in more extended programs. To encourage science centers to use the program in the more extended modes, the project is producing a template based on our experience, and those of the different science centers in running one-week optics camps. This template evolves with each camp we give. For example, four one-week optics camps will be run this summer in Tucson and the template/lessons

Module 5 has ample opportunities for experimentation with ultraviolet light sources and glow in the dark materials (including paper money).

learned/best practices document will be significantly revised after this summer. The program is also producing similar documents to describe our experiences in applying the program to younger audiences associated with the Boys and Girls Clubs.

Each science center has integrated the HOO program in different ways. At Orlando Science Center, it is used in *Dr. Dare's Lab*, *Family Science Night*, *Family Astronomy Night*, *Discovery Labs*, *After-School Workshops*, *Footlocker Science*, *Home School Adventures*, *Ah-Ha Weekend Funshops*, and in summer camps. At the New York Hall of Science, HOO is used in a program called the Extended Learning Series that lasts for several weeks after school. The 'Imiloa Astronomy Center uses it in its *'Ohana Discovery Nights* program. The Adventure Science Center has used HOO in their *Home School Day* and *Family Science Workshops* programs. These different programs take advantage of the flexibility of the materials and also allow the staff to use the skills developed in our professional development program to adapt the materials for different programs and audience. An overview of attendance is given below in Table 8, including the amount of time the materials are used.

Table 8. Sample of attendance at science centers showing age range and range of activities			
Science Center	**Attendance**	**Age Range**	**Time (Hrs)**
Station-based Mode			
Orlando Science Center	5,119	5–18	0.2
Short-Term Time Mode			
Orlando Science Center	1,252	5–18	1.2
Moderate-Time Mode			
Adventure Science Center	55	11–14	4.0
New York Hall of Science	120	12	17.5
Orlando Science Center	71	8–10	4.0
Extended-Time Mode			
Orlando Science Center	71	10–14	40.0
Total Overall	**6,688**	**5–18**	**1.2**

Summary

The Hands-On Optics program as a whole matches well to the *More Emphasis* conditions in how the program supports guiding students in active and extended scientific inquiry. The program also relies on a partnership between the Optics Resource volunteers and the informal science educators in order to best utilize the educational materials. This relationship requires a strong emphasis on the professional development standard of *More Emphasis* on collegial and collaborative learning. The program also supports students engaged in an ongoing assessment of their work and that of other students through an extensive program of embedded assessments and in the use of Module 6 (the culminating module) as an overall assessment for the entire program. The program aligns itself well to the content and inquiry standards emphasizing an array of process skills used in the context of experimentation. Relatively few science concepts are covered in the six modules, but they are covered in depth, and in multiple ways that reinforce each other. The science of optics is also connected strongly to basic mathematics areas useful in optics, such as measuring angles. The Hands-On program is progressing in the areas of instructional materials development, professional development, and dissemination.

Future Plans

Instructional Materials Development

We are modifying the instructor's guides for our modules to reflect the ways that they are being used. First, the modules are being used extensively in programs that serve children younger than the sixth-grade level for which the materials were designed. The appeal of the units is partly responsible for this, but, more importantly, uses in places like Boys and Girls Clubs must appeal to a mixed audience not tightly separated or segregated by age. Thus programs of this sort may serve 8–12 year olds.

We have responded by identifying which units are most appropriate for these younger age children and also by developing some additional materials to appeal to their interest in various topic areas like optical illusions, pinhole camera, and stereo viewing. We have also tried to help the teachers who use our materials in after-school programs, but also use them in the classroom, by creating the linkages to the state standards in the states where they are being used. We are working to make the mathematical connections in our materials more explicit through the use of math boxes that reinforce the connections. Finally, we want to be sure that each aspect of optics covered in the modules has explicit ties to everyday life and devices that use these basic optics principles. For example, the value of fluorescence in detecting counterfeit money and in identifying cancer cells will be made explicit through the use of "Optics All Around Us" boxes in Module 5 and the basics of eyeglasses to correct vision will be added to Module 3, on image formation and telescopes.

Professional Development

Hands-On Optics has the goal of providing high-quality, highly participatory professional development to informal educators. This has been achieved mainly through intensive two-day workshops that each cover three of the modules. The program is currently returning to most of its previously established sites to conduct follow-up workshops introducing the second set of modules to MESA after-school and science center educators. During these two-day workshops, the educators receive assistance with use of the modules, and will receive free modules shortly after the training. Since there is considerable turnover in science center educator positions, one challenge is how to maintain adequate professional development when new educators begin to use the program modules at various science centers.

Like many other programs, Hands-On Optics is beginning to provide professional development online. This material can be used to familiarize new educators with the material, as preparation for face-to-face workshops, or as reference material after a professional development workshop. The material can also be used by the Optics Resource volunteers to familiarize themselves with the modules before assisting an educator or making a visit. The creation of this material is a first step to a complete web-based workshop. We are starting with creating an on-line professional workshop on Module 3, *Magnificent Magnifications*.

Dissemination

The modules were originally assembled at NOAO from parts purchased by the observatory, but the program has partnered with an educational vendor for module assembly and delivery. The consistent use of our materials by after-school educators in their own formal education science classes indicates that the materials will also be ordered and used by many teachers in schools. We expect a broader distribution of the modules in the future with use by many science centers, nature centers, and other informal institutions. Our challenge will be to provide at least the minimal level of professional development and support to enable effective use.

The Hands-On Optics project is a successful model of an informal education project that exemplifies investigations that go deeper and longer; integrate science, mathematics, and technology education; and provide opportunities for collaboration between educators and optics professionals.

Acknowledgements

The Hands-On Optics Project is funded by the National Science Foundation ISE program. Project PI Anthony Johnson, Director of the Center for Advanced Studies in Photonics Research at the University of Maryland, Baltimore County (UMBC), Project Co-I Eugene Arthurs, Executive Director of SPIE—The International Society for Optical Engineering. Project Director and Co-I Stephen Pompea (Manager of Science Education, NOAO). NSF Project evaluators Don Hubbard, Berkeley, CA, and Boys and Girls Club evaluator Erin Dokter (CAPER Team, U. Arizona). Thanks also to Janelle Bailey (UNLV) for her work on compiling standards. NOAO is operated by the Association of Universities for Research in Astronomy (AURA), Inc., under cooperative agreement with the National Science Foundation.

References

Anderson, C. W., and E. L. Smith. 1986. *Children's conceptions of light and color: Understanding the role of unseen rays* (Research Series No. 166). East Lansing: Michigan State University, Institute for Research on Teaching.

Andersson, B., and C. Karrqvist. 1983. How Swedish pupils, aged 12–15 years, understand light and its properties. *European Journal of Science Education* 5 (4): 387–402.

Galili, I., and Hazan, A. 2000. Learners' knowledge in optics: Interpretation, structure and analysis. *International Journal of Science Education* 22 (1): 57–88.

Goldberg, F. M., and L. C. McDermott. 1986. Student difficulties in understanding image formation by a plane mirror. *The Physics Teacher* 24 (8): 472–80.

Guesne, E. 1985. Light. In *Children's ideas in science*, eds. R. Driver, E. Giewne, and A. Tiberghien. Milton Keynes, England: Open University Press.

Hall-Wallace, M., N. L. Regens, and S. M. Pompea. 2002. Design of a professional development and support program for future photonics industry team leaders. *Proceedings of the SPIE: Education and Training in Optics and Photonics* 4588.

Hall-Wallace, M., N. L. Regens, and S. M. Pompea. 2002. University of Arizona's collaboration to advance teaching technology and science (CATTS): Lesson for photonics education collaborations. *Proceedings of the SPIE: Education and Training in Optics and Photonics* 4588.

Humphrey, T., and J. P. Gutwill. 2005. *Fostering active prolonged engagement: The art of creating APE exhibits*. San Francisco: Exploratorium.

International Technology Education Association (ITEA). 2000. Standards for technological literacy: Content for the study of technology. *Technology Teacher* 59 (5) 8–13.

La Rosa, C., M. Mayer, P. Patrizi, and M. Vicentini-Missioni. 1984. Commonsense knowledge in optics: Preliminary results of an investigation into the properties of light. *European Journal of Science Education* 6 (4): 387–397.

National Council of Teachers of Mathematics (NCTM). 2000. *Principles and standards for school mathematics*. Reston: Author.

National Research Council (NRC). 1996. *National science education standards*. Washington DC: National Academy Press.

Pompea, S. M., and T. K. Gek. 2002. Optics in the great exploration in math and science (GEMS) program: A summary of effective pedagogical approaches. *Proceedings of the SPIE: Education and Training in Optics and Photonics* 4588.

Pompea, S. M., and A. Gould. 2003. *Invisible universe: The electromagnetic spectrum from radio waves to gamma rays*. Book in the Great explorations in math and science (GEMS) series. Berkeley, CA: Lawrence Hall of Science.

Pompea, S. M., and I. Hawkins. 2002. Increasing science literacy in optics and photonics through science centers, museums, and web-based exhibits. *Proceedings of the SPIE: Education and Training in Optics and Photonics*, 4588.

Pompea, S. M., and L. Stepp. 1995. Great ideas for teaching optics. *Proceedings SPIE: International conference on education in optics*, ed. M. J. Soileau, 2525.

Pompea, S. M., C. E. Walker, and C. Peruta, 2005. Design and evaluation of optics student competitions and contests for maximal educational value. *Proceedings, ninth international topical meeting on education and training in optics and photonics*. Marseille, France.

Pompea, S. M., A. Johnson, E. Arthurs, and C. E. Walker. 2005. Hands-on optics: An educational initiative for exploring light and color in after-school programs, museums, and hands-on science centers. *Proceedings, ninth international topical meeting on education and training in optics and photonics*. Marseille, France.

Ramadas J., and R. Driver. 1989. *Aspects of secondary students' ideas about light*. Leeds, UK: University of Leeds, Centre for Studies in Science and Mathematics Education.

Robertson, W. 2003. *Light: Stop faking it! Finally understanding science so you can teach it*. Arlington, VA: NSTA Press.

Watts, M.1985. Student conceptions of light: A case study. *Physics Education* 20: 183–187.

Yager, R. E., ed. 2006. *Exemplary science in grades 5–8: Standards-based success stories*. Arlington, VA: NSTA Press.

Zylbersztajn, A. and D. M. Watts. 1982. Throwing some light on colour. Surrey, UK: University of Surrey.

Chapter Appendix

Mathematics and Technology Standards Addressed by Hands-On Optics

Principles and Standards for School Mathematics (National Council of Teachers of Mathematics 2000) for grades 6–8 supported by the HOO modules include:

- Understand measurable attributes of objects and the units, systems, and processes of measurement (Measurement, p. 240).
- Apply appropriate techniques, tools, and formulas to determine measurements (Measurement, p . 240).
- Develop and evaluate inferences and predictions that are based on data (Data Analysis and Probability, p. 248).
- Organize and consolidate their mathematical thinking through communication (Communication, p. 268).
- Communicate their mathematical thinking coherently and clearly to peers, teachers, and others (Communication, p. 268).
- Use the language of mathematics to express mathematical ideas precisely (Communication, p. 268).
- Recognize and apply mathematics in contexts outside of mathematics (Connections, p. 274).
- Create and use representations to organize, record, and communicate mathematical ideas (Representation, p. 280).
- Use representations to model and interpret physical, social, and mathematical phenomena (Representation, p. 280).

Standards for Technological Literacy: Content for the Study of Technology
(International Technology Education Association 2000), grades 6–8, supported by the HOO modules include:

- Design involves a set of steps, which can be performed in different sequences and repeated as needed (Standard 9F, p. 103).
- Modeling, testing, evaluating, and modifying are used to transform ideas into practical solutions (Standard 9H, p. 103).
- Apply a design process to solve problems in and beyond the laboratory-classroom (Standard 11H, p. 120).
- Make two-dimensional and three-dimensional representations of the designed solution (Standard 11J, p. 121).
- Test and evaluate the design in relation to pre-established requirements, such as criteria and constraints, and refine as needed (Standard 11K, p. 121).
- Interpret and evaluate the accuracy of the information obtained and determine if it is useful (Standard 13I, p. 137).
- The use of symbols, measurements, and drawings promotes a clear communication by providing a common language to express ideas (Standard 17K, p. 171).

Science Career Ladder at the NY Hall of Science:

Youth Facilitators as Agents of Inquiry

Preeti Gupta and Eric Siegel
New York Hall of Science

The New York Hall of Science is New York City's hands-on science and technology center, with more than 400 interactive exhibits exploring physics, chemistry, and biology. The Hall also creates and presents demonstrations and programs for students and families, and is the leading provider of professional development in the physical sciences for New York City teachers. The Hall is located in Queens, the most ethnically diverse county in the country. More than 100 languages are spoken within five miles of the Hall, and both its visitors and staff reflect the diversity of the community.

A centerpiece of the Hall's efforts to build and support diversity is its Science Career Ladder (SCL): a program that engages young people in a hierarchy of paid experiences in the museum, designed to cultivate interest in science and science education as possible career paths. The SCL creates a cadre of eloquent, well-informed "Explainers" to serve as a public face for the Hall with its audience. The program recruits, mentors, and pays high school and college students to work as Explainers. Approximately 150 Explainers are employed at the Hall at any one time with the average duration of employment exceeding two years. Because all Explainers are paid, SCL is able to attract and retain participants from all parts of the community served by the Hall.

By 2007, more than 1,800 students have graduated from the Science Career Ladder Program. Approximately 400 are still in contact with us through annual reunions, e-mail correspondence, and participation in surveys.

History of the Science Career Ladder

The Science Career Ladder at the New York Hall of Science began in 1987, initiated in response to a need for staff to support the reopening of the Hall after a lengthy renovation. Initially based upon a high school explainer program at the Exploratorium and a similar college program at the Lawrence Hall of Science in Berkeley, the Science Career Ladder rapidly evolved into a distinctive program addressing the specific needs of the Hall and our audience.

About six months into the program, the Hall realized that "explaining" was really about teaching science, so Hall staff began a series of focus groups to explore the Explainers' interest in science teaching. A majority of the Hall's Explainers come from families lacking a tradition of advanced education; most have parents who did not attended college and many are first-generation Americans. The Hall quickly discovered that these young people were perceived by their families as being important gateways to upward mobility; teaching was not perceived as an appropriate profession for achieving this goal. While many Explainers enjoyed working with children, many told us that their families wanted them to pursue higher-status careers in medicine or business.

In addition, while the Explainers were interested in teaching science, they had little knowledge of training programs or work opportunities, and they did not have money to enroll in extensive training programs. To make informed decisions about their futures, Explainers needed information on opportunities and preparation requirements for careers in science education. And because of family pressures, if they chose to move in this direction, they would need practical support to achieve their goals.

In collaboration with Queens College of the City University of New York, the Hall received a grant to recruit minority teachers. Science majors would work at the Hall as Explainers, take a preservice science education program at Queens College, receive free tuition for all courses required for teaching certification, and, in return, agree to work in area schools for two years as a science teacher. The Hall was successful at recruiting and retaining a few-dozen college students to work as Explainers through this program. As that formal collaboration came to a close, we decided to broaden our reach and recruit all types of college students from different colleges.

To expand our Explainer department and to encourage younger students to consider science careers, the Hall added positions for high school students who could enter the program to assist with public programs. These students participated in basic visitor services especially related to temporary exhibitions, preschool exhibitions, and managing the science crafts areas. This allowed students to become comfortable interacting with visitors, doing simple presentations, and learning the culture of the Hall. Positive assessment led to a promotion into an Explainer position (Siegel 1998).

In 1997 the Hall created the After-School Science Program, where 100 middle school students could participate in fun, thematic, hands-on experiences led by a full-time instructor and assisted by Explainers. Interactions with Explainers inspired many after-school program participants to join the Science Career Ladder. The Hall became proactive about informing after-school students about the program, and the after-school program became the bottom rung of our Science Career Ladder. Each year, approximately 15 eighth graders graduate from the after-school program and about half of them apply to be an Explainer.

As Explainers progressed in their careers at the Hall, many became interested in science education and museum work. In fact, as of 2007, roughly two-thirds (24 out of 39) of the Education Department staff are former Explainers. The Science Career Ladder has allowed the Hall to grow a diverse well-qualified staff that understands the educational philosophy and goals of the Hall.

The Current Science Career Ladder Structure

The Science Career Ladder employs a system of training and assessment leading to increased levels of responsibility, pay, and skill. Active recruitment occurs three times a year although Explainers can be invited to join throughout the year based on need. All paid staff of the SCL work year-round, not just seasonally, approx 5–15 hours/week. Average employment period for an Explainer is approximately two years, after which some graduate from school and go on to full-time careers elsewhere, some go to school outside of New York, and some get promoted into higher positions at the Hall of Science. In a given year, turnover is about 30%. On average, each year about 10% of Explainers are asked to leave because they do not meet requirements or perform up to standards.

Middle school participants from the Hall's After-School Science Program form the first rung of the ladder. Graduates of the after-school program can interview to become Explainer Interns. Explainer Interns learn how to interact with the public, become familiar with the culture of a science center, assist with family programming and gain public engagement skills. After one year, they are eligible to be interviewed for an Explainer position. Explainer Interns who demonstrate proficiency in all of the demonstrations and exhibits and show signs of leadership and initiative are invited to join higher rungs of the SCL; each new rung is accompanied by a pay increase and greater responsibility.

At any given time the Hall employs approximately 15 Program Explainers, the next rung on the ladder. Program Explainers oversee the exhibit floor, and implement special projects. Finally, successful Program Explainers can apply for part-time and full-time positions in various departments of the Hall.

Explainer Recruitment

The Hall is committed to having a staff reflective of the diversity of its community; recruitment from within by climbing the "ladder" represents a key strategy in achieving this goal. For this strategy to work, recruiting the best possible mix of participants into the SCL is critical. All possible candidates for the SCL participate in a group interview. A series of rigorous selection criteria are used to screen the candidates. We made a conscious decision *not* to base selection upon grades in school science since we wanted to avoid just selecting candidates likely to succeed in science anyway. Instead, we favor candidates who are representative of the community as a whole and who demonstrate an interest in working with people, general interest in science, and an outgoing, friendly disposition.

Professional Development

One of the highest priorities of the SCL is providing experiences that guide the personal and professional growth of the youth staff. The NSES have been a key factor in this process. As outlined in the NSES, we have worked to create a cadre of young people who:

- Experience the richness and excitement of knowing about and understanding the natural world;

- Use appropriate scientific processes and principles in making personal decisions;
- Engage intelligently in public discourse and debate about matters of scientific and technological concern; and
- Increase their economic productivity through the use of the knowledge, understandings, and skills of the scientifically literate person in their careers.

These capabilities are relevant to any number of career goals, and the training provided is crucial to the development of these skills.

The NSES Standards on Content and Inquiry emphasize learning STEM content through contextual activity and inquiry. Using multiple process skills are encouraged and the process of learning science is valued as highly as the conclusions of science. All of the Hall's exhibitions have a big idea. Each big idea has a few fundamental messages demonstrated through approximately a dozen exhibits. The exhibits are interactive and some are open-ended with multiple points of entry. Where the nature of an exhibit does not allow for an open-ended design, Explainers are taught to facilitate creative use of the exhibit, add props, and create discrepant events to expand the reach of the exhibit. Writing about constructivist exhibits in general, George Hein (1998) writes, "[Constructivist exhibits] are designed specifically to engage many different active learning modes. Labels and panel texts present a range of points of view. Opportunities are provided for visitors to connect with objects [and ideas] through activities that utilize life experiences." Coupling this approach to exhibit design and interpretation with having Explainers customize experiences for visitors strengthens the SCL's ability to meet the points emphasized in the NSES Content and Inquiry Standards.

From 2004 to 2007, Science Career Ladder developers worked to develop the inquiry-based teaching skills emphasized in the Standards. For example, Explainers now use an "apron of tools," which are small props that staff carry in their aprons and pull out as needed to start an inquiry at an exhibit, or to use opportunistically when teachable moments occur. Explainers look forward to creating multiple points of entry into science concepts for visitors and working alongside them to construct ideas.

The program includes a number of events such as an intensive orientation, informative lectures and seminars with science and education professionals, quarterly department meetings covering topics such as harassment at the workplace or working with visitors that have disabilities, and visits to other museums to learn from their staffs. The most important type of staff development is the ongoing weekly training.

Training and the NSES

Every week, Explainers participate in a one-hour training where they review science concepts; exhibits use; how to use the exhibits to foster inquiry; and generally how to understand and respond to the individual interests, strengths, experiences, and needs of a wide range of visitors. The NSES are at the core of all our training efforts.

Teaching to Transgress by Bell Hooks is a call to action for the renewal and rejuvenation of the teaching practice. "Critical reflection on my experience as a student in unexciting classrooms enabled me not only to imagine that the classroom could be exciting but that this excitement could co-exist with and even stimulate serious intellectual and/or academic engagement" (Hooks 1994, p. 7). Of course, Explainers often suffer in the same unexciting classrooms that Hooks refers to. Through their work at the Hall, Explainers experience the excitement of learning and teaching and see that they must use many different ways to engage different types of audiences. Again according to Hooks, "Fixed notions about teaching as a process are continually challenged in a learning context where students are really diverse, where they do not share the same assumptions about learning" (p. 162). The ability to repeat interactions with many visitors throughout the day allows Explainers to reflect on strategies and techniques that were most successful and on the components of those strategies that made the experience successful.

As Explainers begin interacting with visitors, they quickly realize that the most effective technique for attracting and retaining visitors is to understand and respond to an individual's interests, strengths, and experiences. By testing and refining practices of questioning and inquiry established through the training program, the Explainers are integrating the Teaching Standards that NSES emphasize such as selecting and adapting curriculum (in this case big ideas represented at the exhibits) and sharing responsibility for learning with the visitor. Interactions with visitors at an exhibit are mini-inquiry experiences, ranging from 30 seconds to 15 minutes. The Explainers are trained to use effective interpretive techniques for engaging with the visitor and attempting to address what they perceive as needs and interest of the visitor. Once engaged, the Explainer helps focus the "investigation" by eliciting responses and reactions from the visitor. This helps turn the experience in a visitor-centered inquiry. Throughout this experience, the visitor is in control and the Explainer shares in the experience by assisting as needed, asking appropriate questions, and creating a climate for scientific conversations.

Training of Explainers is an ongoing process. To accommodate the varied schedules of all the Explainers, there are one-hour training sessions scheduled every weekday and two per day on the weekends. Novice and veteran Explainers are intentionally placed in the same training groups. Novice Explainers use this time to learn each exhibit and practice their job, and veteran Explainers use this time to get new ideas, mentor, and share strategies. Training is facilitated by an Explainer Leader or a Science Instructor, but is conducted in a peer-training format that allows for greater sharing of learning responsibility, provides opportunities for scientific discussion and debate amongst individuals, and engenders respect for the learning needs and strengths of each learner. Explainers are each given a weekly assignment to investigate and explain the concepts demonstrated by one or more exhibits. Explainers use the on-site Science Technology Library, internet access, exhibit guidebooks, and interactions with Program Explainers and trainers to prepare for their presentation. During training, Explainers model for each other the strategies that they would hope to use on the museum floor; they give each other helpful hints, encourage inquiry and provide positive reinforcement.

Explainers are trained on all of the exhibits at the Hall of Science. Over a 20-week cycle, which repeats continuously, all of the exhibits are covered. The cycles coincide with the schedule changes for school so that all of the Explainers often shuffle around and get placed in different training groups and with a different trainer. This system generates new ideas and approaches that can be shared with other Explainers. If new Explainers join the program in the middle of the semester, they are added to the training in progress on one of the days they work. Since the cycle repeats, they can have the full experience eventually.

Training facilitators meet once a week for half an hour to coordinate their training sessions, review big ideas, and discuss any challenges they have. These weekly meetings are important to maintain consistency in the training groups, provide professional development across trainers who all bring different strengths to the group and track any difficulties with particular Explainers. The training cycle and material is thoroughly documented in a constantly evolving Explainer training manual.

During the weekly training, the goal is for each Explainer to present their assigned exhibit as if they were doing so for a visitor. The facilitator and peers will take on the role of different types of visitors, "Imagine I am five years old" or "Imagine we are a group of seventh graders." Constructive criticism of the Explainer's presentation leads to the emergence of new ideas, innovative approaches to facilitating inquiry around an exhibit theme, and conversations about learning and teaching theory and strategies. Often the ideas cannot be fully discussed in a one-hour session, but the facilitator remembers to continue the conversation the following week, and may provide an article or website to address an idea that can be useful. These trainings encourage Explainers to be reflective practitioners and producers of new knowledge about teaching. The constructive criticism from their peers helps Explainers see that they are part of a learning community and that they must assist each other in growing professionally.

Types of Assessment

Continuous feedback and assessment is a key component of the Science Career Ladder. Through certifications, training feedback, and periodic assessments, Explainers learn ways to improve their teaching skills, improve their content knowledge and receive positive reinforcement from peers, trainers, and supervisors.

Certifications

Explainers must become certified in public demonstrations. They are expected to learn a new demonstration every 150 hours. In order to become certified in a demonstration, Explainers watch the demonstration, study the script, practice with materials, complete a precertification checklist with a Program Explainer and become certified by a supervisor after satisfactorily interacting with the public and facilitating audience inquiry.

Training Feedback

During the ongoing weekly training, facilitators provide verbal feedback. In addition, there is a formal assessment tool with a rubric that measures quality of the Explainer at engaging the public in active inquiry, the accuracy of any science emphasized, and the ability of the Explainer to relate the exhibit to the personal life and interests of the visitor. Each Explainer has a file with a record of the training "grades" in order to track growth and development.

Periodic Assessments

After every 150 hours of work each Explainer receives an assessment by a supervisor. The supervisor observes the Explainer interacting with regular visitors, and looks for the promotion of inquiry, accurate science, and friendly engagement with the public.

Program Evaluation

Four external evaluations have been conducted on the Science Career Ladder Program. Each evaluation looked at different aspects of the program.

First Evaluation: 1991

The Hall contracted with Inverness Research Associates, who conducted a study of the program under its original program name, Science Teacher Career Ladder (STCL) (St. John et al. 1991). The study examined the effectiveness of the STCL program in expanding the educational role of science museums as teaching centers and in improving the processes of recruiting and training science teachers by describing the program's operations and experiences of the students so that others may learn from this prototype.

Surveys were sent to 318 participants with a remarkably strong return rate of 46%. Thirty-four percent of the former program participants had become teachers, and nearly three-quarters of them taught science full- or part-time. The evaluation examined the inner workings of the program and probed into each aspect of Explainer job responsibilities and related experiences. The results led to several key findings and recommendations for both short-term and long-term program development and resulted in major changes to the program. Two particularly important findings are discussed briefly below:

Finding: Explainer relationships with staff members are not as educationally valuable as they might be.
Recommendation: Explore further how staff member support of Explainers might be improved.

The Hall addressed this recommendation over time by developing a variety of mentorship opportunities and by using Explainers for different roles so they could serve as both mentors and mentees. One program that highlights those changes is Outreach Lesson Modeling, where a full-time instructor goes to New York City school classrooms to work with teachers and students conducting hands-on activities. As modified, an Explainer assists each instructor. Since many instructors are former Explainers, they serve as peer mentors for teaching and learning. As a consequence of this change Explainers were able to see many different formal learning environments and compare teaching styles.

Another example was the After-School Science Program: programs for middle school students that were taught by an instructor and assisted by Explainers. The middle school students received mentorship from Explainers and the instructors. They saw the Explainers as smart, cool people who are slightly older than them, but came from the same backgrounds and liked science. This was very reinforcing for the Explainers as well as the middle schoolers.

Finding: The relationships between the university courses and the STCL experience are inconsistent and tenuous.
Recommendation: Find ways to enhance the university-STCL connection.

To accommodate this recommendation the Hall timed the STCL experience so that it coincided with or preceded the students' college physics and/or biology courses. By allowing Explainers to first be introduced to ideas about teaching learning, they were better able to see how the content of their science courses could be applied to instructional contexts; both in school and at the science center.

In 2006, a National Science Foundation–funded project began at the Hall entitled Collaboration for Leadership, Urban Science Teaching, Evaluation, and Research (CLUSTER), which allowed the Hall to directly address the recommendations made by Inverness Research Associates. In CLUSTER, the Hall is working with City College of New York and City University New York Graduate Center to test a model of teacher preparation designed to incorporate 1,000 hours of Explainer experience into a preservice teacher curriculum and to measure whether those students are more confident and comfortable with inquiry-based teaching at the onset of their career as secondary science teachers compared to students in a traditional teacher preparation program, which wouldn't be able to provide such an intensive field experience. CLUSTER Fellows take required coursework for secondary science certification while working as Explainers; the three partner institutions coordinate college course work with Hall-based Explainer experience. The flexible schedule for Explainers allowed them to take the required science and education courses at their schools while working at the museum. The curriculum for the CLUSTER project is set up so that students take the science methods course at the onset of the program as they are first beginning their Explainer experience. The course is cotaught by a college faculty member and a Hall educator who is well prepared to teach college-level education courses. The Hall becomes a teaching laboratory. Field Experiences are required for the other education courses for the CLUSTER Fellows. All of the professors who teach those classes require one-third of the fieldwork to be conducted at the Hall.

Second Evaluation: 1994

Ten years after the inception of the SCL, Ilona E. Holland and Associates conducted our next external evaluation (Holland et al. 1994). This report was commissioned as part of the Hall's effort to disseminate best practices of the existing SCL to 12 science centers around the country and demonstrate success in meeting program goals. The goals of this evaluation were to assess the overall appeal of the program, determine its usefulness of specific elements of the programs related to alumni employment, assess the impact or lack of impact of the program on the perceptions of science and science-related careers, and to determine the contribution of the program to those who have elected to pursue a career in education.

Ninety-one alumni (approximately one-fifth of the total at the time) responded to the written survey administered by mail and 34 alumni participated in a focus group. Over three-fourths of those who completed the survey rated the program as being valuable to their professional lives. This rating included 81% of those alumni who were teachers and 71% of those in science-related careers. They also stated that the program provided practical experience for teaching, improved communication skills, developed their ability to work with diversified groups of people, enhanced self-confidence, developed a base of knowledge in science, and addressed various personal needs. Almost half (49%) stated the program had positively influenced their career choice while the rest surveyed said that the program did not have a direct influence on their career choice. Recommendations for improvement included providing a better structure for Explainers to be able to voice their concerns, enhance and increase training of Explainers, and provide a vehicle through which Explainers could assume greater responsibility while remaining within their parameters of a given "rung" of the ladder. The Hall spent many years after receiving this report strengthening the program, improving in areas recommended by the evaluator and continuing and growing practices that led to such high appeal by the Alumni Explainers.

Third Evaluation: 2002

An external evaluation conducted by the Institute for Learning Innovation (ILI) documented and analyzed the long-term impact of participating in the NYHS Science Career Ladder program in the areas of personal attitudes and personal lives; perception of science and scientists; academic career goals and directions; and leisure time choices (Storksdieck, Haley-Goldman, and Jones 2002). Specifically, the evaluation attempted to address four primary areas of interest:

(1) The short-term and long-term effect of the program on participants' knowledge and skills (self-reported), specifically their problem-solving and critical-thinking skills; their math literacy; and the transfer of those skills to everyday and professional life.

(2) The ability of the Program to shift participants' perception of science and scientists.

(3) The influence of the Program on participants' career planning, including the ability of the Program to evoke interest in teaching and science.

(4) The influence of the Program on participants' leisure time choices, with respect to lifelong learning and cultural enrichment.

Surveys were mailed to 570 alumni Explainers (there were more Alumni, but only 570 had good addresses.) The return rate on the survey was 19%. In addition, an abbreviated survey was administered to a control group of 67 young adults who participated in various activities at the Hall, but were not affiliated at all with the SCL program. ILI researchers also conducted semi-standardized, open-ended telephone interviews with a stratified sample of 16 Alumni Explainers out of a pool of 81 who were willing to be interviewed.

Institute researchers concluded that the SCL is a highly successful program that fosters personal development in various major areas. Specifically, the SCL impacts participants in the following different areas:

• Participants developed self-confidence and communication and teaching skills, and generally seemed to have been positively influenced in their personal development during a critical phase in their lives. In fact, personal growth is strongly facilitated by the program, either by fostering existing predispositions, or by exposing program participants to new challenges in a challenging and supportive environment.

• Participants were more willing than the average college graduate to consider a career in teaching (inasmuch as they did not consider it before they joined).

• Participants acquired an appreciation for science in all its diversity, and for teaching.

- Participants developed a lifelong appreciation for, and a personal connection to science and learning, and likely developed above-average science knowledge.
- Some evidence suggests that participants generally developed an interest in other cultural arenas outside science (art, for instance).

A key recommendation by ILI was to continue developing inquiry-based training approaches for Explainers. The Advanced Explainer Training was initiated in 2004 to serve two purposes. The first was to investigate whether an inquiry-based approach of exhibit interpretation for visitors in a science center was even feasible if Explainers were given the proper training. The second was to create excitement and renew energy levels in the Advanced Explainers who have worked at the Hall for many years.

Advanced Explainers are defined as Senior Explainers, Program Explainers, and high school and college Explainers who have not yet reached a higher status on the ladder, but demonstrate leadership and expertise in key areas of the museum. At a given time, there are approximately 20 Advanced Explainers. During this training, Explainers were asked to work in teams and categorize Hall exhibits in one of four categories: constructivist, orderly, discovery, and systematic. Once they categorized the exhibits, they had to think of props and related questions that they could use to bring exhibits that were *not* in the constructivist category more toward it. The goal was to take more directed exhibits and use inquiry approaches to create open-ended experiences for visitors.

Results from this evaluation convinced us that the program had best practices in place and while there were areas of growth, we were in a position to consider replication and dissemination of our best practices into other science centers and museums.

Fourth Evaluation: 2005

Kim Sabo Consulting was contracted to conduct an evaluation of the Advanced Explainer Training. Specifically, she investigated how and to what extent had the Advanced Explainer Training enhanced the quality of service the Explainers are able to provide to visitors. In particular, do the Explainers exhibit an increase in the following characteristics or outcomes after the completion of their advanced training?

- Enthusiasm about their work
- Knowledge of exhibits and curiosity about the subject matter
- Understanding of and ability to identify multiple learning styles
- Ability to teach to a variety of learners and to facilitate dialogue with visitors
- Capability to elicit questions from the visitor in order to better meet their needs
- Ability to refer visitors to other exhibits that address their questions and needs

Findings through survey and observations of 14 Explainers demonstrated an increase in all of the characteristics listed above. All Advanced Explainers stated that they gained knowledge and further developed their skills during the Advanced Explainer Training. They stated that the training made their jobs more enjoyable, gave them more confidence, helped them feel more knowledgeable about the exhibits, enhanced their teaching skills, and supported them in future work environments.

Benefits of SCL to the Hall and Its Stakeholders

Visitors

Science Centers, like all institutions, are being forced to accommodate to a changing marketplace. The historic, one-size-fits-all museum of old is no longer acceptable. According to Falk and Sheppard (2006), 21st century visitors require more individual attention and customization. Staffed with a team of well-trained Explainers, the Hall is now capable of creating an efficient and effective way to help customize the public's learning experience.

The Hall attracts a stunningly diverse population of visitors: diverse in age, income, and ethnicity. The structure of the SCL, in particular that Explainers are paid, allows us to employ an equally diverse group of youth in the program, which in turn means that we can offer our widely varied audiences many different styles of interaction and interpretation. Explainers who are close both in age and background to our visitors demonstrate to our visitors that science is accessible, and that they too can be expert and eloquent.

Youth in the SCL

The Science Career Ladder benefits the participants in multiple ways. In addition to building knowledge and teaching skills, the Science Career Ladder provides training in interpersonal relations; skills that are invaluable for careers in communications, the arts, law, business, and health. Explainers benefit from increased content knowledge of science and technology concepts through interactions with scientists and educators. They gain access to career information, opportunities for different levels of advancement within the program, information about science teaching programs with tuition waivers and other benefits. Through their work and through guided training, they learn job success skills such as cooperation, timely attendance, and reliability.

Through training, evaluation, and a rewards system, youth employees are mentored into leadership roles. Senior Explainers conducting training sessions for the newer students alleviates the burden of full-time staff while building the capacity of all individuals in the program. With increasing frequency, upon graduating from college, former Explainers are hired as full-time employees at the Hall. Essentially the Hall is growing its own staff—people who already understand our mission, exhibits, educational philosophy, and audience.

Finally, Explainers form strong social bonds, the foundations of a learning community and a professional network that is a model for advancement in their lives. In essence, participants in the SCL join a "community of practice," a place where individuals of varying expertise collaborate around efforts to achieve shared goals (Lave and Wenger 1991). As is typical of a community of practice, there are levels of expertise among Explainers, ranging from senior to novice Explainers. There are also full-time instructors who serve as mentors and trainers. While there is always an assumption that individuals at higher levels have greater expertise, there is also a clear atmosphere of peer respect and appreciation that everyone can learn from everyone else. As suggested by Lave and Wenger and supported by the SCL, "The effectiveness of the circulation of information among peers suggests, to the contrary, that engaging in practice, rather than being its object, may well be a condition for the effectiveness of learning" (p. 14). Explainers are learning about science and the intricacies of effective instructional practice not just because someone told them to do so, but for personal enrichment and to accomplish their job. This gives the SCL the qualities of an apprenticeship model; a proven effective model for learning as well as for creating relationships and bonds that are capable of lasting a lifetime.

Institutional Commitment and Funding

Why has the Science Career Ladder at the New York Hall of Science thrived and expanded? Institutionally, the Hall's leadership is thoroughly committed to the program's vitality. The Hall is a service-oriented institution, and the SCL reaches an important constituency. The program is funded through a variety of sources, including private and corporate foundations, individuals, and state and federal agencies. Most of these sources are interested in supporting science education, career development, and college preparation programs for disadvantaged and at-risk women and minority youth. Because Science Career Ladder Explainers, Public Program Assistants, and Volunteers are intricately involved in all aspects of the Hall's Education Programs—from outreach to schools to exhibition interpretation—virtually any program for which the Hall seeks funding will include an Explainer salary line, which, in turn, helps us reach our financial goals for supporting the program.

Current Challenges and Future Directions

A key area that presents a challenge for the Hall of Science is the training regime for the Explainers. Over the past 20 years, training has moved from an informal, exploratory component of the SCL to an extremely formalized, structured one. In addition, throughout the existence of the SCL, different staff have led the development, growth, and design of the training. We found that left to their own devices, staff will focus on what is most important to them in leading the training team. Therefore, training has gone through changes where historically leaders emphasized presentation and inquiry while, more recently, the head trainer emphasized accurate science content. Through the evaluation we learned that all of the Explainers were extremely knowledgeable about science concepts and knew many details about how things worked in both the natural and physical world and they were excited to share that knowledge with visitors. However, the last two years of Explainers lacked skills in good questioning techniques and fostering inquiry. We are currently involved in re-evaluating the training rubric and creating a better balance between process and content. This re-evaluation and opportunity for improvement comes at an important time when we are ready to move the program with all of its exemplary practices to the next level.

The Science Career Ladder has demonstrated great results and has the potential for national impact. We believe that the Hall's Science Career Ladder program could potentially represent an important mechanism for helping to alleviate the national shortage of well-qualified science teachers. We continue to conduct evaluations that help us improve the program at the Hall, but also provide the foundation for creating a generalizable program that could be exported to other informal science institutions nationally and internationally.

With funding support from the Institute for Museum and Library Services and the Noyce Foundation, the Hall is currently assisting 16 informal learning institutions internationally that are interested in growing and improving their youth employment program or starting one. All selected museums are receiving a manual to use as a guide to help develop the logistical detail and policies for their program, participating in a four-day Hall-run training institute designed to immerse museum staff in the practices of the SCL and foster creation of a community for learning and discussing best practices. Each participating museum also has the option of receiving complimentary on-site technical assistance in implementing key aspects of the program. A formal external evaluation by MEM Associates is examining whether key components of this program are in fact replicable in other cities, which characteristics can be transplanted, and which will be modified during replication.

Over the years we have worked to make the Science Career Ladder an exemplary youth and workforce development program. While there are many challenges that still exist, we continually strive to search for innovative solutions. Key to our past and future success is the involvement of each new cohort of participants in the process of reinventing the program. By embodying the spirit of the NSES we have been able to not only improve the learning experiences of our visitors but also ensure that each year a new crop of youth will begin a reflective and transformative learning journey.

References

Falk, J. H., and B. K. Sheppard. 2006. Thriving in the knowledge age: New business models for museums and other cultural institutions. Lanham, MD: Altamira Press.

Hein, G., and M. Alexander. 1998. Museums: Places of learning. Washington, DC: American Association of Museums.

Holland, L., B. Flagg, H. Davies, and D. Slechta. 1994. New York Hall of Science career ladder evaluation final report. New York: Ilona Holland and Associates.

Hooks, B. 1994. Teaching to transgress: Education as the practice of freedom. New York: Routledge.

Lave, J., and E. Wenger. 1991. Situated learning: Legitimate peripheral participation. Cambridge UK: Cambridge University Press.

Sabo. K. 2005. New York Hall of Science advanced explainer training evaluation report. New York: Kim Sabo Consulting.

Siegel, E. 1998. The science career ladder at the New York Hall of Science. Curator, (Dec): 246–253.

St. John, M., F. Tibbitts, B. Heenan, and B. McClaskey. 1991. A study of the science teacher career ladder program. Inverness, CA: Inverness Research Associates.

Storsdieck, M., K. Haley-Goldman, and M. C. Jones. 2002. Impact of the New York Hall of Science career ladder program on its former participants. Annapolis, MD: Institute for Learning Innovation.

Copies of the full reports of the four evaluations can be obtained by contacting the Vice President for Education at the New York Hall of Science.

Curious Scientific Investigators Solve Museum Mysteries

Elizabeth Wood
Indiana University-Purdue University Indianapolis

Rick Crosslin, Michele Schilten, and Jean Deeds
The Children's Museum of Indianapolis

Dinosaurs bursting out of the front of the museum, fireworks of glass exploding through the building, a giant water clock ticking away the hours—these are just some of the amazing icons we see each day at The Children's Museum of Indianapolis. For 80 years (60 at the same site) the museum has delighted children and families in immersive and interdisciplinary exhibits and inquiry-based family learning and school programs. With more than 110,000 objects in the collection, 11 permanent gallery spaces, a 350-seat theatre, planetarium, public library, and classroom space, our museum can rightfully claim to be the largest children's museum in the world.

The museum's mission is to create extraordinary learning experiences that have the power to transform the lives of children and families. Over the years the museum emerged as a leader in the children's museum field and is noted among all museums for its excellence and creativity in exhibits, educational programming and community outreach (AAM 2004). The museum strives to uphold its mission to educate the public through its exhibits, educational programming, and collections. Serving more than 1,000,000 children and families annually, the museum attracts over 100,000 students and teachers each year, while approximately 280,000 children and families visit the museum through free or reduced admission prices. The museum provides free memberships to museum neighbors and hosts four free days annually, plus a monthly free evening for families. While the museum's primary audience is children through age 11, museum staff implement family learning strategies into new exhibits and programs to expand audiences. In addition, the museum has special opportunities for the grades K–8 audience, educators, neighborhood residents, and adolescents.

A Vision for Strong Science Education

Most museums and science centers operate within a free-choice learning framework (Falk and Dierking 2002), which promotes choice and control by visitors to learn and experience in their own way. We believe that providing this type of environment for school visitors is critical in helping to highlight and model key National Science Education Standards (NSES). In developing our programs for students and teachers, we are keenly aware of the need to demonstrate the ways in which teachers can "change emphasis" in their science programming. We support this awareness by modeling strategies around teaching, demonstrating an intentional orientation to content and inquiry standards, and offering staff development to support the implementation of these strategies. The museum is uniquely positioned to demonstrate free-choice, inquiry-based learning as a new way for teachers to do science in their classrooms.

The vision for the *Curious Scientific Investigators* (CSI) program is to support learning by all members of a classroom community, stimulate a lifelong interest in science, and demonstrate the museum as a place of investigation. We designed a program that mixes the best the museum has to offer with classroom instruction. We want to see kids and teachers doing real science. The program targets three areas of emphasis: (a) guiding students in active and extended scientific inquiry, (b) developing teacher skills in integration of science knowledge, and (c) helping teachers implement inquiry strategies. The program combines the strong informal learning orientation of the museum with these elements of the NSES standards into a cohesive program that incorporates professional development, small-group inquiry experiences, student-centered learning, and content-rich experiences. These learning opportunities are grounded in the inquiry-based environment of the museum that promotes interaction and collaboration.

Developing the Program

In developing the CSI program, we worked closely with partners in local school districts. Through multiyear collaborations with area schools, the museum staff identified strategies to support educators in the integration of science content knowledge and practices. Details that can hinder both visits to the museum and doing real science in the classroom were also addressed. Elementary teachers needed a model for building inquiry-based science experiences in the classroom. They needed a way to gain professional development that promotes an integration of theory and practice—one that worked with their schedules. Educators and administrators wanted us to find a way to support student visits to the museum when few chaperones could be found. Our partners in the local school districts wanted to improve science instruction in the classroom with the ultimate goal of increasing student science achievement.

To respond to these needs, the museum created a science education liaison position. The person hired for this position is an employee of one of the local school districts but also serves on the staff of the museum to build the partnership. Our goal for the pilot program was to build a strong inquiry-based, guided science program that exemplifies scientific enterprise and can be used as a "focused science experience" highlighting one section of the science curriculum. Museum staff and district partners anticipated that individual teachers would use these investigations as a template to create similar experiences in their school or classroom with the other areas of the science curriculum. We worked with school-based teams of teachers from the same grade level to support learning and development of curriculum that extended the museum format and experience and built their interest in teaching science.

Using museum exhibits and gallery spaces allowed us to demonstrate ways in which teachers and students can better practice and apply the use of tools, the scientific process, data collection, and analysis of results. The use of hands-on learning, open-ended situations for discovery, and learner-directed activity gave a strong basis to create programs that clearly model critical areas of the NSES standards, and it allowed us to build strong, high-quality programs that support the needs of teachers and promote lifelong interest in science for both children and adults.

A primary goal of the program was to create student-centered experiences that emphasized developing skills and concepts rather than knowing specific facts and information. It was important to offer multiple activities throughout CSI that would require students to implement skills and strategies learned, use process skills, and analyze data in as many real-life situations available in the museum setting. Furthermore, it seemed critical that the program center on a series of extended investigations using science concepts and process through the use of tools, analysis, and synthesis of data.

Perhaps one of the most noteworthy challenges for teachers is the lack of other adults to help students in inquiry-based experiences. The CSI program had to build a cadre of well-trained volunteers to support positive adult-child interaction through discussion, exploration, and application of ideas and science concepts. We were fortunate to attract many retired scientists, engineers, and educators to participate in the program. Training our volunteers is as critical as the work we do with teachers. We work continuously to build science literacy in all participants in the program—teachers, volunteers, and students.

Above all, we continually encourage all participants to own their investigations. "This is science. Don't take my word for it, try it yourself," is the main theme of CSI's concept and design. Says one volunteer in a written survey: "I've learned even more the power of discovery as related to learning and retention in children. If they can explore and question themselves, they will remember not only the results, but also the process." We strive to generate opportunities for the adult volunteers, the teachers, and the students to learn what science is all about.

The Curious Scientific Investigators Program

Curious Scientific Investigators (CSI) began at the museum in 2004 as a focused learning investigation combining classroom-based activities, on-site teacher professional development and small-group museum-based activities that take place over time in the classroom and at the museum. While the museum is the primary point of contact for the experience, the program is divided into three parts: in-school activities and preparations, data collection at the museum, and follow-up activities back in the classroom. Using the museum galleries and resources as a learning lab, the program models a realistic scientific investigation that reflects best practices in science education for students and teachers. These activities exemplify many of the NSES content and inquiry standards, including: (a) the ability to understand scientific concepts and developing abilities of inquiry, (b) investigating and analyzing science questions, and (c) recognizing science as argument and explanation.

Centered on a mystery at the museum, students spend a series of previsit class sessions learning how to use the scientific processes and use tools to solve problems. During a museum visit, trained museum volunteers (called Museum Friends) help teams of students use tools and scientific strategies to solve the mystery. While students are collecting data throughout the museum, their teachers are simultaneously receiving professional development. These workshops support teachers in learning science content and show them how to guide students through the inquiry process, providing direction for selecting and adapting science-based experiences and curricula. Teachers are encouraged to promote student ownership of the scientific process. The program makes use of web-based videoconferencing and a course delivery system to disseminate CSI materials to students, teachers, and volunteers.

This is not your ordinary field trip. Most museums provide enrichment materials that are highly supportive, but not germane, to the success of the project. This program is unique because the pre-and postvisit activities are essential—not extracurricular—to the project. The process of incorporating lessons before, during, and after the museum visit is intended to meet the NSES standards to use investigations over extended periods of time. The next sections outline the activities that happen throughout the program.

PreVisit Classroom Activities

The CSI program includes two types of previsit activities—one for teachers and the other for students. Classroom teachers attend orientation sessions with museum staff to receive materials and training on the core activities necessary to support the student experience in the program. Prior to visiting the museum, students receive information about a mysterious stain left by a visitor at the museum (see box). They are told that the stain could have come from one of five places in the museum: the Water Clock, the Pond, the Watering Hole, The Dock Shop, or the Aquarium. During the first day of classroom activities students practice with the skills and processes needed to solve the mystery. They examine the evidence (a mysterious stain) and view a series of short video programs with information necessary to complete the investigation.

The Case of the Mysterious Stain

"Sorry, We Caused A Leak At One Of Your Exhibits And We Have To Leave The Museum!"

The Children's Museum needs your help to solve a strange science mystery at the museum. We need two things to unravel this mystery. First, we need a curious group of students to work on the problem. Second, we need students to conduct a real investigation using scientific methods. What we need is CSI—Curious Scientific Investigators! Your class has been selected to take the CSI challenge where you use real science to solve The Case of the Mysterious Stain. Get ready to ask questions, make a hypothesis, collect data, make observations, test ideas, determine results and draw a conclusion.

The museum had a liquid or water leak out of one of the exhibits. The problem is we do not know where the leak came from! A museum visitor turned in a piece of paper that contained a stain. The visitor said it came from a leak, but they left the museum before we could ask the location of the leak. There are many places that could contain liquids in the museum. We need your help to use science to examine the stain and the museum exhibits to find the source of the leak before we have a big mess on our hands. You will need to come to the museum to complete the investigation. Your class will also need to use science skills to solve the mystery.

Students inspect an evidence card that contains a sample of the stain and begin to review the existing physical evidence. Students familiarize themselves with the areas of the museum that contain liquids. In class sessions, they learn about scientific methods and science tools they will need to make their investigations. They discuss problems and questions, hypotheses, procedures, data collection, results, and sharing.

Students then review key principles of liquids and states of matter that may help them in their search for the origin of the stain. In addition to the main idea of liquids and states of matter, they learn to recognize and practice using tools such as a thermometer, graduated cylinder, pipette, and hydrometer. Following their preparations, students form teams to begin the initial process of hypothesizing. Class teams meet prior to their museum visit to attempt to determine the source of the stain and clarify the primary question, problem, and hypothesis.

Museum Visit

The CSI program targets all third-grade classes at a given school. On "CSI museum day," all classes come to the museum to do their data collection. There, we provide opportunities for students that parallel the content and inquiry standards—groups of students working together to analyze and synthesize data, implement inquiry strategies, and use evidence to develop explanations—and we give them the chance to evaluate their work and to apply it to new situations. This cycle repeats itself throughout the entire program.

Proudly bearing their color-coded team badges, the student investigation teams meet up with a Museum Friend who will work with them throughout their visit to the museum. These five-person teams and their Museum Friends review key tools and safety procedures and talk about their team hypotheses. They also get to know each other a little bit. The small-group approach is a distinctive element of the program, not usually found in museum settings. We believe it is a crucial element for modeling inquiry strategies, building the adult-child relationship, and helping build a bond within the group around solving the problem.

Students are told that they will need to make keen observations and ask lots of questions during their visit—both qualities of a good scientist. Each team heads to the particular exhibit where they will collect data. There, they study and learn about the exhibit, looking particularly at the liquids. They make observations and estimate the flow of the liquid. The teams collect temperature readings, hydrometer readings, and a liquid sample at their exhibit location and then visit all the other possible leak sites to make additional observations. Students love using their tools and equipment to scrutinize all aspects of the museum's galleries. It is not uncommon to see small groups of begoggled students closely examining the floor with a hand lens!

The museum is full of immersive exhibit experiences, many of which are full-scale dioramas. One in particular, the *Dinosphere* Watering Hole, poses an immediate problem—there are no actual liquids used in the exhibit! Museum Friends encourage the team to think critically about the evidence and where within the exhibit water may have come from. Eventually the groups determine that a nearby water fountain may be the source of the leak and are able to collect a sample. This is a great opportunity for us to work with students on their observation skills and ability to think critically about information. It also provides a reference point for the follow-up activities at school, where students will apply what they learned at the museum to conduct a study of water from the school's drinking fountains.

We work continuously throughout the students' visit to instill critical questioning and a scientific way of thinking. Even during snack time we look for opportunities to talk about science. Our snack time inquiry focuses on the different properties and states of matter. We provide all students with a hand lens to keep. We ask them to closely examine their snacks and ask, "Is your goldfish snack made of matter? Is it a solid, liquid, or a gas? Is your glass of water made of matter? Is your drink mix a solid, liquid, or gas? What other observations can you make?" These investigations reiterate key concepts, allow for a more informal use of science between Museum Friends and students, and provide more opportunities to engage and explore.

Before the end of the museum visit, the teams review their data collection experience and complete their team data sheets. This process of review and application of ideas supports student learning and helps to demonstrate for students the ways in which they were able to conduct an experiment with tools and good scientific thinking. The Museum Friends encourage the groups to think about all the observations and data collected. Eventually they will be sharing their data with their classmates, just like real scientists. In the end, we encourage students to recognize that they have been doing science all day long.

Program Conclusion and Follow-Up Activities

When students return to their classrooms, each team presents their data to the class. The information is recorded on a classroom data sheet. The class then tests their hypotheses. Each teacher has received a set of tools and materials from the museum to do their final testing of the hypotheses. Students use samples collected at the museum along with examples of the stain to verify their results. The class attempts to reach consensus on their hypotheses based on the data collected. Groups create a final data sheet, class results, and conclusion information and generate additional questions. Each class assembles a CSI Investigation Board to display its results to other classrooms at their school. These data boards, not unlike a poster presentation, allow the students and their teachers to demonstrate their process and results to others.

In addition to the final testing, students complete follow-up enrichment activities to further apply what they learned in their museum data-collection process. The students conduct a study of liquids at their school using the same process of collecting a sample and taking temperature and hydrometer readings. They create simple "water detectors" to continue their development of observation skills and determine whether water was placed in an apparatus overnight. Finally, students create written descriptions of their process and procedures for data collection and their experience at the museum.

Teachers regularly send us examples of new ways they are applying the information in their classrooms and extending the learning. These include small-group activities to practice using and recognizing tools and to practice parts of the scientific method. Teachers also use reading and writing activities to stimulate student thinking about their experiences. They regularly send us enthusiastic updates about the program:

"By incorporating the CSI Stain into my curriculum, it has made me aware of how the scientific method approach improves the children's understanding of how science works. It hits on higher-level applications. Now, all my science experiments incorporate the scientific method."

"[CSI] has helped the students to realize that science isn't all about how 'smart' you are, it's about investigating on your own or discovering with a group how something works, why salt water leaves a residue when it dries, or which objects sink and which ones float."

"Since my students have gained real-life science experience through this project, I have been able to do more hands-on scientific thinking and investigating in my classroom."

The museum hosts a CSI website where we invite all classes to post their findings from classroom to school. They are able to submit questions and writing samples, as well as meet with museum staff over IP videoconferencing to discuss their results and conclusions. The website allows for greater communication among students both within their own school as well as with other schools around the city. This is an area we hope to expand and build with the classroom teachers as another aspect of increased public discourse and debate.

Assessment Results

Our assessment of the learning that happens in the CSI program emphasizes key inquiry standards, including: (a) implementing inquiry strategies; (b) processing skills in context; (c) using evidence and strategies for developing or revising an explanation; (d) applying the results of experiments to scientific arguments and explanations; and (e) communicating science explanations. Our goal is to provide an opportunity for young people to gain basic skills in the use of science questioning and processes, tools and measurement to learn the states of matter, and to understand the elements of the scientific process. We want them to be able to recognize different ways that scientists develop hypotheses, make observations, collect data and arrive at conclusions (Wiggins and McTighe 2005). Here, our objective is to create a situation where students conduct a science investigation to collect evidence that supports *their* explanation and see that they can do science. What is perhaps most critical is that we provide students with an opportunity to interpret, apply, and gain perspective on the scientific process. One of our biggest challenges is in working against the tendencies caused by standardized testing to have students simply recall facts and information.

Our evaluation process takes into consideration the multiple ways in which students can demonstrate what they understand and know. We created a series of measures that would provide this information both for our program as well as in support of the classroom teachers' needs. This includes student presentations of their team hypothesis and results, opportunities for writing and discussion, pre- and posttests, and application of processes. Clearly, this is an area in which we are continually refining and revising based on the experiences in the program, our interactions with teachers, and national standards.

The national standards for assessments in science education call for a focus on measuring what is most highly valued: rich, well-structured knowledge, and learning what students do understand. In each of these areas we are working with the teachers to collect data and assess student achievement. In our program, we use these criteria to develop a variety of measures that will help identify student achievement toward content and inquiry standards. These assessments are collected by both museum staff and classroom teachers. Each of the components reflects an

NSES standard:

- A student readiness inventory during the museum visit assesses *student abilities to use inquiry strategies*;
- Pre-and posttests measure *process skills in context*;
- Museum follow-up data testing gives a *process for using evidence and strategies for developing or revising an explanation*;
- Writing samples show students *applying the results of experiments to scientific arguments and explanations*; and
- Public displays and presentation provide *opportunities to assess student ability to communicate science explanations*.

The two primary sources of student assessment used by the museum include a student readiness inventory and pre-and posttests. These strategies allow us to focus on student use of inquiry strategies and the process skills in context. This information is collected by the museum and shared with the classroom teachers. Each is described in detail below.

Student Readiness

The Museum Friends are trained to work with students using inquiry-based strategies. They work with a set of questions that focus on scientific process, use of tools, and critical observation skills. The Museum Friends review the use of tools and terminology as a way of assessing the readiness of the group to perform the data collection process. During the second year, we asked the Museum Friends to complete a brief inventory at the end of each session that rated each group's readiness on these items. The initial data show that on a scale of 1 (students know little or nothing) to 4 (students are very well prepared), we found students to have moderate to good preparation with the tools (Thermometer use 3.5; Hydrometer 3.3; Graduated Cylinder 3.3) and the least amount of preparation with scientific process (2.9). Comments from Museum Friends also point to the level of familiarity students have with tools and process:

"Had obviously been introduced to the vocabulary, but could only define hypothesis. They knew basics about the thermometer, but needed reminders. It was the same about the graduated cylinder and the hydrometer. The kids knew about the stain, but they were confused about its significance. The kids had heard about the hypothesis but a bit confused about meaning. They had not been introduced to the scientific concept. They obviously did pretrip work, but needed reminders and prompting."

"Group had not made correct hypothesis, but had excellent reasons about their decision."

"This was a super group. Well informed, conscientious, worked well together. Asked good questions. Had lots of questions about the water clock. "

"Group was interested in the investigation and appeared somewhat well prepared for their day. They knew what the tools were and what they were used for. (Esp. the hydrometer.) They seemed to really understand density. They understood a lot of the science concepts even if they didn't know all the terms."

"The kids were not at all familiar with the vocabulary. They were somewhat familiar with the tools. They knew the name of the thermometer and how it works, but didn't know hydrometer or what it measures. They didn't know the name of the graduated cylinder but they understood it measured "how much." The kids had not heard of scientific method. They did make reference to the [previsit] video…. They were very excited to solve the mystery."

One challenge we discovered is a need to refine this inventory to hone in on skills and process development rather than on student behavior. We are investigating new ways to work with the Museum Friends to help gather assessment. As we continue to develop this program we look forward to revising this process so that we can better understand the relationship between the preparation of the students and the previsit activities, as well as the key areas of inquiry that challenge the students most.

Pre- and Posttests

The pre- and posttests provided to teachers are a more typical measurement of knowledge, and they are also a way for us to see what kind of impact the CSI program may have on the overall learning of students. The pre-and posttests also help to show students and teachers the extent of their learning through the CSI program.

Following an orientation to the program and before beginning the unit, teachers give students the CSI pretest. After the completion of the full program (previsit activities, museum visit, postvisit activities) teachers give the posttest. Test items refer specifically to scientific tools and processes used throughout the activities in the classroom and at the museum.

We found that the teachers like to use these as a way for students to assess their own work and see their progress. Teachers report that students like to see tangible results of their progress. Most students make fairly large gains from pre- to posttest. In our first two years of data collection, 752 students took the pretest and 713 students took the original posttest from all participating schools. The vast majority (87%) of students from both districts correctly answered fewer than 5 out of 20 questions on the pretests. Scores on the posttest show a remarkable difference in the student achievement: Students scoring 5 or fewer correct items dropped to 15%. The number of students scoring more than 10 correctly increased to 66%.

This process has been useful for us in working to develop systems and measures that help us gauge the value of the museum visit and the overall classroom experience. Still, we must continually revisit and revise our pre-and posttest questions so that we are focusing on the most highly valued knowledge and build our own understanding of what students are really learning. The results from the original test format and changes in the program suggested by teachers and Museum Friends prompted us to review what we were really measuring, and we have changed the test to better reflect the national standards. We designed the new test around the use of tools and scientific process. The new test consists of questions that measure the student's understanding of when to use certain tools, how to make measurements, and how to identify parts of the scientific process. We ask questions such as

- Use the picture of the thermometer to answer these questions: What is the temperature shown in Fahrenheit? What is the temperature shown in Celsius?
- Match the science tool with its name.
- "Mary took the temperature of the water and recorded the results in her journal." Which part of the scientific method does this describe?

Though we have not yet completed the 2006–2007 CSI program, the results from initial pre- and posttests suggest that while students are scoring slightly higher on the redesigned pretest, they appear overall to be scoring as well or better on the new version of the posttest. In the new test version, students are scoring an average of 5 of 13 correct answers on the pretest and 11 of 13 correct on the posttest. We are confident that our continued evaluation of the assessments toward student learning and understanding is helping us build a better program.

Impact

After two full years of implementation we are beginning to see the real impact of the CSI program. At a time when schools are plagued with an overwhelming pressure to "teach to the test," the CSI program is thriving. While CSI is clearly a departure from the scripted pacing guides that many districts now favor, our two district partners, the Indianapolis Public Schools and Wayne Township Schools, have made a commitment to continue the program and increase the number of schools and students involved. The district support for the school liaison will continue, as well as an increased level of support for four new pilot programs, technology support, and teacher release time for increased participation.

Teachers respond very well to the program because it provides them with focused instruction on both logistics and science content. We provide all the materials, forms, and museum-day supervision—which greatly decreases much of the "science anxiety" that comes with a hands-on science investigation. We provide content support that greatly improves "content expertise" for the teachers. In addition, our highly trained volunteers allow the teachers to focus on the preparation and follow-up learning. The teachers who participate in CSI are seeing a program that models and applies strong science instruction. Teachers have responded positively to exploring science inquiry methods that they use and build upon throughout the year.

For the students, this guided investigation changes them from casual learners to committed learners. Students ask questions, plan strategies, collect data, and communicate findings. For most, this is the first experience with the science enterprise. Prior to this program most students participated in literature-based science reading with very little hands-on measurement or inquiry. They have not participated in any science-based investigation where they make findings based upon the data they collect. The CSI program requires students to communicate and defend their findings in postvisit class discussions. For most students, this may be the only time they are exposed to these experiences until the upper grades.

The third group for which the impact is real and observable is the Museum Friends. Many are senior citizens who have discovered a new comfort level in working with children and with science concepts, and thus a new zest for living in a multigenerational culture. These volunteers look forward to Tuesday mornings when they need to be sharp and focused and compassionate in dealing with children, many whom are from underserved families. Other volunteers are young mothers whose enhanced knowledge of science through CSI gives them a basis for conversation with their own children and a better understanding of the work their children bring home from school. As one volunteer lamented last year when summer arrived, he missed coming and had "the Tuesday morning CSI blues!"

Future Directions

The success of the CSI program with third-grade classrooms across the city has been tremendous. Each year we work with 22 different schools in two districts and more than 1,500 students. We will soon begin piloting new programs for Grades 4, 6, and 7. Each of these programs will employ similar formats, with professional development for teachers and authentic experiences for students both in the classroom and at the museum, particularly around topics of biotechnology and dinosaurs.

In addition we continue to look for ways to strengthen and support our professional development activities and increase student science literacy. Further, we are exploring the options available through web-based learning to include families in their own CSI investigations. Each of these avenues provides us with the opportunity to showcase the museum as a pivot point for learning activities. These kinds of free-choice learning activities provide young people and adults the opportunity to be in charge of their own learning and set the direction for their inquiry. We can provide authentic experiences that demonstrate the best opportunities for science learning.

While we work to create new versions of the program, we are still focused on refining and building our evaluation and research of the student and teacher learning. The museum's partnership with Indiana University-Purdue University Indianapolis provides us with the opportunity to work closely with science education and informal learning specialists who can help us increase our assessment capacity and assist in the ongoing research and evaluation of the program. We work closely with preservice science educators from Butler University, offering a way to build their own science literacy while working with children. Finally, our continued partnership with the Wayne Township school district gives us opportunities to work closely with teachers in developing curriculum and testing ideas.

Our ultimate goal is to create opportunities in our community where the museum serves as a resource and a destination for science-based learning for children and adults. We want to create extraordinary experiences in lifelong learning that stimulate an interest in science and ultimately contribute to scientific literacy. As we like to say in CSI: "This is science. Don't take our word for it, try it yourself."

References

American Association of Museums (AAM). 2004. *Accreditation report of The Children's Museum of Indianapolis*. Washington, DC: Author.

Falk, J. H., and L. D. Dierking. 2002. *Lessons without limit: How free-choice learning is transforming education*. Walnut Creek, CA: AltaMira.

National Research Council (NRC). 1996. *National science education standards*. Washington, DC: National Academy Press.

Wiggins, G., and J. McTighe. 2005. *Understanding by design, expanded 2nd edition*. Alexandria, VA: Association for Supervision and Curriculum Development.

Science With Attitude:

An Informal Science Education Experience

Dean Jernigan, Dana McMillan, Katherine Patterson-Paronto,
and Elaine Ceule
Union Station Kansas City

A middle-American city in the middle of the United States, Kansas City is the epitome of America's heartland—a place where average "Joes" and "Janes" abound. Its reputation for normalcy is such that it has long been a testing ground for consumer attitudes about new products and services.

The metropolitan area's population of more than 1.7 million is more diverse than some would expect, breaking down as follows: 80.80% White, 12.80% Black, 5.2% Hispanic, 1.6% Asian and 0.50% Native American. Public school districts in the area include some of the nation's highest ranked as well as some of its worst.

Union Station in 1917.

Grand Hall of Union Station.

There are actually two Kansas Cities—the larger is in Missouri while its much smaller cousin is in the state of Kansas. The state divisions end at Union Station, completed in 1914 as one of the nation's largest rail passenger terminals and reopened through a bi-state tax initiative in 1999 after years of decline and neglect.

Today, a fully restored Beaux-Arts masterpiece operated as a 501(c)(3) corporation, Union Station Kansas City (USKC) is home to a permanent rail exhibit with vintage rail cars (*KC Rail Experience*) and an interactive science center (*Science City*), as well as theaters, restaurants, shops, and meeting spaces. Today the station is once again a busy Amtrak stop.

Interior of Grand Hall.

Since its renovation, Union Station Kansas City often is referred to as the area's "Little Switzerland," or "Kansas City's front porch," bringing together a diverse and far-flung metropolitan population for civic, social, and community events.

Central to the mission of USKC is the presentation and interpretation of Kansas City's regional history and the promotion of science and technology (the latter has been identified as a high priority by the area's business and civic community). This is accomplished through the development of collections, exhibits, and educational programming.   .

It is in the spirit of USKC's role as the Kansas City area's connecting point that we developed the Science City Summer Camp program, "Science With Attitude." The attitude in this case is one of inclusiveness and diversity of purpose, methodology, and participation. This "attitude" is accomplished through the program's goals:

- Involve children ages 6–12 years from a wide range of socioeconomic backgrounds.
- Train and employ young adult teaching assistants, one-half or more of whom are from the area's urban core.
- Promote a cooperative teamwork approach among the staff, with special emphasis on

child development and pedagogy.
- Involve and combine science, technology, engineering, and math with other disciplines such as art and music in order to promote maximum participation and address diverse learning styles.

Science City Summer Camp Structure

The staff design of the successful science program requires many levels of leadership and encourages development of leadership skills with practical and engaging interactions with science and people.

The support staff of Informal Science Educators (ISE) begins with a *Director* whose responsibilities include liaison with community partners and local funders, and who also provides leadership and direction for the overall function of the program. A *Child Development Specialist* (CDS) works with all child participants and staff personnel in the program. The CDS is especially helpful with interviewing, training, and transitioning students selected from community organizations into leadership roles within the program. An ongoing function of the CDS is to maintain the integrity of the program, intervening as necessary to keep the emphasis on best practices.

The *Camp Manager* also assists with hiring and training staff, but primarily plays a supervisory role in the daily function of the program.

The *Registrar* organizes the enrollment procedures, responds to parent inquiries and performs much of the recordkeeping throughout the planning and implementation of the summer program.

The *Instructional Team* of ISEs consists of licensed teachers who develop and facilitate the activities in the five subject matter–specific learning centers. These centers are:
- Investigative Science (Life Science emphasis)
- Investigative Science (Physical Science emphasis)
- Active Expression (Writing, Drama, Music emphasis)
- Creative Arts (Visual Arts emphasis)
- Science City (Science Center programs)

Each center has a dedicated space and equipment. Each lead teacher receives $18 an hour for development and instructional expertise, and is responsible for managing the use of $2,000 for instructional supplies throughout the program.

Teaching Assistants (TAs) support the centers' learning activities and model behavior for the younger students. Twenty TAs were hired to assure each camper could participate in small group activities—each with its own leader. Ten of the TAs are *specialists,* providing support for the lead teacher and performing specific responsibilities within the center as each group visits that activity. Ten additional TAs are *generalists* who lead their small group through the rotation of centers and encourage small group interaction and enjoyment of the day in general.

The TAs may be given the opportunity to switch roles from generalist to specialist, or specialist to generalist, during the course of the summer.

Half of the TAs were selected from those recommended for interviews by our community partners. The other half were selected by interviewing high school and college students who independently sought summer employment, and indicated an interest in science and education. All TAs receive $8 an hour in wages. For many of these young people, it is their first job.

The eight-week summer program features four weekly themes that repeat after the first four weeks. Weekly themes for 2006 were:

- Fur, Feathers, and Scales (nature theme)
- Concoctions, Cooking, and Reactions (chemistry theme)
- Stars, Planets, and Astronauts (space exploration theme)
- Dinosaurs to Terror Cranes (the ancient world)

In 2007 the themes will change to:

- Fur, Feathers, and Scales (nature theme, including the ancient world activities)
- Concoctions, Cooking, and Reactions (chemistry theme)
- *New!* Catapults, Bridges, and Robots (design and build theme)
- Stars, Planets, and Astronauts (space exploration theme)

Science City.

A Day at Science City Summer Camp

Children are greeted by a samba band each morning as they arrive at the program. The band is a participatory and welcoming activity that sets the mood for an active daily program. Five brightly colored flags provide visual assistance in grouping the children into the five age-level groups. At the morning samba band performance, each of the five groups is accompanied by two TA generalists who remain their group leaders throughout the week's activities. Science experiences take on a whole new dimension for the 750 children, ages 6–12, enrolled in this one-of-a-kind summer camp with regular programming from 9 a.m.–4 p.m., and optional early/late care 7:30 a.m.–6:00 p.m.

Drawing on the knowledge that people have different learning styles, Science City introduces science concepts each day of the eight-week camp through creative art projects, active expression (dance, music and drama), active play, or investigation. Students have a true "camp" experience, but learn about science in ways not typically available even in their school classrooms. Perhaps the best way to showcase Science City Summer Camp is through the eyes of one of the participants and the dedicated people who made this camp a reality. Let's follow Maddie as she grows and learns throughout the 2006 summer program.

Meet Maddie

Maddie is a nine-year-old girl whose mother enrolled her in Science City Summer Camp because Science City at Union Station is near her place of employment. She would be able to drive Maddie to camp each morning and pick her up after work. She felt secure that Maddie would be near her during the day and even allow her to occasionally have lunch with her. Maddie's mother also has concerns that her daughter's science education may be lacking. Like many younger elementary school students, Maddie has had limited science instruction. With the emphasis on reading and math and the high-stakes testing that have become too familiar under the federal mandates of No Child Left Behind, Maddie's suburban elementary school is able to provide very little time for a science curriculum. Just as in many other neighborhood schools, the science instruction is provided by an elementary school teacher who may lack skills and resources to offer much more than basic science facts without hands-on applications. Typically, children like Maddie receive science instruction about 30 minutes per day for three to four days per week. In some cases, the science instruction is shortened due to rotation with social studies classes.

But Maddie likes science. She has been on school field trips to the zoo and visited an aquarium with her family. She is curious about dinosaurs and asks her parents difficult questions about how things work. She enjoys working in the garden with her grandfather and loves to search for insects when she plays outside. But this nine-year-old suburban dweller has likely never considered a career in science. Her stereotype of a scientist is an old man in a white coat doing something mysterious with funny looking tubes. Additionally, Maddie has spent very limited time with children outside her neighborhood; she has never explored a vast space like Union Station in midtown Kansas City, nor had opportunities to pack her days being challenged to think beyond standard rote questions. All of that is about to change.

Samba band greets children.

When Maddie arrives on the first day of Fur, Feathers, and Scales week, she is feeling a little overwhelmed. Standing just outside the entrance to Science City at Union Station she is greeted by a large number of adults in matching polo shirts playing an amazing collection of drums and other unusual instruments. The Samba band opens Maddie's senses to an electric beat as it fills the large space. Other children are arriving. Some come with their parents, just as Maddie has with her mother, but others are arriving on a large school bus.

Maddie is provided a nametag with a color dot. She is told to join a group standing with several teenagers and a flag of the same color. All of the other children in the pink group look to be about her age but she does not know any of them. For a moment, Maddie has a feeling of fear and shyness. She looks to her mother for reassurance and when she has received it, she takes the plunge, kisses her mother goodbye, and joins the group.

Quickly, a teenager introduces himself as her "TA" (Teacher's Assistant) Dane. Dane is a high school senior. He joined the staff at Science City Summer Camp for a fun summer job. He has worked other summer jobs with children at the swimming pool and in recreational camps, but this is his first job that includes the responsibilities and challenges to make each child's day an amazing success. Dane realizes he must quickly find the skills for being leader. Maddie may not believe it but Dane is at least as nervous as she is about how this first day of the first week of camp will go.

Dane has learned during the staff training days, prior to the opening of camp, that his priority is to shepherd his group of children throughout their day. He must navigate the vastness of Union Station, keep the group on schedule, and attend to their personal needs. Beyond that, he is expected to participate in each of their planned activities. He has received training on child development, diversity, inquiry-based instructional theory, and constructivist's behavioral practices.

Dane's partner Terah is also nervous. This is her first job. She is just 15 years old and sometimes looks and acts closer to Maddie's age. Terah competed with more than 30 other young people to receive a spot on the staff. She was selected because of her infectious personality. She is not all that happy with the required uniform nor the expectation to be at work at 8:00 a.m. This may cramp her usual sleeping routine, but Terah knows this job is important to more than just her. She has a

plan that so far, she has shared with no one. As soon as she receives her summer wages, Terah will use her first-ever paycheck to make the family car payment. Her mother is in the hospital and may not get out for a long while. If Terah can make the payment, they will be able to keep their family's only transportation. But Terah is not thinking about all of that right now. She must concentrate on how to perform her job this first morning. She received the same training as Dane and the 25 other staff members, and now besides all that, she has learned she is trying to form a meaningful partnership with Dane. She takes his lead and introduces herself to Maddie too.

Children with instruments.

When the pink group is formed and the band has set aside their instruments, everyone begins the trek through Union Station to the fourth floor of the east wing where camp is headquartered. Maddie has been to Union Station before but somehow it looks different when she is following along with the 25 other eight and nine year olds. As she walks across the Grand Hall, this Kansas City icon appears bigger and brighter than she remembers. Her eyes and mind are suddenly open to seeing this place as more hers than she ever thought about it before.

Along the trip Dane and Terah explain to the children that they will be following a schedule that begins their week in the Investigation Center with Miss Betty. When they arrive, the children are immediately thrust into an in-depth exploration of animals. Miss Betty begins by asking the children to print on chart paper what they know about vertebrates and invertebrates. Along with Dane and Terah, two additional TAs have been assigned to help Miss Betty throughout the week with the small group projects. During the morning hours in the Investigation Center, Maddie and her new friends settle into activities such as dissecting an owl pellet, creating a food chain, and examining

Teacher's Assistant leads small group.

plankton from a pond under a microscope. With a midmorning snack, the children are getting to know each other and their TAs.

Maddie's biggest fear that Science City Summer Camp would feel like school has been forgotten. She and her now best friends find they not only can talk in "class"—they are encouraged to! Dane stays with the small group to model his interest in their activities, ask probing questions, and actively listen to the girls as they express their opinions on the topic. They laugh, relax, and learn so much that by noon they can hardly believe its' time for lunch.

Lunchtime is held in a room along Sprint Festival Plaza (the former Union Station North Waiting Room). All five groups, 125 students in all, and half of the TAs, gather to eat their packed lunches. This is not a typical school lunchtime. Children eat and chat with other students and TAs who have learned a more effective form of supervision by interacting with the children informally, serving as both a role model and an interested friend. Maddie and her friends discuss the contents of their lunches, occasionally trade food, and make their best nine-year-old jokes about what owl pellets really are. After lunch they return to the fourth floor to play games in an area called "The Park" stocked with books on the topic of the week, puzzles, Legos, and bean-bag chairs to relax. Again, the

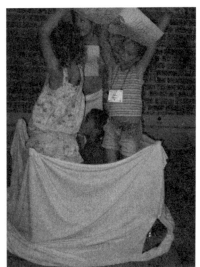

TAs play games and talk with them. TAs guide small groups of children to the Inquiry Wall to record the children's questions about the week's topic on animals.

After lunch, the Pink Group is scheduled with Miss Hallie in the Creative Expression Center. Quickly Maddie discovers a new aspect of science by exploring issues and attributes of animals through drama. As a practicing artist and director, Miss Hallie has developed interesting scenarios connected to the week's topic of animals. Using the simplest recycled materials such as scarves, yarn, and old boxes, she focuses the children using theater terms and a fully engaged student-centered approach. The children are divided into small groups, each assigned one TA. In her group, Maddie takes the role as the top carnivore in a living food chain. The afternoon flies by quickly culminating with each group performing their productions for the others.

By the end of the first week of Science City Summer Camp, Maddie has completed two rotations in each of the five centers. She has spent two sessions with Brad in Cooperative Games, another two with Trevor in Science City, two sessions with Kathleen in the Art Center, and returned to Investigations and Creative Expression. All the centers

Children perform.

emphasized the science concepts chosen to match that week's theme. She has also made amazing friends she wants to keep in touch with beyond the summer. Most importantly for Maddie, her mother has signed her up for the remaining three weeks of this cycle of summer camp, convinced that Maddie is learning and growing beyond her highest expectations.

Dane and Terah have also learned much this week. Before the week is completed they have put into practice how to keep their charges engaged in each of the activities, keep everyone on schedule and learned to work together as a team. After several visits with Dana, the Learning Specialist, both Dane and Terah have been challenged in different ways. Dane had a meeting to talk about strategies for keeping the children involved during Cooperative Games without taking over the game for the children. Terah has been shown some "tough love" in conversations about remembering her responsibilities. During one of those discussions, Terah also shared with Dana her family situation. It was insightful for both of them. Weekly TA meetings, informal conversations with teachers, and bonding between TAs helps to keep everyone growing in their jobs. What was learned in the initial training days has become a reality for the entire staff as they face each day's challenges and rewards.

Child with flower pot.

The Scientific Attitude Prevails: The Challenge to meet Science Education Standards

Science City Summer Camp was developed as an innovative way to connect science with a child's world. The program planners incorporated hands-on, inquiry-based learning as the guiding principle in developing each summer camp activity. Campers would become aware that science is all around us. "Does it engage participants in investigation?" was the key question to be asked for each phase of the camp's development. What followed was programming that naturally fit the spirit and the letter of the changes recommended in the National Science Education Standards in the planning and implementation.

Teaching Standards

In preparation for the camp activities, the staff created the goals and learning objectives. Teachers were then given creative reign to develop themed lessons within that framework. Each teacher adhered to the ideals of interactive, small group-based learning activities in their planning. The children were to be considered active participants in their own science learning, and their natural inquiry and verbalized thoughts used as topics for scientific debate and discussion.

Students in creative expression class.

Revitalized Standards:

- Understanding and responding to individual student's interests, strengths, experiences and needs
- Selecting and adapting curriculum
- Guiding students in active and extended scientific inquiry
- Providing opportunities for scientific discussion and debate among students
- Supporting a classroom community with cooperation, shared responsibility, and respect

Students predict and discuss outcomes.

Assessment Standards

The programming for the summer was designed in such a way that informal assessment of student learning and understanding is part of the activity itself.

Teachers adjusted lessons to help students understand the concept, or modified the lesson to the level of the child's under-

A teacher assesses prior knowledge.

standing. Inquiry-based learning provides a rich environment for observing and assessing the student's understanding.

The learning specialist observed each activity and discussed them with the teacher to ensure they were age appropriate and engaging—and packed with learning objectives.

Revitalized Standards:
- Assessing to learn what students do understand
- Assessing achievement and opportunity to learn

Small-group activity with a 1:6 ratio.

Content and Inquiry Standards

Weekly themes were explored in each of the five learning centers. The teacher assigned to the learning center used scientific principles to guide the creation of that week's activities. Children were assigned to a three-hour morning or afternoon session, giving teachers an opportunity to develop in-depth activities. Children explored science through art, theater, games, the science center, and investigation. Sometimes participants were guided through several activities, each building on the knowledge and concepts gained in the previous activity. In some centers, students did one comprehensive activity for the entire morning or afternoon. Inquiry, small-group, and investigation-based activities were the norm for all sessions.

Small team works to redesign a Lego machine.

Revitalized Standards:
- Learning subject matter disciplines in the context of inquiry, technology, science in personal and social perspectives, and history and nature of science
- Integrating all aspects of science content

Test kitchen activity reaveals effect.

Students perform life cycle of a butterfly.

Students analyze a mystery substance.

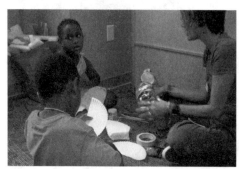

Creative art teacher works with students.

- Implementing inquiry as strategies, abilities, and ideas to be learned
- Processing skills in context
- Using multiple process skills—manipulation, cognitive, procedural
- Doing more investigations in order to develop understanding, ability, values of inquiry and knowledge of science content
- Communicating student ideas and work to classmates

Staff Development Standards

A two-day preservice learning session was conducted for the entire summer staff. This training encompassed the same principles that governed the activities of the children. Specifically, small-group discussions and activities on the topic were the norm for all sessions. Teachers and the TAs were assigned together in groups where they interacted as peers. The small groups then reported back to the large group what they had learned and gathered in their discussions. Participants were encouraged to share personal expertise and knowledge, expanding the potential interaction with the group.

Revitalized Standards:
- Collegial and collaborative learning
- A variety of professional development activities
- Staff developers as facilitators, consultants, and planners
- Teacher as producer of knowledge about teaching

Science City Summer Director and Manager participated in a two-day training conducted by the Institute for Inquiry (based at the Exploratorium in San Francisco). This preliminary preparation was organized for informal science programs funded by the Kauffman Foundation. Activities learned were used in the preservice training with the summer staff to teach them inquiry-based science techniques.

Staff members participated in staff development sessions addressing learning theory and constructivist approaches to learning and discipline. The discussions led to practical application of these new approaches that were implemented into inquiry-based science activities. The benefits also included confidence among the staff in addressing and anticipating common issues with groups of children, and subverting behavior that could negatively impact the group's experience.

Theater T.A. guides participants.

Revitalized Standards:

- Learning science through investigation and inquiry
- Integration of science and teaching knowledge
- Integration of theory and practice in school settings
- Teacher as source and facilitator of change

Assessment and Results

Science City Summer Camp's primary goal was to offer area young people—especially those representing underserved populations—exciting, engaging, and challenging science learning experiences that could also serve as a foundation for future school and out-of-school success stories. A secondary goal was to determine what kind of infrastructure and resources would allow existing science education organizations to expand their reach on a sustained basis to students from high-poverty populations.

In 2006, the Kansas City–based Ewing Marion Kauffman foundation, the 26th largest foundation in the United States, funded seven informal science education initiatives in the Kansas City metropolitan area. The foundation's investment totaled $685,000, of which $175,000 went to Science City Summer Camp, the largest of the programs. In February 2007, the foundation received the evaluation reports on those seven initiatives they had commissioned from the Program in Education, Afterschool and Resiliency (PEAR) at Harvard University and McLean Hospital, in collaboration with the Exploratorium in San Francisco.

PEAR evaluators used multiple methodologies of assessment, including program observation, interviews, and qualitative surveys. They did *not* reveal individual programs in their written report, citing the "trust" developed during the process of data collection and site visits. However, they concluded that the summer initiatives were "highly positive for both the young people and the organizations that offered the programs." They further noted that organizations responded in a remarkably short time frame to expand and alter their program offerings, having started a development trajectory that will take some time to further mature.

The success of the initial 2006 offerings has led to funding for 2007 and beyond. The participating organizations are now forming a coalition to assist with program development, marketing, and sustainability. With much of the formative evaluation completed, the emphasis is shifting to a longitudinal, summative evaluation of outcomes for each program.

Prior to the Kauffman Foundation funding, the Science City Summer program was funded by enrollment fees, which excluded most underserved children. The Kauffman Foundation support has allowed the Science City Summer program to emphasize diversity by merging teaching staff and participants in a variety of ethnic and socioeconomic groups.

Science City Summer Internal Survey to Parents

An internal evaluation survey was conducted to assess participant satisfaction. These surveys were mailed to 186 families (participants not sponsored by the grant), and received 50 returns. The results provided invaluable feedback for program adjustment, as well as indicating a high degree of program satisfaction, with marks averaging between 4.0 and 5.0 in all categories.

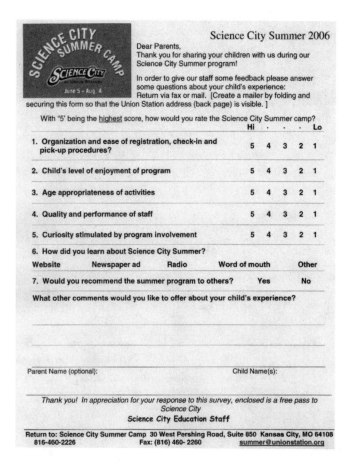

Internal evaluations were addressed at weekly staff meetings. All staff members were encouraged to contribute to the evaluation and discuss program concerns. Staff morale was enhanced through guest speakers for both inspiring and informing staff in effective teaching behaviors.

Lead teachers met separately each week to discuss and evaluate the program and assess teaching assistant performance. Meetings were scheduled throughout the summer with community partners to coordinate programming and gather feedback, then making changes as appropriate.

This ongoing assessment resulted in comments on the parents' evaluation forms, such as Maddie's mother who wrote, *"Maddie had a wonderful time. I think she learned more in one day than she did all last year in school! She had a great summer. Thank you!"* Other parents wrote:

"My kids went to several different camps this summer, but this one was by far their favorite. They were so interested in all of the activities. We will definitely be back next summer. P.S. We loved the music in the morning!"

"I thought the summer program was excellent! Allison loved the program and the staff. I truly hope you will have this next summer."

"John described this camp as the best camp he ever had gone to. He loved it!"

"Excellent camp. High ratio of instructors to students was very good. Very well organized."

"Bryanna said 'It was awesome! I loved it!' Really enjoyed making fossils. Thought all the teachers did a good job."

"He loved it! He cried on Friday because he would miss it!"

"Elise enjoyed her camp experience. She came home very excited about what she had done each day. Elise also commented on how much she liked her group leaders and TA from Creative Expressions."

This year, in addition to the ongoing Kauffman evaluation, a more structured research component being conducted by the University of Kansas Center for Science Education has been added to the program to define intended outcomes for the summer program and to assess the degree to which these stated goals and outcomes are achieved.

Program Goals and Outcomes for Science City Summer 2007

Goal 1: To provide a wide range of inquiry-based, hands-on learning activities imbedded into real-world issues.
- **Outcomes will be evidenced by:** well-developed inquiry-based STEM program material and lesson plans implemented within a clear scope and sequence

Goal 2: To provide engaging learning experiences for each child addressing a wide range of learning modalities.
- **Outcomes will be evidenced by:** inquiry-based STEM program material and lesson plans built on a learner-centered curriculum model.

Goal 3: To develop in all students a deeper interest and understanding of the natural world through the scientific process.
- **Outcomes will be evidenced by:** students who actively engage in the scientific process on their own initiative.

Goal 4: To enhance social skills that promote student social development; including the citizenship skills to live and work in a democratic society as informed decision makers, rather than just activists.
- **Outcomes will be evidenced by:** students who are actively and effectively engaged citizens.

Goal 5: To serve all segments of society by insuring participation of economically and academically underserved populations of students through partnerships with community organizations.
- **Outcomes will be evidenced by:** sponsorship through scholarship funding from community partners who serve children in the lower socio-economic groups while increasing the appeal for families who self pay.

Goal 6: To continue the development of young people through an instructional/mentoring program for teaching assistants.
- **Outcomes will be evidenced by:** well-established students as teacher models for high school and post secondary students.

Goal 7: To determine the value of these informal learning strategies by assessing the impact of this experience on their interest in science and science careers as well as their achievement/testing scores in their schools.
- **Outcomes will be evidenced by:** (proposed) a longitudinal study following these students through school and later as they make career choices.

Evaluation—A Work in Progress

Personnel with the Center for Science Education at the University of Kansas will be conducting the external summative evaluation of the stated program goals and outcomes for the 2007 period. Preliminary interviews and surveys will establish an assessment baseline.

A major goal for Science City Summer Camp is to introduce and inspire elementary-age students to consider advancing their education and select careers in science. Students and TAs in the program will be exposed to science through nontraditional, hands-on, inquiry-based experiences. The evaluation will measure the long-term effect of this informal summer education program. The summative evaluation design will recognize the impact of this opportunity for students at several levels: (1) Student participants will be between the ages of 6–12 years; and (2) the TAs range from high school to early college age. The evaluation will explore changes in attitude toward science, career interests, and school success with both student participants and TAs. To that effort, the children in the program will be surveyed and interviewed for their attitudes toward science and mathematics and the likelihood that they will consider a career in these areas. Those children that continue in the program for multiple years will be tracked for changes in these attitudes having experienced the enrichment classes.

The TAs will be assessed for the impact that the *students as teachers* curriculum models on their attitudes toward science and math, and school achievement in those areas. The leadership role experienced by the TAs will be factored into attitudinal changes and confidence in pursuing careers requiring higher education.

Parents of all the participants (students and TAs) in the study will also be surveyed for changes in their child's behaviors concerning science and mathematics over the course of these informal science experiences.

The Next Step

This type of enrichment camp experience, delivered in an informal setting, goes well beyond the expertise and abilities of most schools' educational programming. The question becomes: What is the educational value of such summer science and math enrichment experiences? The real answers, for now, remain unknown. There are several important requirements for a definitive baseline study aimed at determining the value of these programs. A longitudinal study, spanning a period of at least 3–5 years, would assess the following:

(1) How do children involved in enrichment informal programming compare, educationally and developmentally, with their peers who do not attend such programs?

(2) How can we obtain data from populations that are significant, but not easily available for study, such as children attending care centers?

(3) How does the experience of being Teaching Assistants affect their career and higher education choices?

(4) How does teaching in informal enrichment programs affect teachers' instructional behavior and outcomes in formal education settings?

The answers derived will be very important in developing effective models for educational change and reform. If found to help achieve significant educational gains, for example, informal education programs could partner with schools to provide a very cost-effective means of boosting student learning and teacher effectiveness.

The future of Science City Summer is as exciting as the past few years. There is a natural niche for informal programs to exist alongside traditional summer school programs and in after-school programs. The development team is already planning how to disseminate the program by partnering with other informal and formal education settings to deliver a new attitude of science and education for Kansas City's children—and beyond.

Forecast—Cloudy With a Chance of Educational Reform:

New Weather & Water Partnership Offers Some Relief From the Drought

*Harry Helling, Susan Magdziarz, Jennifer Long,
Melissa Laughlin, Jacqueline Kasschau,
and Jessica Camp
Ocean Institute*

To be clear, there were not any exemplary weather education programs available in our area before this tale began to unfold. While lesson plans existed for other content areas from the fifth grade, the weather and water cycle components, representing almost a third of the required content standards, had virtually no quality curriculum, teacher professional development, materials support, or models for inquiry and constructivist teaching. As California began counting fifth-grade standardized science test scores in the ever-important school API scores, teachers began reacting to the combination of increased requirements and limited resources with anxiety and distress. District science supervisors began creating "emergency curriculum," a euphemism for quickly produced, untested, and unsupported teacher materials.

At the same time, the Ocean Institute had an emerging set of initiatives seeking to increase the contribution of informal science education centers to the systemic reform of science education. With several decades of offering elaborate and well-integrated field trips, the Ocean Institute sought to leverage that success into broader impact and in 2002, created the Center for Cooperation in Research and Education (CORE) to address these objectives. In 2003, an 11-university collaboration called Southern California Coastal Ocean Observing System (SCCOOS) approached the CORE group with NOAA funding and a mandate to link a complicated network of buoys, satellites, and shore-based weather sensors to classrooms. The Arnold and Mabel Beckman Foundation saw even larger potential and invested in our informal science education center to broker into existence a new Weather & Water Fifth-Grade Partnership focused on reform and best practices.

Setting

The Ocean Institute is a nonprofit educational organization dedicated to increasing awareness and understanding of the ocean environment. The Institute was established in 1977 and currently serves 109,000 K–12 students per year with innovative science and social science field and lab programs. The Ocean Institute engages students with 60 standards-based programs and a philosophy that encourages small-group learning, trained professional science instructors, and inquiry methodology. In 2002, the Ocean Institute built a modernized Ocean Education Center that offers fully equipped At-Sea, Ecology, and Surf Science Learning Labs supported with a collection of local marine life in over 60 tanks, a Coastal Ocean Observing Station, 16-foot Oceanography Test Tank, Digital Video Analysis Lab, Center for Technology and Communications, and the Center for Cooperation in Research and Education. In addition, the Ocean Institute operates three seagoing vessels including the 70-foot research and education platform *R/V Sea Explorer,* brig *Pilgrim,* and topsail schooner *Spirit of Dana Point.*

The Ocean Institute has emerged as a leader in developing innovative solutions to improving science education with a particular emphasis on linking university research to formal and informal education settings. The Center for Cooperation in Research and Education (CORE) has become a think tank for addressing challenging educational projects and currently manages a range of developmental programs that build stronger and more effective bridges between the research and education communities. CORE has specialized in providing education and outreach solutions for research projects funded by public agencies such as NSF, NOAA, NASA, JPL, and California Coastal Conservancy. Projects range from creating exhibitions, developing educational curriculum and products, conducting teacher professional development, to improving technology and media applications.

In 2003, SCCOOS approached CORE with a request to assist with their education and outreach efforts. Their research project is part of a large-scale national program to establish an integrated ocean observatory. SCCOOS is responsible for the development of a system of California buoys, satellites, and shore-based sensors that can report immense amounts of current local weather and ocean data. Some public data products were available on the web, but none were applicable to the needs of schools. CORE's challenge was to create effective links between a multimillion-dollar sensor network and both formal and informal education community needs.

Specifically, our challenge as an informal science center was to find a way to interface the very frontier of ocean science with the needs of fifth-grade teachers and classrooms.

Weather & Water and the National Science Education Standards

Weather & Water's First Grade: Fail

While the initial Weather & Water design team was experienced and capable, there were some early errors when mapped against the National Science Education Standards' *More/Less Emphasis* conditions for reform (NRC 1996). The intentions were, of course, pure in trying to allow eight classes of fifth graders to meet fourth- and fifth-grade standards with an interesting interface with a cutting-edge ocean research program. What science educational designer would not have been seduced by that promise? The problem emerged, however, as the design team wrote a 2–3 week curriculum on waves and weather that used existing web-based data products to help students learn how ocean sensors work and to provide meaningful access to current and forecast information about the ocean. Teachers were involved with learning, students accessed (albeit somewhat complicated) research websites, technology was linked (somewhat) to standards, the curriculum was student-based (where students used raw data and primary sources to classify, analyze, and predict weather), the researchers were happy, and all should have been well. And all was well, until the pilot teachers reported that students were frustrated and the project had spent too much time on too few standards and, as a result, they would not have time deal with the balance of the required standards. The well-meaning first effort failed to provide teachers with what they really needed.

In retrospect, the curriculum was not particularly constructivist in its approach and, in terms of the *More/Less Emphasis* conditions, it went in a few wrong directions. Certainly in the teaching of standards where there should have been more emphasis on "focusing on student understanding and use of scientific knowledge, ideas and inquiry processes" there was, in fact, an emphasis on "focusing on student acquisition of information." Students learned about technology, waves, and science but did not learn about applications to understanding weather, which was the nature of their content standards. Assessment was minimal, violating the NSES reform tenets of "assessing rich, well structured knowledge," and "engaging students in ongoing assessments of their work." Perhaps the biggest violation under the reform indicators for content and inquiry standards was that the emergent curriculum failed to offer "management of ideas and information" and could not efficiently advance teachers' objectives of improving standardized test scores while maintaining science teaching's best practices. Finally, rather than creating a pool of well-armed and confident teachers, we impeded progress by not providing "long-term coherent plans." The balance of this chapter will explore the overlay of NSES standards onto the now successful Weather & Water Partnership.

Weather & Water Emerges Stronger

The second attempt was far more strategic and mindful of NSES reform standards. There was recognition that there were no easy solutions for integrating current science into classrooms and that success would be a "roll up your sleeves" intensive development effort. The design team doubled (to four) and, armed with active teacher and scientist advisory panels, set forth to create a comprehensive Weather & Water Partnership that could increase student performance on standardized tests and model best practices in science inquiry. The solution for interfacing with current research was to embed it deeply into a comprehensive new student-based curriculum. In 2005, after a year of redevelopment, the Weather & Water Fifth-Grade Partnership invited 105 classroom teachers in 16 school districts in Orange County, California to be part of a new collaborative and developmental process. This time the project demonstrated many of the key tenets envisioned by the NSES's blueprint for change.

Weather & Water, now in its third year of development, has become a good example of NSES reform, helping teachers change the way they teach, the way they continue to communicate and grow as teachers, the way that content and context are defined, how learning is assessed, how science programs are built, and how collaborators can nurture improved achievement. The chart below shows examples of Weather & Water activities mapped against NSES *More Emphasis/Less Emphasis* conditions. Standards highlighted with an asterisk are further elaborated later in the chapter.

More Emphasis On...	*Weather & Water* Examples
Teaching Standards	
Focusing on student understanding and use of scientific knowledge, ideas, and inquiry processes	Weekly student investigations where learners are active in questioning, thinking, and collecting evidence.
Guiding students in active and extended scientific inquiry	Weekly student investigations that use science notebooks and include inquiry and testable questions.
Providing opportunities for scientific discussion and debate among students	Investigation teams discuss conclusions and contribute to an all-class discussion after each investigation.
Continually assessing student understanding*	Student-based assessment strategies—preassessment and various formats of formative worksheets, class discussions, science notebooks, and quizzes—allow teachers to monitor student progress.
Working with other teachers to enhance the science program*	An active teacher advisory team, tested in a core group of eight classes, 100 teachers invited into project as partners in a research project, a Listserv connects teachers as a community.
Assessment Standards	
Assessing what is most highly valued	Assessments measure teacher confidence in teaching inquiry; students' attitudes; skills and content mastery; and effectiveness of investigations at driving questioning and analysis.
Assessing scientific understanding and reasoning	Student-based science notebooks.

Assessing to learn what students do understand*	Carousel brainstorming, KWL Charts, GIST summaries, one-minute paper, and science notebooks help establish a starting point for construction of new knowledge or skills.
Content and Inquiry Standards	
Understanding scientific concepts and developing abilities of inquiry	Eight weekly student investigations and three field trip experiments involve learners in questioning, thinking, and collecting evidence.
Integrating all aspects of science content	Science notebooks encourage the synthesis of content.
Activities that investigate and analyze science questions*	Eight weekly student investigations and three field trip experiments allow students to develop and test questions.
Process skills in context	Process skills are applied in the context of weekly student investigations, field experiments, and a real-time weather website.
Public communication of student ideas and work to classmates	Investigation teams discuss conclusion questions and teams contribute to an all-class discussion after each investigation.
Staff Development Standards	
Teacher as a member of a collegial professional community	Teachers treated as partners in a research project; active Listserv allows for effective communication between all partners.
Mix of internal and external expertise*	Teachers, informal science centers, and science researchers partner to contribute to program according to their areas of expertise.

Building Better Partnerships Between Education and Research Communities

The Weather & Water Partnership defines optimal roles and responsibilities for teachers, school districts, informal science centers, and science researchers in cooperatively increasing student performance on standardized tests and modeling best practices for science inquiry. The program addresses the appropriate balance for external and internal expertise in properly empowering teachers with curriculum that interfaces with today's science.

NSES: More/Less = Less emphasis on reliance on external expertise and more emphasis on a mix of internal and external expertise.

Role for teachers: Teachers contribute to the design, testing, and reporting on effective components of the curriculum. They are responsible for representing science as an exciting frontier replete with new investigations and for bringing students close to that frontier. Teachers are responsible for implementing student investigations with high-quality inquiry pedagogy and an emphasis on NSES. Teachers agree to participate in the evaluation effort and to enrich the development process by suggesting ways to improve the program for all teachers and students. Teachers communicate obstacles and solutions within their school teams and to the community of Weather & Water teachers via the Listserv.

Role for informal science centers: In the case of Weather & Water, the Ocean Institute contributes by facilitating the participation of partners at critical times; monitoring the flow of information between partners; creating new approaches to inspire teachers and students; leveraging Ocean Institute staff and facilities to support teachers; synthesizing evaluation data; coordinating remediation efforts; and managing budgets, timelines, and production staff.

Role for science partners: Scripps Institution of Oceanography scientists serve as the primary representatives for the SCCOOS network in the development of Weather & Water. The science team provides access to personnel, data, systems, and equipment. The multimillion-dollar network of sensors provides students with real-time access to wind, temperature, and ocean data. Data managers and web designers incorporate modifications to their website in response to needs of the design team. Scientists critically review emerging drafts of the curriculum for scientific accuracy.

The Weather & Water Fifth-Grade Program

Program Structure and Description

Weather & Water is a comprehensive nine-week program that aligns tightly with California Science Content Standards. Weather & Water seeks to improve test scores on standardized assessments and model best practices in inquiry science. The Weather & Water Partnership developed, tested, and implemented a program with the following components:

- Seven hours of teacher professional development and a Train-the-Trainer Program shows teachers how to participate and contribute to a broader collaboration
- Weekly lesson plans for 60-minute direct instruction and 60-minute student investigations
- Weather & Water Science Kit with all materials required for seven simultaneous (small group) in-class student investigations
- English Language Learner and Gifted and Talented Education modifications
- 30 custom transparencies (also provided as a PowerPoint)
- A full suite of formative and summative assessment instruments
- Supporting documents: weekly organizer, storyline, glossary, student and teacher background sections, homework, parent involvement strategies, and science skills activity suggestions
- Technology-based lesson plans that link curriculum to SCCOOS weather and ocean research; this is supported by a customized website and a stand-alone CD-ROM
- A 2½ hour field trip at the Ocean Institute with student-run, inquiry-based lab activities exploring differential heating, water cycle, and weather mapping

Weather & Water has four primary components, each of which employed NSES and *More/Less Emphases* to guide their development and implementation: Teacher professional development, the curriculum, the field trip, and the research collaboration are examined in detail below.

Teacher Professional Development

Teacher professional development is the foundation for the Weather & Water Partnership's success. Weather & Water teachers receive seven hours of collaborative exploration of the content, are offered ongoing in-class support from the Ocean Institute, and are connected via an Ocean Institute moderated listserv as a community of teachers. During the professional development day, teachers are introduced to their role and responsibilities in the Weather & Water Partnership. They learn that as a partner in this program they have the opportunity to test the curriculum in their classroom and inform their community and the design team of its effectiveness. Teachers agree to evaluate the program and make suggestions for improvements that may be incorporated into the following year's curriculum. Their input is critical to the success of the program.

The project models several of the NSES reform standards including more emphasis on guiding students in active and extended scientific inquiry; focusing on student understanding and use of scientific knowledge, ideas, and inquiry processes; and supporting a classroom community with cooperation, shared responsibility, and respect. In addition, Weather & Water, consistent with the NSES, allows teachers to "learn science through inquiry, having the same opportunities as their students will have to develop understanding" (NSES, Professional Development Standard A).

NSES: More/Less = Less emphasis on working alone and more emphasis on working with other teachers to enhance the science program.

Example: Teams of Teachers

Teachers in the Weather & Water professional development program work in small teams to set up and test every direct instruction and student investigation lesson plan. Teachers share their teaching approaches, perform every lab experiment, and together tackle the web-based technology lesson plans. In addition, teachers ask questions and discuss important "need to know" weather content. Teachers working in small teams are better able to understand and anticipate the obstacles and challenges in inquiry learning pedagogy before they attempt to implement it in their classrooms. By putting teachers in the role of the students in a friendly and collaborative atmosphere, they are able to share their different approaches and gain a collective confidence toward teaching effective inquiry-based science. Teacher teams work together within grade levels at their schools and through a Weather & Water Listserv moderated by the Ocean Institute.

> I wanted to let you know that my students and I have just started working on the Weather & Water program and are extremely excited about all the learning to come. In my 18 years of teaching I have never felt as enthusiastic and empowered about teaching science as I do right now.
>
> —*Response from a participating teacher*

The Curriculum

The Weather & Water curriculum captures the spirit of the NSES in allowing students to experience the richness and excitement of understanding the natural world by linking activities in the classroom and on field trips with big-picture ideas on weather. Students learn the science concepts associated with weather patterns and the water cycle by being engaged by scientific questions; making predictions based on their existing knowledge; and participating in activities, investigations, and discussions that allow them to explore the concepts and construct knowledge based on their experiences. Weather & Water provides a fresh way of looking at collaborations and the way they can leverage resources for teachers and students; it provides a workable plan for teachers who are not comfortable with teaching inquiry science and guarantees that each week students will be involved in at least one high quality, student-centered investigation. Inquiry activities go beyond hands-on and align with the definition in the NSES by allowing students to "begin with a question, design an investigation, gather evidence, formulate an answer to the original question, and communicate the investigative process and results" (NSES, Science Content Standards, Standard A). A number of evaluation tools are carefully integrated into the program and allow teachers to continuously probe for student success.

The following is a one-week excerpt from the Weather & Water Table of Contents:

Week 3: Uneven Heating of the Earth

Weekly Organizer	
Storyline	3 -- 1
Direct Instruction: *Uneven Heating of the Earth*	3 -- 5
Homework: *Convection Currents Detector*	3 -- 15
Student Investigation: *Uneven Heating of Playground Surfaces*	3 -- 21
Homework: *Uneven Heating of Playground Surfaces Story*	3 -- 35
Homework: *Sea Breezes and Land Breezes*	3 -- 43
Website Activity: *Sea Breezes*	3 -- 48
Weekly Quiz	3 -- 67
Question Bank	

Example: The Use of Science Notebooking

The NSES standards are emphatic about allowing students to take responsibility for their own learning. Weather & Water uses a notebooking program to support responsibility for student learning both individually and as members of teams. Teachers are able to build upon student ideas and questions with a vehicle that encourages development and reflection. Notebooking allows teachers to give individual students active roles in designing and implementing investigations, in preparing and presenting student work to their peers, and in assessing their own work. Science Notebooks provide a vehicle for consistent, high quality inquiry science instruction and allow teachers to assess continually what their students understand.

> NSES More/Less = Less emphasis on testing students for factual information at the end of the unit or chapter and more emphasis on continuously assessing student understanding.

The Science Notebook format supports the constructivist pedagogy by giving students the opportunity to track new knowledge that is developed as lesson plans, student-based investigations, and class discussions evolve. The Science Notebook approach reflects the essential features of classroom inquiry as defined by the National Research Council in *Inquiry and the National Science Education Standards: A Guide for Teaching and Learning* (2000). Students are engaged with a scientific question and make a prediction based on their understanding of the concept. They work with their team to perform an investigation and collect data. Students analyze this data to develop an explanation for what they observed during the investigation. They answer conclusion questions to help them develop their explanation and then share their explanation with the class in an all-class discussion. This discussion allows the students to evaluate their own explanation and make any necessary revisions based on the findings of their classmates and the scientific information provided by the teacher. They record any new information that they learned from the discussion in their Science Notebook.

During the investigation that focuses on the evaporation rate of water, students are asked if heat and wind affect the rate of evaporation of water. They make a prediction based on the knowledge they gained from previous lessons and design the procedure that they will follow in order to test their prediction. They use a fan, a lamp, or a hairdryer to evaporate water, and they record their data in their Science Notebook. As a team, they answer the conclusion questions, which helps them create an explanation for their observations and apply their understanding to situations in the real world. Each investigation team uses a different piece of equipment during the investigation, so they share their data and compare results with the other teams during a class discussion. This gives the students the opportunity to use the input from their classmates and teacher to evaluate their explanation and adjust their understanding of the concept.

The Field Trip: How an Informal Science Center Can Fill in the Gaps

The Ocean Institute field trip includes a 2½-hour laboratory program with three 50-minute student investigations. The field trip reflects NSES focus on "inquiry into authentic questions generated from student experiences is the central strategy for teaching science "(NSES, Teaching Standard A). Each investigation is inquiry-based and engages students in hands-on activities that are not easily duplicated in a classroom. Students continue to use their Science Notebooks to explore convection currents, the water cycle, and weather maps. Students build on their previous understanding and link outcomes of lab activities to observations in nature (sea breezes, clouds, etc.). The Weather & Water Partnership provides a new definition of the role that an informal science center can play in supporting teachers in their classrooms. Of the more than 60 field trips offered by the Ocean Institute, Weather & Water is the only one that is precisely, almost surgically, inserted into a comprehensive nine-week curriculum. The field trip is designed to fall around the seventh week of the curriculum and serves to reinforce previously learned concepts of differential heating and the water cycle and introduce the difficult concept of weather mapping. Finally, Ocean Institute instructors, all with science backgrounds and specialized training in inquiry teaching, serve as valuable role models for visiting teachers.

NSES: More/Less = Less emphasis on activities that demonstrate and verify science content and more emphasis on activities that investigate and analyze science questions.

Example: Convection Currents Investigation Station

Students work in investigation teams to conduct a tabletop investigation to explore the relationship between air temperature and air movement. They use their prior knowledge from activities

Students study convection current.

they have completed in the classroom to make a prediction about the direction of air currents. Using hot and cold sources to drive air currents in cylinders, students use smoke to test their prediction and collect data. After they have mastered the basic concepts of differential heating, they use sensors to measure the speed of currents and play with parameters of heat and cold to maximize measured wind speeds. Students use their data and conclusion questions to develop an explanation for their observations. They discuss the conclusion questions with two other investigation teams and an Ocean Institute instructor, which allows them to share their results and make any necessary adjustments to their explanation to ensure that it is scientifically accurate. Finally, students apply their new knowledge of convection currents to the real world by labeling the diagram and discussing the origin of sea breezes.

Example: Water Cycle Investigation Station

Small teams of students explore the phenomena of condensation, precipitation, and evaporation in a laboratory setting. During the experiment, students investigate the role that temperature plays in various parts of the water cycle. Students build on their knowledge from classroom activities to make and test a prediction about how water moves through a system of heated and cooled flasks. Student teams work together to explain what is happening and enter their observations and conclusions into their Science Notebooks. Finally, a diagram is used to stimulate a student discussion on how the phenomena might be expressed in nature.

Water cycle investigation.

Example: Weather Maps Investigation Station

During the pilot year of the program, teachers informed the design team that weather forecasting is a difficult concept for them to teach in the classroom. This resulted in the development of the weather maps investigation station during the field trip. This station introduces the students to the basics of reading weather maps and weather forecasting, so that they have prior knowledge on which to build when they study weather forecasting in the classroom. During the field trip, students work in investigation teams to interpret symbols used on weather maps and then use their new knowledge to correctly place weather symbols on a magnetic map of the United States. They learn about the weather conditions that accompany pressure systems and temperature fronts and that weather systems travel from west to east across the United States. They take this information and apply it to a real-world situation by making a pre-

Student examine weather maps.

diction on the direction a pressure system will move. In order to test their prediction, the investigation teams review the weather maps from the three days before their field trip. They choose one system to track over the three-day period and use a map scale, ruler, and a calculator to determine how far it travels each day. Using this information, they predict where the system will be on the current day and use the weather symbols to illustrate the weather conditions they would expect to find in that location. They then check the current day's weather map to determine whether they were correct.

Investigation teams work together to answer conclusion questions that they discuss with two other teams and the Ocean Institute instructor. The students' answers to these questions allow the instructor to assess if the students have successfully integrated all of the concepts that they learned throughout this station.

Example: Weather & Water Technology Strand

Weather & Water offers a technology strand with a series of 60-minute lesson plans that use the SCCOOS network of sensors and related real-time and archival data products to support standards and assessment-based learning objectives. All of the partners had a role in creating an effective student experience.

Students access user-friendly websites specifically designed by Scripps Institution of Oceanography to provide student access to data from buoys and shore-based observation stations. Students work in small teams at computer terminals and use archival or real-time data to reinforce the weather concepts that they learn during the week. For example, students learn about sea breezes through a homework activity during the week and then use archival data to connect this concept to the real world and see the air temperature conditions that are necessary for a sea breeze to form. In this activity, students select one inland weather station and one buoy station and collect wind and air temperature data at each location for four different times of the day. Students compare wind patterns along the coast over the course of the day and determine how temperature differences affect wind patterns. The activity supports classroom and field trip lessons on differential heating and allows students a different approach to standards' mastery.

The development of these activities required careful coordination between all the partners. Teachers reported a low success rate in early versions, which necessitated more work by the web designers to refine the web-based activities. Lack of internet access required a solution to use a freestanding CD-ROM for the archival data activities. Real-time data needed to be presented in a format that was student-friendly and included listing the data in the familiar Fahrenheit and local time while still introducing students to Celsius and UTC as the units used by scientists.

Weather & Water Assessment

Assessment Strategies

Weather & Water incorporated evaluation planning into the earliest design and development phases. As a result, the program now offers a broad range of integrated and tested assessment tools that can inform teachers about student performance and program developers about program effectiveness. Results from surveys, observations, pre- and postinstruments, and the embedded assessments play an integral role in program revision, teacher professional development, and student success. Compilation of data, data analysis, and remediation represented significant efforts by the Ocean Institute during year 1 and led to numerous modifications, explained at the end of the chapter.

Weather and Water Fifth-Grade Program Assessment Summary

Area of Assessment	Tool	Use
Students • Acquiring science knowledge • Acquiring science inquiry skills • Developing positive attitudes	Pretest/ Posttest	Students complete the same 10-question test before beginning the unit and after completing the unit to measure science knowledge acquisition. The test contains multiple-choice, matching, and labeling questions.
	Weekly Quizzes	Students complete weekly content quizzes so teachers can monitor student progress through content.
	Science Notebooks	Students record all procedures, data and observations, and conclusions in their Science Notebooks. Teachers evaluate the Science Notebooks to measure student progress in building knowledge through inquiry.
	Embedded Assessments: • Carousel Brainstorming • KWL Chart • GIST Summaries • Class Discussions	Embedded assessments allow teachers to monitor student acquisition of science knowledge and inquiry skills. Teachers can make minor adjustments to lessons as well as provide individual students with additional support.
Program • Meeting science standards • Implementing the program • Changing student attitudes	Interviews With Teachers	Program designers conduct interviews with focus groups and individual teachers to provide assessment data on teacher and student attitudes, program success in helping students meet science standards, program flow, and ease of implementation.
	Classroom Observations	Program designers observe students engaged in program demonstrations and investigations in the classroom. Observations include student time-on-task; number, type, and level of student questions; use of Science Notebooks; and teacher facilitation of investigations.
	Weeks 1–4 Survey Weeks 5– 9 Survey	Teachers complete a survey on the first half and on the second half of the program to provide data on student/teacher/parent attitudes, program flow, program effectiveness, Science Notebooks, and student investigation teams.
	Field Trip Observations	Program designers observe students engaged in field trip investigations. Observations include student time-on-task; number, type, and level of student questions; use of Science Notebooks; and instructor facilitation of investigations.
	Teacher Field Trip Survey	Teachers complete a survey on the field trip to provide data on student experience, student attitude, program alignment with science standards, program structure, and overall program quality.
	Ocean Institute Field Trip Survey	Instructors complete a survey on the field trip to provide data on student/instructor attitudes, program flow, program quality, use of Science Notebooks, and student investigation teams.

Teachers	Surveys	Teachers complete a survey before participating in the Weather & Water professional development and after teaching the unit to measure the effectiveness of the program in changing teacher knowledge of, skill in, and attitude toward teaching inquiry-based science. Teachers also complete a survey on the effectiveness of the professional development in providing teachers with a variety of activities that allow the integration of science and teaching knowledge.
• Acquiring science knowledge • Acquiring skills in teaching inquiry • Developing positive attitudes		

Student Assessment: Teacher Tools

The variety of assessment tools empowers teachers with the tools they need for continuous assessment. There is enough variety and flexibility of evaluation tools that teachers can choose or modify instruments to suit their needs. For example, they can select from preconstructed quizzes or use question banks to make their own tests.

NSES More/Less = Less emphasis on testing students for factual information at the end of the unit or chapter and more emphasis on continuously assessing student understanding; and less emphasis on assessing to learn what students do not know and more emphasis on assessing to learn what students do understand.

Teaching teachers to continuously "probe" for success is an important outcome from the teacher professional development workshops. The training covers the use of instruments and strategies as well as how to react to formative evaluation results. Some of the instruments that are employed include standards-based pretests, activities (carousel brainstorming, described below), student Science Notebooks, quizzes with question banks, KWL (Know, Want to Know, Learned) Charts, 1-minute papers, GIST (Generating Interactions between Schemata and Text) summaries, class discussions, homework assignments, and standards-based posttests.

Example: Carousel Brainstorming Activity

Carousel brainstorming offers a powerful tool for assessing both teacher and student foundational understandings of weather concepts. The approach is enjoyable and can be the basis for a constructivist approach. Carousel brainstorming starts with seven large sheets of butcher paper posted around the room, each with a weather or water topic (weather forecasting, water cycle, etc.) clearly labeled. Investigation teams rotate to each of the topics and write down everything they know about that topic. After two minutes, the teams rotate to the next topic, trying to add something to the growing string of knowledge. Teachers can use this activity to quickly assess student understanding and identify any misconceptions held by students before instruction begins.

Example: Embedded Assessment Linked to Standards

Weather & Water offers numerous embedded assessments that allow teachers to see how students would do on comparable standardized test questions. The Ocean Institute produced numerous drawings and charts that teachers could use to test for understanding of important concepts. This drawing offers students the opportunity to personalize their interpretation of differential heating. Students color in the drawing adding people and flags on the boat and flagpoles to illustrate the wind direction during sea breezes and land breezes.

Example: Standardized Pretest and Posttest Results—Students

Detailed standardized test performance data were collected from eight Weather & Water classes and demonstrates an increase in performance across all classes on a 10-question standardized-style test. Some of the questions were taken directly from the California Department of Education's STAR (Standardized Testing and Results) program's released questions. "The fifth-grade test covers grades 4 and 5 science content standards; the fifth-grade test was field tested in 2003, and the test that was administered in the spring, 2004, is now operational and will be included in a district's API. The fifth-grade test is comprised of approximately 40% grade 4 standards and 60% grade 5 standards. The Investigation and Experimentation standards comprise 10% of the test items" (CSTA 2006). Released questions provided the best analog for standardized test readiness. The range of increase across the tested classes was from 15% to 42% with an average of 26%. Some of the greatest percentage improvements were in the Santa Ana district, indicating the curriculum works well in ELL (English language learner) environments. Another interesting indication from the data was that the highest percentage increases in student performance came from teachers who had scored the highest in the five confidence categories. This is really a surprise, but verification of the importance of strong professional development.

Program Assessment: Design Team Tools

Continuous assessment allowed program development staff to understand the effectiveness of strategies against stated goals. Weather & Water was tested in 105 classrooms in 16 districts in Orange County, California, from September 2005 to April 2006. The design team collected data from surveys and conducted a series of focus sessions, intensive teacher interviews, and extensive classroom observation before developing a remediation plan for year 2.

Example: Pre- and Postsurvey Results From Teachers

A summative survey was administered to teachers participating in the Weather & Water Partnership. The data represents 21% of teacher participants. Areas of particular strength included the fact that 95% of teachers attending training actually taught the program, 89% of the teachers planned to participate again the next year, 84% rated the program as high quality and a valuable addition to the classroom, 74% felt the program addressed science content standards, and 80% found the Science Kit to have met the needs of the Unit. The pre- and postsurvey data yielded the most impressive impact for Weather & Water with increases in teacher confidence across all metrics: 23% in teaching science as inquiry, 24% in teaching weather content, 25% in using technology, and 36% in teaching scientific process. The data also shows some areas for improvement.

Since 37% of the teachers were unable to complete the entire unit, there was a need to increase efficiencies in the classroom. Over 89% of the teachers did not successfully use the website activities, indicating a need for increased professional development and classroom support. The use of the Science Notebooks and effectiveness of conclusion questions were not as successful as we would have liked (51% and 37% success, respectively) indicating some need for rewriting. Finally, only 3% of the teachers felt that the curriculum increased involvement of parents, indicating the need to redevelop effective strategies.

How Assessments Informed Program Development

The design team ended up identifying and responding to over 175 modifications in the eight-month interim period from May to December, 2006. Examples of problems identified from teacher and student surveys and classroom observations are provided below.

Identified problem 1: Assessment showed that 37% of Weather & Water teachers were unable to complete all nine weeks of the curriculum.

Solution: Part of the low completion rate, verified through focus sessions, was because the curriculum was new and teachers had not yet practiced teaching all of the components. However, efficiency became a primary objective for Weather & Water and the design team queried teachers on how to improve efficiency. One of the responses was to reorganize the curriculum to make it easier for teachers to use. For example, a weekly organizer was created to assist with navigation and preparation. Also, the Student Notebook was modified by adding student worksheets for direct-instruction demonstrations, adding testable questions in addition to the inquiry questions. For example, one of the student investigations was completely revised because student data led to incorrect conclusions. The simplified investigation more efficiently addressed the science content standard for that week.

Identified problem 2: Teacher surveys and interviews indicated an unacceptable number of teachers (<11%) had success with the technology strand designed to provide students with access to the SCCOOS network of weather sensors. The three major reasons cited were lack of time, problems with access to computers, and low confidence in using the lesson plans.

Solution: The primary modification that resulted from this finding was the creation of a stand-alone CD-ROM that allowed teachers to implement the activities even when access to the web was limited. In addition, the SCCOOS web designers modified web pages so that real-time data would be available in a teacher- and student-friendly format.

Identified problem 3: The design intent for Weather & Water was to support, not supplant, science textbooks by referencing appropriate background sections. However, poor access to textbooks across the districts presented a major obstacle for using the curriculum.

Solution: The Weather & Water design team responded by writing independent student background sections for all nine weeks. This allowed the curriculum to work as designed even when teachers did not have access to referenced textbooks. The process took an entire summer and required considerable input and approval from our SCCOOS partners.

Identified problem 4: Classroom observations by Ocean Institute staff showed that students were struggling with basic science skills, such as reading a thermometer and using a ruler.

Solution: The design team responded by developing an addition to the Introduction section that included suggestions for science skills activities that teachers could use to improve student measuring, charting and graphing, conversions, observation skills, following written directions, and using latitude and longitude. For example, we included an activity called "Measurement Marathon," where student investigation teams rotate through stations measuring a variety of classroom objects and volumes using different types of equipment and tools (rulers, graduated cylinders, pipettes, tape measures, thermometers). Students select the right tools to measure the height of a table, the length of a classroom, length of a paper clip, temperature of cups of water. A weekly organizer shows teachers which skills will be required each week so they can better prepare their students for success.

Future Forecast for Weather & Water: Sunny With a Chance of Change

Weather & Water lessons:
- Partnerships are important and can help to improve science instruction in schools. Informal science centers offer potential to broker effective solutions into existence and support them with financial and personnel resources not available to teachers. This aligns with NSES calling for the identification and use of resources outside the school. "The classroom is a limited environment. The school science program must extend beyond the walls of the school to the resources of the community" (Teaching Standard D).
- There are no easy solutions. Incomplete curriculum efforts will not likely address the needs of teachers or students and, as we found in our pilot, has the potential to drive results in the wrong direction. Meeting the NSES will require hard work, time, resources to develop effective lesson plans, ample support materials, and adequate teacher professional training.
- Continuous evaluation is critical for successful science instruction. This is true for teachers who constantly need to adjust for understanding; for curriculum developers who need to improve program effectiveness; and for parents, administrators, and funders who need accountability.
- It is possible to design effective curriculum that both prepares students for standardized assessments and models best practices for science inquiry.

- The real gift to teachers is a comprehensive curriculum that is consummately efficient and allows teachers to build competency in all required standards in the allotted time. And, of course, the real challenge is to do that without compromising NSES objectives of inquiry, minds-on, teaching pedagogy.

> NSES More/Less = less purchasing of textbooks based on traditional topics and more on adoption of curriculum aligned with Standards and on a conceptual approach to science teaching, including support for hands-on science materials.

Some findings relative to our goals of building facile and effective links between SCCOOS and fifth-grade classrooms are:

- Complex data products can be useful to formal K–12 education when properly integrated into curriculum.
- The process of integrating data products into formal education is time and labor intensive and involves a careful analysis of where and how to make effective linkages. In the end, SCCOOS products could not be effectively integrated using stand-alone lessons but rather required embedding them into a comprehensive nine-week curriculum.
- Achieving broader impact requires effective partnerships, strong project management, awareness of formal education needs, and a team of qualified curriculum developers and education-savvy researchers.

Weather & Water's Future Is Bright!

Weather & Water is currently in its third year of development and will host over 3,500 students in 16 school districts throughout Orange County, California, during the 2006–2007 academic year. This year, the project also moves into the dissemination phase with the initiation of a Train-the-Trainer Program designed to empower districts to provide professional development for their own teachers. To date, six districts have trainers and free access to all curriculum resources. The Weather & Water field trip will become a formal offering in the Ocean Institute's course catalog in 2007–2008. The SCCOOS program will continue to fund the refinement of the web-based student activities and the Arnold and Mabel Beckman Foundation has agreed to fund a new two-year effort to develop a fourth-grade Earth science unit built upon the successful emergent strategies from Weather & Water.

Weather & Water has helped define a role for informal science centers to contribute to systemic science education reform. Most important, perhaps, are the functions of assisting with teacher professional development, building confidence in teachers to use inquiry teaching in the classroom, coordinating program development, building bridges with scientists, and hosting field trips that have meaningful and direct support of classroom curriculum. Beyond program development, informal science centers can play the vital role of teaching content standards that are difficult for teachers to teach in the classroom and modeling good science inquiry pedagogy. Two informal science centers in our region will be adopting Weather & Water in 2007 and testing these assumptions. The California Science Center in Los Angeles will be collaborating with their museum school and the University of California Santa Barbara's Marine Studies Institute will begin working collaboratively with the Santa Barbara Office of Education.

The National Science Education Standards seek to create a scientifically literate nation. The document describes an educational system where all students demonstrate high levels of performance, in which teachers are empowered to make the decisions essential for effective learning, in which interlocking communities of teachers and students are focused on learning science, and in which supportive educational programs and systems nurture achievement. "The school science program must extend beyond the walls of the school to the resources of the community" (NSES, Teaching Standard D). The Weather & Water Partnership, in addition to focusing on student performance and building teaching communities, can be a model for catalyzing a broader educational system that supports science literacy. Weather & Water demonstrates the value of strong buy-in from principals, funding agencies, non-profit organizations, research agencies, individual scientists, parents, and teachers all working toward the NSES vision of science literacy.

> Thanks to you and to the Ocean Institute now I'm curious about science. Maybe someday I will become a meteorologist. You opened my mind to science.
>
> —Omar (fifth-grade Weather & Water student)

References

National Research Council (NRC). 1996. *National science education standards*. Washington, DC: National Academy Press.

National Research Council (NRC). 2000. *Inquiry and the national science education standards: A guide for teaching and learning*. Washington, DC: National Academy Press.

California Science Teachers Association (CSTA). 2006. *STAR tests*. Sacramento, CA: California Science Teachers Association. Available online at *www.cascience.org/STAR.html*.

Omaha's Henry Doorly Zoo Academy:

Where Science Education Comes to Life!

Elizabeth A. Mulkerrin
Omaha's Henry Doorly Zoo

Fundamental to the Omaha's Henry Doorly Zoo's mission is the education of 1.35 million visitors and 80,000 students who visit each year. This commitment to education has driven the zoo to become a strong and active supporter of education in the state of Nebraska for over 30 years. The zoo has become a leader in both informal and formal education by leading many math and science initiatives. To accomplish this leading role we have partnered with educational institutions on a variety of math and science partnership programs and provide expertise in curriculum development, teacher content development, long-distance learning, university classes, K–12 formal education programs, and a home-school science program.

The Zoo Academy is one example of an effective nontraditional teaching model for science education. The academy has become an excellent work-based learning model and demonstrates how to collaborate and form partnerships successfully between school districts and the nonprofit/business world. From the Zoo Academy model, over 24 academy programs and five informal summers career camps have been developed and used with students in the Omaha Metropolitan area.

The Zoo Academy model is a prime example of science education reform in action. It removes the teacher and the students from a traditional classroom and places them into a nontraditional learning environment where they observe, learn, and apply scientific knowledge to real-world situations. It also becomes a safe environment where the teacher is given the opportunity to freely guide students through active scientific inquiries, establish a community-learning environment, and emphasize student understanding as the final goal to achieved learning. The combination of these components leads to the establishment of a perfect learning environment for students to demonstrate their understanding of scientific concepts, freely investigate, experience real research, analyze, and communicate science explanations to peers and professionals.

National Science Education Standards in Action

The National Science Education Standards (NSES) are incorporated into every facet of the Zoo Academy program. The secondary science teacher selected is required to have a degree in zoology or biology, including field research experience and experience managing animals. This requirement is very selective but guarantees the teacher will have the necessary educational background, interest, and experience needed to guide the students through an inquiry-based program. These teachers are given a variety of professional development opportunities to increase their understanding of the facts and concepts presented in the zoology portion of the academy. The selected Zoo Academy teacher spends three months interning at the zoo to develop current curriculum, develop conceptual connections between zoology and zoo business, develop an understanding of conservation issues facing zoos and the community, and establish a working relationship with zoo employees. Building this relationship with animal area supervisors and animal curators is a key component to assure the experiences the students receive are positive and educational.

Every day of the Zoo Academy is a new science education adventure for the teacher and students. The academy teacher teaming up with the expertise of the zoo staff provides a very rich inquiry-based learning environment for students. The teacher plans the curriculum goals around inquiry-based experiences. In doing this, the teacher constantly evaluates his or her own knowledge and expertise and determines where he or she needs assistance to meet the needs of the students. This allows the teacher to guide the students successfully through a variety of inquiry processes. The zoo staff becomes the resources needed to help the teachers guide their students through scientific investigations and experiences with zoo conservation scientists. This experience establishes a relationship between the students and the zoo staff by giving everyone the opportunity to communicate their findings and to discuss the impact of new discoveries and how they relate to current conservation issues.

Throughout the year, students witness how rapid changes and scientific discoveries quickly outdate information found in textbooks. The teacher is continuously adapting curriculum to ensure the students are receiving the most recent scientific information and skills needed to address new topics developed from student experiences.

The expertise of the teacher is limited to his or her educational background and experiences. It is crucial for the teacher to utilize zoo staff as a resource and incorporate their expertise in the total curriculum. The combination of teacher and zoo staff expertise can be seen as simple presentations in the classroom as well as elaborate laboratory experiences behind the scenes that one needed for guidance through an inquiry experience.

The Zoo Academy concept is a combination of three major educational components: career exploration, classroom experiences, and scientific research opportunities. Career exploration allows for students to explore freely their career goals through internships. The internships give students the opportunity to work directly with horticulturists, nutritionists, veterinarian staff, and animal management teams. The students are given a chance to discover new scientific careers that may start the career decision process.

The Zoo Academy coursework is developed to give students a variety of learning opportunities and daily experiences by taking advantage of access to zoo professionals, research laboratories, animal exhibits, and behind-the-scenes areas. All of these opportunities are used to establish a living laboratory setting. This concept of a living laboratory is very successful and important to the whole concept of the program. The interaction between the teachers and zoo staff allows for more opportunities to apply scientific concepts and to see live examples from the animal kingdom.

Student working with a zoo conservation researcher.

Building off of the living laboratory concept, students are given multiple scientific research experiences. Throughout the year, students actively participate in a variety of inquiry-based projects. These projects range from helping animal supervisors or "vet techs" determine why an animal is behaving differently to asking their own questions and designing scientific investigations.

Through a variety of assessments we have discovered that when students are given the opportunity to participate in the inquiry process they are more willing to

Second year student working on DNA sequencing.

commit their own time to investigate questions developed through their experiences. To accommodate the students' need and desire to investigate, Zoo Academy teachers are encouraged to expand their program by providing additional learning opportunities. For example, the Papillion La Vista Zoo Academy has incorporated a Zoo Academy research course for second-year students. Students who have successfully completed the Zoo Academy and would like to continue their exploration of scientific research in more detail are given the opportunity to spend a year in the Grewcock Center for Conservation Research. This gives the students the opportunity to conduct their own inquiry-based research in one of the zoo's state-of-the art labs.

Omaha's Henry Doorly Zoo Academy Program

In 1996, Omaha Public School District (OPS) received school-to-career funding to design and implement a science career academy. Administrators from OPS and the Henry Doorly Zoo established a solid collaboration and agreed the concept of a zoo academy program was innovative and would become an ideal model for a nontraditional student learning experience. The Zoo and OPS jointly developed the ideal zoo academy model, curriculum, and a student selection process.

The uniqueness of the academy program allows for the selection of a wide range of students with varying academic abilities. Students who are ranked low academically do extremely well in the rich educational environment at the zoo and have shown improvement and success in all of their core classes and their whole lives outside the school.

To be eligible for the Zoo Academy, students are required to have completed their sophomore year, and have successfully met all their biology, chemistry, and algebra graduation requirements. These requirements are to ensure the students have a basic knowledge of the science applications needed for the internship component of the Zoo Academy. Students who meet these requirements will complete the application process by submitting a student essay, parent letter of support, and teacher recommendations. The final component of the selection process is a panel interview. The panel consists of the Zoo Academy teacher, school career counselor, and a zoo education curator. At the end of the process 18 students are selected to participate in the program. In the last five years an additional partner has been added, which has allowed us to increase the number of Zoo Academy students to 40.

To ensure the best possible experience for the students, an educational agreement for success has been developed between the school districts, students, parents, teachers, and zoo officials.

Academy Research Experience

Conservation research is a major part of the zoo's mission. Because of our commitment to conservation research, we felt it was very important to incorporate inquiry-based research into the curriculum. The research component becomes an excellent opportunity for the students to participate actively in a scientific investigation, formulate scientific explanations, and work side-by-side with field researchers. The teacher and zoo researchers mentor and guide the students through the scientific process.

Students are given the opportunity to explore their interests, identify questions, and develop their own scientific study to answer their questions. Over the years students have conducted animal behavior studies, genetic analysis, nutritional studies, breeding pattern studies, and researched the ideal incubation temperature for bamboo sharks.

At the beginning of the school year students start generating scientific questions through observations and experiences during their internships. The students are asked to formulate their questions, propose testable hypotheses, develop a research hypothesis, develop a research plan, and conduct scientific investigations. At this time we start to see students establish relationships with zoo researchers. The guidance of the zoo staff helps the students successfully design a study and collect needed data.

During the first five months of school, students develop a research plan, collect and analyze data, and draw conclusions with guidance from zoo scientists. The end result is a written scientific paper to communicate results and defend their hypotheses. The students are given the opportunity to discuss and defend their scientific findings effectively to the zoo director and staff, a panel of university professors, and their peers. Students complete the scientific communication process by presenting their findings at the Metro Science and Engineering Fair and Nebraska Junior Academy of Science.

Results of the student scientific inquires have given the zoo insights for developing a variety of exhibits while also increasing knowledge of behaviors. These have all led to exhibit changes, animal moves, and changes in animal management protocol.

Several students have become coauthors on scientific papers in the field of genetics and reproductive physiology. It has been very rewarding to see the students succeed in the research component of the Zoo Academy.

Papillion La Vista student presenting genetic research at MSEF.

Academy Classroom Experiences

Zoo Academy teachers are given access to a vast number of endangered animals to use as examples in the survey of the animal kingdom course. Utilizing the zoo's animal collection and the constant communication with zoo staff leads to a variety of learning enrichment opportunities for the students. For example, the aquarium supervisor was aware of the Zoo Academy studying cephalopods. The aquarium supervisor scheduled a necropsy to be completed on an octopus at the same time as the Zoo Academy class. The aquarium supervisor was able to provide learning opportunities for students by bring the octopus necropsy to the classroom. The students were able to participate in the procedure under the direct supervision of the aquarium supervisor, ask their own questions, and explore the internal structures of the octopus.

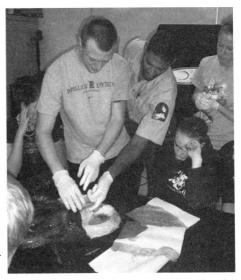

Students performing a necropsy under the direction of the aquarium supervisor.

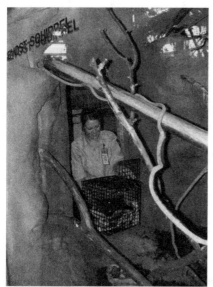

Student releasing animals into a Lied Jungle exhibit during internship experience.

The students learned how to identify abnormalities, the importance of recording observations for zoological records, and how to draw appropriate conclusions. Opportunities similar to this occur on a daily basis.

Academy Internship Experience

Internships are designed to give the students a chance to really experience a zoo career. Before the student internship rotations begin, students are required to complete the zoo's employee safety training program. During this program the students learn how to work with a variety of animal species and how to report and record any out-of-the-ordinary behaviors, food consumption, and water chemistry. The need for safety and responsibility is continuously reinforced with the students. Once the training is completed, the students complete a two-day exploration rotation in the following areas: Scott Aquarium, Hoof Stock, Children's Petting Zoo, Horticulture, Penguins, Desert Dome, Kingdoms of the Night, Lied Jungle, Nutrition, Birds, and Genetics lab.

At the completion of this experience student assessment is in the form of a resume, cover letter, and an elaboration of scientific skills required to work in three different areas for the remaining school year. Zoo supervisors complete the assessment process by evaluating the students' scientific literacy and work skills at the end of each rotation. Throughout this process the zoo staff is seen as teachers while also serving as role models and mentors for the students.

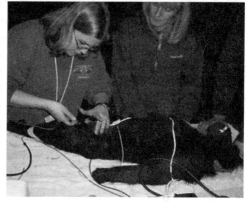

Former student working as a full-time vet.

Post–Zoo Academy Opportunities

The Zoo Academy program has become a valuable resource for hiring future zoo employees. Zoo Academy students spend nine months developing the scientific skills needed to become a zoo employee. Many of these students become summer keepers, volunteers, and interns. Many participate in the eco-adventure summer career academy. Several Zoo Academy alums have completed their postsecondary education and returned as veterinarian externs and full time employees.

Zoo Academy Effectiveness

The Zoo Academy is seen as a very successful program by the partnering school districts and the Henry Doorly Zoo. To measure the effectiveness of Zoo Academy, the number of students who pursue science degrees and science careers is tracked and measured. To determine this effectiveness, the Omaha Public Schools research department collected data from the OPS Annual Graduate Study to analyze the postsecondary activities of Zoo Academy alumni. From this survey it was found that 61.9% of the Zoo Academy students reported their career goals, as categorized by the Nebraska Career Education Career Fields, as agriculture and natural resources, health services, or scientific research and engineering. When compared to all the 2002–2005 graduates, only 26.7% reported similar career clusters as a career goal. This provides evidence that the Zoo Academy students continue to have an interest in science-related careers.

When asked about their plans for college majors, 53.6% of the Zoo Academy students reported their majors to be agriculture and natural resources, health services, or scientific research and engineering. This high percentage compares to only 25.5% of all graduates reporting the above career clusters as a college major for all the 2002–2005 graduates. The results are very promising, showing that the Zoo Academy students are pursuing science-related careers in animal management, research, engineering, and health services. The school districts and the zoo will continue to track the students through postgraduate studies.

Through the data collected by OPS we were not able to answer the question "Do high school experiences cause a change in student career goals?" To answer this question, we collected data from the Papillion La Vista School District to see if experiences in the Zoo Academy program changed career goals. Looking at results from career interest surveys given to Papillion La Vista students in ninth and tenth grade, Zoo Academy students were found to be interested in the following career clusters: agricultural and natural resources (24.5%), health services (24.5%), scientific research and engineering (30%). All of these figures differ from the total student body where 67.9% were reported *not* to be interested in a science-related career.

After graduation, these students were given a postsecondary survey to find out what college majors they are pursuing. From this survey we found students were majoring in fields related to the following career clusters: agricultural and natural resources (35%), health services (17.6%), and scientific research and engineering (35%). Only 11.7% of the students surveyed reported that they would not pursue a science-related major. Comparing student survey results before participation in the Zoo Academy to the majors Zoo Academy alumni are currently pursuing, we can see the students have increased their interest in science career fields. This sample is an indication that career choices do change as a result of their high school experiences. To determine a change in student career interests generally much more data must be collected.

Over the last 10 years the zoo has hired 7 full time employees, over 30 summer keepers, 2 veterinary

Former students working a full time animal management job at the zoo.

externs, and multiple interns from the Zoo Academy. Through continuous contact with past graduates, we know students have become successful veterinarian technicians, veterinarians, science educators, informal science educators, naturalists, animal management experts, and a variety of other science-related professionals. The Zoo Academy is one example of a very successful collaboration with formal education. This innovative program is an effective nontraditional teaching model for science education.

Summary

In its 10 years of existence, over 200 Zoo Academy students have been given a unique opportunity to witness and work with the zoo's state-of-the-art medical and research capabilities in reproductive physiology, nutrition, genetics, genome resource banking, conservation programs, and animal management. Not only are these students witnessing and participating in the rapid changes in science, they are also exploring scientific career options for their own futures. Through externship experiences and interaction with zoo staff on zoo grounds, students are provided daily learning opportunities and given challenges to solve animal management issues, answer research questions, and apply scientific concepts learned.

Students have the opportunity to become certified divers through the summer career academy.

The zoo continues to make a positive impact in the education community through a variety of collaborations at the local, state, and national level. Adopt-a-School and district partnerships have formed to help local educators develop and implement new math and science teaching techniques. This is accomplished by providing professional development workshops at the zoo and area schools, through a joint math and science partnership with the state of Nebraska.

Zoo educators are providing science enrichment through long-distance learning and curriculum support. The zoo's education department has a voice at the state level through the "Building a Presence in Science" board and a Math-Science Partnership advisory committee. Nationally, the zoo is working with educational representatives from Alabama, Florida, Illinois, and Montana to replicate the Zoo Academy model and full-day kindergarten program. In the future we are hoping to design and implement a similar middle-school program.

The Zoo Academy program is the ideal model to demonstrate science education reform in action. All three components demonstrate different facets of the *More Emphasis* visions from the NSES. This unique opportunity places students in a rich learning environment where they can make discoveries about the natural world and apply the knowledge gained to real-world situations.

"MITS" You Each Summer

Mary C. Nash and Emily V. Wade
Museum Institute for Teaching Science

At a meeting of seven Boston-area museum directors in 1983, Dr. Paul Gray, then President of Massachusetts Institute of Technology (MIT), spoke about the declining percentage of students electing to go into science and engineering as a career and the danger this posed for the future of the United States. This discussion led to the beginning of the Museum Institute for Teaching Science (MITS). In turn, the mission for MITS was formulated: To promote the teaching of participatory, inquiry-based science, mathematics, and technology at the elementary and middle school level (K–8), through collaboration among informal science education institutions. This mission recently expanded to include engineering.

To accomplish this mission, MITS developed three programs to advance inquiry-based, hands-on, minds-on teaching of science, technology, engineering, and mathematics (STEM) at the K–8 grade levels: a two-week Summer Institute; a quarterly K–6 publication, *Science Is Elementary*; and three winter seminars for museum educators.

The first program, begun in 1986 and funded for five years by the National Science Foundation, was the two-week Summer Institute for K–8 teachers taught by informal educators from seven museums. Becoming incorporated in 1992, MITS is now funded by foundations, corporations, individuals, and occasionally by the state. The museum educators use inquiry-based, hands-on, minds-on activities that the teachers can use as a model for their classroom activities to implement curriculum. With these activities students become engaged and excited, realizing that science is a participatory process and that it is stimulating and fun. Since 1993, this program has evolved and expanded and is now in nine regions of Massachusetts, from Cape Cod to the Berkshires. More than 2,500 individual teachers, many of them returning several times, have participated in these Institutes. The Summer Institutes are organized with educators from four or more museums in each region, one of whom is the lead educator and is responsible for organizing the program in their region. The lead educators form the Museum Educator Advisory Committee under the chairmanship of Dr. Mary Nash, Program Director for MITS.

The second program, developed by MITS and a teacher who attended one of the first Summer Institutes, is a quarterly resource publication for K–6 teachers called *Science Is Elementary*. It was originally linked to the National Benchmarks for Science Literacy and in the past few years, linked to the National Science Education Standards also. Each issue presents ten hands-on activities, pertinent background information, and reference resources. Each volume of four issues is themed on the prior year's Summer Institute, presenting the topic from four different points of view. The publication is free to participants in the prior year's Summer Institute and on a subscription basis around the country.

Realizing that museum educators also need help in keeping up-to-date with education reforms and with the latest methods, MITS provides three one-day professional development seminars (PDS) during the winter for museum educators. This third program developed by MITS uses experts from New England and New York to present pertinent seminars on topics suggested by the Museum Educator Advisory Committee.

From 1997 through 2001 MITS, in cooperation with the Eisenhower Regional Alliance for Mathematics and Science Reform, organized the Northeast Informal Science Education Network (NISEN) for educators from informal science education organizations in New England and New York and presented two-day professional development conferences for them.

From 1997 through 2002 MITS partnered with the Massachusetts Department of Education to provide science and mathematical activities and kits for their National Science Foundation Parent Involvement Project (PIP). This involved using museum educators to develop activities for parents and children to do together and designing informational booklets and kits for distribution to parents. These activities were developed into a booklet, *Creating Family Friendly Activities in Science and Math*, available from MITS.

In the 20 years that MITS has been offering the Summer Institute, the office for MITS has been housed at various locations, including office space at the Museum of Science, the New England Aquarium, and now at the Boston Children's Museum. Our classrooms and workshop areas are the cooperating museums throughout Massachusetts.

Standards

Through the years, MITS Summer Institutes have strived to move their program to the *More Emphasis* side of the recommended standards. This is not an easy feat to accomplish and one that educators emphasize throughout the Summer Institute with participants. Teachers have thought and even now think that if they do not dispense "words of wisdom" to their students, the students will not know how to answer questions on standardized tests. The problem with this method is that students then only answer what they have been told and not what they have researched, reasoned, and critically thought out. Once teachers utilize more of the *More Emphasis* side, both they and their students find science exciting, interesting, and challenging to do as a group and as individuals. It leads to *Less Emphasis* on directed, didactic teaching and a greater understanding of the concepts being addressed.

Changing Emphasis

Teaching Standards

In the "Blueprint for Change" the changing emphasis on Teaching Standards is addressed. It gives great emphasis to working with students in all aspects of their experience in the classroom whether it is interaction with each other, with the teacher, or with the curriculum. It is through inquiry methodology that teachers and students learn content in many disciplines. This is really the essence of what MITS is trying and succeeding in doing. The teachers at the MITS Institute are treated like a class of students, thus modeling how they should treat their students. Often the class will start with an open-ended question such as: "Why are there no whales in New Bedford Harbor?" After a general discussion the class will be divided up into groups of four or five to explore ways to find an answer and will be provided with a table of resources that can be used to help find the answer. Working together, the teachers have to learn to respect each other's ideas and learn that some of them are stronger in certain aspects of researching the answer to the question than others. They have to learn to cooperate with each other and to listen to someone who may have different background knowledge than they do. Time and again in the reflective journals kept by the teachers, they mention how they have learned about classroom dynamics from being back in a class situation. In all the Institutes there is an emphasis on being a facilitator rather than a know-it-all who lectures to a submissive class. Interaction, questioning, and exploration are the important parts of each lesson and are what lead teachers and eventually their students to gain greater understanding and retention of the principles being taught.

Assessment Standards

Most teachers are under the impression that assessment is a factual measurement of what the students are taught. This fits in very nicely with "factual" teaching, where the student receives information and answers "factual" test questions by regurgitating what was taught. When teachers are introduced to inquiry-based methodology, they are also shown various ways for measuring learning—as learning takes place. The students' work on a project should be an ongoing assessment and one that will test their achievement as they process their work. During the Summer Institute, assessment is modeled in differing ways for the participants, particularly when they develop their lesson plans and units, assessment plans for their classes, and when they take their pre-and posttest, as it may be a question on thinking about a solution rather than just answering a question. Once shown how to assess students' knowledge and understanding, teachers are very open to implementing the various methods with students.

Content and Inquiry Standards

The MITS museum educators are the facilitators for the teachers' development of activities and methods to advance an understanding of science concepts through inquiry-based methodology. One of the major goals of each Institute is to introduce to the teachers and have them understand three methods of inquiry—directed, guided, and open—through discussion and modeling during the various activities using the different forms of inquiry teaching. Part of every activity is a report, developed as a consensus of the group's work or as a single comment if that is the way the question was addressed. The activities used in the Institutes are developed in such a way that the teachers can apply them to their own classes, adjusting as necessary for grade-level differences and students' level of understanding. They often are extended over a period of two days or more and always have a component where the teachers have to defend their results and look at the results as extension of further research, utilizing the science processes. By having the teachers exposed to the methodology that MITS models throughout the Summer Institute, the teachers learn by doing and also learn some of the feelings that their students undergo in a similar situation. "I don't like to work in groups," or "The other people in the group aren't listening to what is being said" are comments often heard.

During class time, educators are encouraged to accept questions from the teacher/participants and to address them with the whole class. After working on a question—by developing an experiment and implementing the science processes or researching the web and books, or visiting a laboratory to find an answer—each groups' answer is shared with the whole class, often leading to unanswered questions raised by the earlier ones. Future unanswered questions lead to further ways to answer these questions and allow teachers to think critically of ways to arrive at content knowledge. This is an example of a fully engaged class and one that is encouraged by the museum educators. It is easily transferred to the teachers' classrooms. When developing their lesson plans and or units for their future classroom work, teachers are asked to identify in each lesson the type of inquiry to be implemented. This is an extension of what the teachers have been observing and commenting on throughout the Institute. Their comments are frequently expressed in their reflective journals.

Staff Development Standards

Under the staff development standards, MITS puts its emphasis on learning science through inquiry and experiential methods. This is what the museum educators model for the participating teachers in the Summer Institute. They show the teachers how to link their lessons/units to the Massachusetts Frameworks, how to adapt them for inquiry-based methods, and how they can develop their curriculum utilizing an inquiry approach. Another asset of the Summer Institutes is that they provide an opportunity for teachers from different school systems and schools to work together and to learn from each other. Teaching is a lonely profession with many teachers, closeted with their class for most of each day and with no chance to exchange ideas and techniques with other teachers. Since our Institutes mix teachers from grades K–8, from different school districts and sometimes even different states, there is an opportunity for great exchanges of ideas and methods amongst the teachers and good collaborative learning. MITS encourages teachers from the same school to come together to support each other when back in the classroom, to be able to develop complementary plans for their classes, and to influence their school to adopt more inquiry-based learning methods. This point was stressed by the evaluation team at Lesley University's Program Evaluation and Research Group, who did an evaluation on the MITS program by visiting teachers at schools and speaking with them.

Mits Summer Institute Program

MITS Summer Institute programs are held the first two weeks of July in nine regions of Massachusetts. Each region has 4–7 cooperating museums in that region, with each institution teaching one or two days during the institute. With the variations in museums: art, aquaria, nature centers, science centers, botanic gardens, zoological parks, stamp museum, and preserved forests, the settings and materials used are different each year.

The difference in the materials used is also the result of the theme of the institute and the concepts addressed changing each year. Some of the institute titles and themes addressing various concepts are given as examples of the wide variations of content covered over the past 10 years. Even though there are as many as 44 museum educators involved during a given Summer Institute, the teaching of many activities are similar at all the different sites.

- 1996: "Getting Physical." Teachers focused on physical science content and activities during this institute, only to realize that they were teaching physical science in their classes without knowing it.
- 1997: "Science All Around Us." Activities during this institute focused on everything around them such as home, schoolyard, and classrooms that could become a source of science learning.
- 1998: "Tools of the Trade." Emphasis was put on using technology activities to enhance and engage students. Introduction to many tools and technology not used by the teachers was accomplished.
- 1999: "The Everyday Scientist." Teachers were shown that the world is science and we are all scientists and everyone should have a great curiosity about our living world.
- 2000: "21st Century Science." What great changes in students' science thinking and use of science discoveries from the last century will affect students in the new century?
- 2001: "Form and Function." Teachers in this institute looked at manmade and natural structures, machines, birds, fish, and habitats to gain knowledge of their form and function.
- 2002: "Modeling Makes the Abstract Tangible." To better understand concepts, teachers were introduced to the use of models.
- 2003: "Integrating Science With Mathematics, Literacy, and the Arts." The importance of integration was accomplished by looking at nature through the power of words, art, and mathematical equations.
- 2004: "Design: A Context for Learning." Participants explored design as a context for learning science, engineering, mathematics, and art.
- 2005: "Exploring the Science and Math of Change." Teachers took part in activities that pinpointed environmental changes, technological changes, plant population changes, and engineering changes.
- 2006: "CSI: Cycles, Systems, and Inquiry." Some of the activities involved teachers observing and measuring geologic changes in rocks, sand, soil, and fossils as well as the chemistry and mathematics of cooking.

- 2007: "Measuring up to STEM." With emphasis on measurement, teachers will center their activities on how measurement is used throughout the teaching of STEM.

In the following paragraphs, an introduction to the museum sites in the different regions will be highlighted along with a description of activities. The lead museum will be identified. The lead Museums change regularly so the lead museums at present are the ones labeled. Each lead museum educator is responsible for developing a syllabus for their region with their cooperating museum partners that addresses the topic for that year and includes objectives to be met with described activities that are referenced to the Massachusetts State Frameworks. A reference bibliography is also attached. The syllabus from each region is further submitted to the various colleges that will award graduate credit to the teachers who have registered for the credit. MITS works with five different colleges that service different regions to award graduate credit to the teachers. Some teachers register for Professional Development Points only that satisfy their re-certification requirements, which is on a five-year cycle in Massachusetts.

Boston

The largest group of teachers attends the Boston region Summer Institute. Usually, the teachers are divided into four separate groups according to grade level of teaching. The museum educators have a two-day session with each group, addressing the activities to their grade level. Museums in the Boston region include: MIT Museum (lead), Boston Children's Museum, New England Aquarium, and Franklin Park Zoo. The teachers meet as a group on the first day, have a "taste" of the inquiry-based activities to be done in the next two weeks, are given directions to the other sites, gain insight into the path that led to a woman scientist choosing a science career, and have the opportunity to sign up for college credit. The teachers are told of the requirements for Professional Development Points (PDP), college credit, and completion of the course. (This is the same format in each region for the first day.) For the Institute "Exploring the Science and Math of Change" the MIT Museum had teachers develop their own system of measurement by giving each team different sized plastic containers, having them name them, then determining how many of what measurement filled the largest container. Each group exchanged their method of measurement and tested to see if the measurement worked for the other group. This led to a wonderful discussion amongst the teachers. The seven remaining days were filled with inquiry-based, hands-on activities that culminated in the last day of pulling the learning all together.

Berkshires

During the Summer Institute "CSI: Cycles, Systems, and Inquiry," the Berkshire Museum (lead), Berkshire Botanical Gardens, Center for Ecological Technology, Samson Environmental Center, Antioch New England Graduate School, and Hopkins Memorial Forest were the museum sites for western Massachusetts. Teachers were involved in numerous activities with the cyclical changes in the succession of the forest being identified and discussed. During the hands-on activities, teachers were able to experience the canopy of the trees by climbing up and crossing over the canopy walk that is part of Hopkins Forest. With more than four cooperators, teachers spent one day at some sites and more than one day at other sites.

Cape Cod

The Cape Cod region has some interesting sites. The Ocean Quest, a boat-based education site, is the lead for this area. Waquoit Bay National Estuarine Research Reserve, Cape Cod Museum of Natural History, and Thornton Burgess Society are the cooperating museums. During this past Summer Institute, Ocean Quest concentrated on bacteriological systems found in the ocean. Teachers determined the large number of microbes in the ocean and described characteristics of plants and animals as they relate to marine plankton and the seasonal/physical changes that impact their life cycles.

Essex

Teachers in the Essex region experience inquiry-based, hands-on activities at a number of Museum sites, spending one or two days at Essex Shipbuilding Museum (lead), Massachusetts Audubon Society Endicott Regional Center, H.O.B.B.E.S. (Hands-On Boat-Based Education and Science), Peabody Essex Museum, Schooner Adventure, and Gloucester Marine Heritage Center. During this past Summer Institute, the program at H.O.B.B.E.S. explored the mechanisms and cycles of phytoplankton growth and distribution, the relationship to global climate change to the recent increase in red tides and related harmful algal blooms in Massachusetts Bay coastal waters. Participants collected and identified plankton and measured and evaluated related water-quality factors. Participants tried inquiry-based activities to reinforce plankton cycle concepts with their students.

Lowell

The Lowell region offers a unique experience to the teachers, as it was an old textile area with unusual factory buildings. Involved in this area are Tsongas Industrial History Center (lead), New England Quilt Museum, American Textile History Museum, Lowell Heritage State Park, and Amoskeag Fishways in New Hampshire. Participants in the Summer Institute of 2006 explored the cyclical nature of natural plant and animal fibers' growth and our use of them (including flax, cotton, wool, and silk) at the American Textile History Museum. They explored how science has replicated this process to produce manmade fibers, including the "extreme fabrics" of today and the fantastical possibilities of current research. Teachers made charts and graphs of synthetic fabric production from recycled soda bottles (Polartec). Hands-on learning included flax processing, felting wool, unraveling silk cocoons, extruding, and microscopic and scientific fiber testing to discover physical properties. Many mathematical extensions were applied to their acquired knowledge.

Metro West

In the Metro West region, there is an exciting mix of museums. The Massachusetts Audubon Society Drumlin Farm (lead), along with the New England Wildflower Society/Garden in the Woods, DeCordova Museum and Sculpture Park, and Spellman Museum of Stamps and Postal History complete the group of museums in this area. During the Summer Institute of 2005, teachers in three different groups developed a sculpture of various materials that the DeCordova Museum put in their sculpture park so that when the teachers returned in the spring, they could assess the strength, durability, and sustainability of the materials and form that they had made into the sculpture.

Southeast

In this region, there are four very different sites that offer a unique experience for the teachers. The museums include Massachusetts Audubon Society Oak Knoll Wildlife Sanctuary (lead), Lloyd Center for Environmental Studies, Buttonwood Park Zoo, and New Bedford Whaling Museum/ECHO Project. At the New Bedford Whaling Museum, teachers looked at the South Coast region's (especially New Bedford's) prominent place in the history of global whaling and the region's current variety of whale research relating to many themes in the state curriculum frameworks. They figured out the oceanographic reasons why whalers that were based in New Bedford didn't catch whales in local waters. The investigative skills helped teachers learn the biological and economic reasons why certain whale species were targeted. Classifying marine (and terrestrial) organisms will become much easier. Using different whale drawings to practice various math skills will be a great activity to bring to the classrooms.

Springfield

In the Pioneer Valley of Massachusetts, the Springfield Science Museum (lead), Children's Museum of Holyoke, Mount Holyoke College Botanic Garden, and Hitchcock Center for the Environment offer an unique opportunity for teachers to learn activities that can be brought back to their classrooms and the wonderful resources for their students. For "CSI: Cycles, Systems, and Inquiry," during the two-day sessions at the Children's Museum of Holyoke, teachers used a series of questions as the starting point for tiered engineering inquiry, to explore energy, power, gears, mill architecture, and the implications of industrialization. Industrial Holyoke of the late 1800s demonstrated an almost perfect system for translating water power into products. Teachers will be able to bring that system into their classroom. Each stage of inquiry began with a challenge question and teachers were asked to explore alternative strategies to test their answers. One set of questions lead to the next set and ended with a culminating project demonstrating all phases.

Worcester

In the Worcester region, some of the sites had one day of teaching and some had two days to teach. This is a result of having more than four sites. The Massachusetts Audubon Society Broad Meadow Brook Wildlife Sanctuary (lead), EcoTarium, Tower Hill Botanic Garden, Massachusetts Audubon Society Wachusett Meadow Wildlife Sanctuary, Higgins Armory Museum, and Worcester Art Museum are the museums in this region. During the Summer Institute "CSI: Cycles, Systems, and Inquiry," teachers at Wachusett Meadow studied the milkweed plant and the effect of the planting area on its growth. Measurements were made and estimations on the number of sprouted blooms in these areas were made. Along with plant studies, teachers looked at the sites where different small animals could be found and why they were found in those areas. The activities were easily transferred to learning in the classroom.

Requirements and Materials

While each region has many different types of museums that take part in the Summer Institute, the procedures, course requirements, and materials are similar. On the first day, teachers receive the requirement list for the Institute. Here the teachers have a choice of receiving 60 Professional Development Points (PDP), 90 PDP, or 90 PDP plus graduate credit from one of five colleges associated with MITS. If teachers choose to receive 60 PDP, they must complete two grade-level lesson plans that they can utilize during the school year. If they choose 90 PDP, they must complete a unit of study plus a completed lesson plan for their grade level, and if they want college credit plus 90 PDP, they will be graded by the lead educator for the completed unit and lesson plan. Teachers are asked to identify the form of inquiry used in their lesson plan and throughout their unit plans. If they have chosen to receive graduate college credit, they are graded according to the grading rubric that was shared with all teachers on the first day of the Institute. The MITS Program Director and the lead educators determined the grading rubric and the unit/lesson plan format to be implemented. Teachers receive these materials along with a completed lesson plan and unit outline on the first day of the Institute. Included in these materials is the outline for keeping a daily reflective journal, one of the major requirements for completion of the institute. Each region includes pertinent activity materials for their region, while resource material and informative reprints are included for all teachers from the MITS home office.

Pedagogy

The overall methodology applied by all the museum educators is to model and involve the teachers in activities they can transfer to their classroom setting. Teacher participation in all the activities, whether in groups or singly, give them good insight and understanding of inquiry-based, hands-on teaching methods. Teachers are asked to identify the form of inquiry used during each activity at the Institute. For many of the teachers the interaction in the group is as much a learning experience into how their students feel in class as the content and the methodology. The ability to interact on a two-week basis with teachers has proven to be an important benefit of the Summer Institute. Time and again the teachers comment on how much they learn from other teachers in the group.

Assessment

One of the best assessments for the MITS program would be to visit the participants' classrooms throughout the school year to determine the level of inquiry-based learning taking place. Over the years, at different time intervals, Lesley University's Program Education and Research Group has evaluated a random group of program alumni classrooms and found very positive results linked to the MITS Summer Institutes. To determine the learning of the content offered during the Institute, teachers are given a pre-and postinstitute-questionnaire on the first and last day of the Institute. It is a great measure for the teachers and for the museum educators to see how the participants have gained content knowledge as well as inquiry-based knowledge. In each region, the cooperating educators submit two questions for this assessment. The same questions are used on the first and last day and the results are shared immediately with the teachers. This is invaluable feedback for these teachers.

A second method of assessment includes the lesson plan and units developed by each participant. With a prescribed outline for the lesson plan and the unit, teachers' understanding of inquiry by identification, content, and frameworks are readily pinpointed in the finished products. These products are their own work and should be for their grade levels and easily implemented in their classrooms. With testing results being a large part of their consideration for instruction, teachers' identification of the frameworks for their lesson plans and units indicates their understanding of the curriculum that should be addressed. As mentioned earlier, teachers who have opted for graduate credit are assessed on their units/lesson plan according to a developed rubric.

While reading the daily reflective journals for each teacher, the museum educators and MITS program director can assess the teachers' understanding of inquiry-based instruction and any difficulties that stand in the way of their understanding. The reflective journals only strengthen the implementation of future modeling by the museum educators in future Institutes and are used to continually refine the requirements and provided materials.

During the school year, teachers are given an opportunity to share their implementation of the inquiry-based methods they have employed in their classrooms. Each spring during a callback day in each region, teachers are invited to bring displays, materials, and stories about their implementation of inquiry-based lessons. One teacher of learning-disabled students related how implementation of inquiry-based learning in the classroom improved the process of engaging the students. During this time, if there are questions concerning "how" to implement inquiry-based methodology, they are addressed and discussed. A new questionnaire for teachers at the callback further addresses the use of inquiry-based instruction practices in their classrooms since their involvement with the Summer Institute.

Professional Assessment

MITS has employed PERG (Program, Education, and Research Group) at Lesley University to determine the overall impact that the MITS Institutes have had on implementing inquiry-based instruction in schools. During the last assessment of a randomly selected group of teachers from earlier Summer Institutes, researchers visited classrooms and interviewed teachers. To quote from their report: "Although a single workshop has important and sustained influences on teachers, there are clearly significant and additional advantages to repeated enrollment and attending with colleagues." The findings also indicated that when more than one teacher from a school attended an institute, the implementation of inquiry-based learning in that school was enhanced.

Following one of the suggestions in the report, MITS now offers teachers a discount in price if more than one teacher from the school attends a Summer Institute.

Future

MITS is constantly in the process of evaluating and improving the Summer Institute program to fit the educational needs of the time. Consultations with educators and staff at TERC, at the

Museum of Science, and knowledgeable individuals to investigate how best to align MITS with the needs of the teachers in addressing the "No Child Left Behind" requirements is an ongoing process. At the MITS November Board meeting, the members discussed at length the inquiry-based, hands-on approach that MITS uses to teach the STEM subjects. They felt strongly that by teaching process methodology, MITS was providing a unique opportunity to K–8 teachers in Massachusetts. MITS Summer Institute is a unique professional development program modeling inquiry-based, hands-on methods, by engaging the museum educators as facilitators. Their modeling and involvement with the teachers enables the teachers to apply these methods to whatever science curriculum their school uses and to integrate it into other disciplines.

MITS is investigating how to get the teachers to assess the effect of their newly learned approach to science teaching on their students. Last year MITS developed a survey for 2005 participants to assess how they used the inquiry-based methods with their students. Those that returned the survey predominately stated that their students were more engaged, spoke up more in class (even the normally quiet ones!), interacted more with their classmates, and understood the concepts better. This year MITS will have the survey at all callback days and will send it to teachers who are unable to attend the callback with the hope of getting 100% answered. During the planning sessions with the Lead Museum Educators and the MITS Program Director, MITS will rewrite the reflective journal requirements to increase the teachers' insight and thoughts of the material to be implemented as inquiry in their classrooms once they return to school. More emphasis will be put on identifying the type of inquiry used with activities and how it can be transferred to their individual classrooms. Each year, the MITS Program Director and lead museum educators discuss and improve the requirements and outcomes of the Summer Institute.

MITS has plans to participate in meetings and conferences such as the Massachusetts Science Supervisors and Massachusetts Science Teachers Conference, the Association for Science Teacher Education New England Conference, and local educational group meetings. MITS is an active participant in the Massachusetts STEM Pipeline. Attendance at these conferences and meetings advances the professional development necessary for improvements to the Summer Institute. MITS museum educators will have an opportunity to engage in professional development at the three Professional Development Seminars that MITS organizes during the winter and that are pertinent to the Summer Institute. These Professional Development Seminars are offered during the winter months of January, February, and March in different regions of Massachusetts so that educators from the museums will be able to attend during an off-season at their museums. The presenters at these seminars are experts in their fields. MITS runs the all-day seminar at a very reduced rate so that educators from small museums will be able to attend. The topics chosen for these seminars are decided by the lead educators, MITS Board of Directors, and MITS Program Director.

The model of the MITS Summer Institute program can easily be transferred to museums in different states throughout the United States. If anyone would like further information needed for establishing a program similar to MITS, please contact the MITS office at 617-695-9771.

References

Books
Massachusetts Department of Education. 2000. *Massachusetts mathematics curriculum framework*. Malden, MA: Author.

Massachusetts Department of Education. 2001. *Massachusetts science and technology/ engineering curriculum framework*. Malden, MA: Author.

National Research Council (NRC). 2000. *Inquiry and the national science education standards*. Washington, DC: National Academy Press.

National Science Foundation, Division of Elementary, Secondary, and Informal Education. 2000. *Foundations, vol. 2: Inquiry, Thoughts, Views, and Strategies for the K–5 Classroom*. Washington, DC: National Science Foundation.

Articles
Colburn, A. 2000. An inquiry primer. *Science Scope* 23 (6): 42–44.

Inquiry Based Science: What does it look like? *Connect*, March-April, 1995, p.13.

Rossman, A. D. 1993. Managing hands-on inquiry. *Science & Children* 31 (1): 35–37.

Valadez, J., and Y. Freve. 2002. Teaching hands-on/minds-on science improves student achievement in reading: A Fresno study. *FOSS Newsletter*, (Fall) 20.

Ward, C. 1997. Never give 'em a straight answer. *Science & Children* 35 (3): 46–49.

Evaluations Reports
MITS Summer Workshops Evaluation Reports, Lesley University Program Evaluation and Research Group, 1990, 1991, 1993, 1994, 1995, 1996, 2000.

Splash, Flash, Crank, Slide, Alive!

Interactive Standards-Based Science Experiences for Grades PreK–2 at Discovery Center

Bonnie T. Ervin, Discovery Center at Murfree Spring
Kim Cleary Sadler, Middle Tennessee State University

Created for the children and families of Middle Tennessee and the surrounding area, Discovery Center at Murfree Spring is a hands-on museum and environmental education center. The museum's goal is that everyone who visits the museum will be engaged and will grow in knowledge and appreciation for themselves, their families, the community, and the environment. Objectives are to provide daily high-quality and unique programs through exhibitions about science and technology, the environment, conservation, arts, culture, health and safety, and to ensure availability of these programs to the entire community. The Standards-based educational school tours use these existing hands-on exhibitions and are supplemented with activities as needed.

Discovery Center is located in downtown Murfreesboro, Tennessee, 25 miles southeast of Nashville. Rutherford County has a high percentage of school-age children receiving free or reduced lunches: Murfreesboro City Schools has 40% of the student body in this category, while the Rutherford County School system has 30%. The local community is moderately diverse, with 15% of the population in Rutherford County comprised of underrepresented members. Participation in museum programs by non-dominant students is higher than the county average population with 18% African American, 2% Asian American, 1% Hispanic, and 1% of the students identified as "Other," attending museum programs. English Language Learner (ELL) classes regularly visit Discovery Center for applied and kinesthetic reinforcement of science concepts. The Nissan Foundation generously donates program scholarships to students on free and reduced lunch plans.

Chartered in 1986 as Children's Museum Corporation of Rutherford County, Discovery House expanded in 2002 to Discovery Center at Murfree Spring, an 18,000 square foot museum on 20 acres of restored urban wetlands. By the fall of 2007, an additional 7500 square feet of gallery space will be complete. Working in partnership with the U.S. Army Corps of Engineers, the State of Tennessee, the Tennessee Wildlife Resources Agency, the City of Murfreesboro, local corporations, and numerous civic groups, the new museum serves over 82,000 visitors a year, with 15,000 visitors enjoying free admission.

Specific Visions for Change

Prior to NSES, the museum offered a single tour program that was scientific and thematic but not based on grade appropriate National Science Education Standards; with age appropriate modifications, all school groups received the same basic "one size fits all" science tour.

Although it has been a process, integration of the National Science Education Standards has been an essential component of the museum's mission to promote excellence in education. Since 1986 Discovery Center has always kept the natural curiosity of the child in mind when planning programs and exhibits. Time-tested favorites in the museum have been experiences with water, construction activities with blocks and sand, investigations with microscopes and magnifiers, interaction with a variety of animals, exploration of cultural diversity, and creative expression through multimedia. It is not a coincidence that the most well received tour programs and exhibits have been those that enhanced basic science-process skills (which are also life skills) such as observing, measuring, counting, comparing and contrasting, classifying, predicting, and communicating. When the National Science Education Standards (NSES) were introduced in 1996, followed by the Tennessee Science Curriculum Standards in 1998, museum administrators responded with staff education sessions. Working closely with the university and public school system, Discovery Center hosted teachers and informal educators for several of the initial NSES professional development workshops and continues today to collaborate and provide professional development on a variety of topics related to inquiry-based learning. Close partnerships with educational institutions enabled the museum to continue to promote quality science programs that clearly met national and state standards. The introduction of "No Child Left Behind" (NCLB) legislation in 2001 placed further emphasis on standardized testing but restricted school field trips by classes dramatically. Teachers were soon limited to curriculum-guided field trips, forcing the museum to think critically about the content and format of museum tour activities.

After NSES, the museum staff developed multiple tour programs based on the context and content of the National Science Education Standards for regional schools; each program is now uniquely age appropriate for content and inquiry.

The introduction of "No Child Left Behind" provided the business incentive for Discovery Center's programs to meet the legislated needs of the students, teachers, and school systems. The NSES and the Tennessee Science Curriculum Standards provided the essential documentation and support for truly meeting the science education needs of the same audience. After relocation to Discovery Center's new facility, a science tour was created for grades preK–2, called "Splash, Flash, Crank, Slide, Alive Tour." Using Tennessee Standards and NSES as the guiding parameters, the tour was designed for younger students to experience science interactively in the context of inquiry with materials found in the museum's new permanent exhibits. Rather than a lecture-based, show-and-tell experience, "Splash, Flash, Crank, Slide, Alive Tour" embodies the NSES, giving the students the opportunity to learn skills in context of the each exhibit's unique features. The tour was developed to support students' natural curiosity in scientific exploration across several aspects of the K–4 science curricula. Attention was paid to Content and Inquiry Standards, Teaching Standards, and Assessment Standards as the tour was formulated. Facilitated by experienced staff members, individual classes of students rotate in small groups through a series of hands-on learning centers.

More…Attention to Content and Inquiry Standards

The learning approach of the "Splash, Flash, Crank, Slide, Alive Tour" is guided by Inquiry and Content Standards. The students are the investigators. To assess prior experiences of the station topic, students' ideas are explored through leading and probing questions. Revision of introductory information and questions about the impending investigation are responsively posed to the individual or the small group. During the investigation of the exhibit, students, in teams or individually, are encouraged to do more as they are asked, "What else can you do/find? What does that result mean? Does that result change what you thought before? Are you able to repeat it?" Students are praised for their competence, their discoveries, and their collaborative work. They are asked to share their experiences and defend their findings during wrap-up minutes at each station.

Designing the standards-based tour for grades preK–2 learners required planners to consider not only developmental appropriateness but experiences that provided meaningful learning with deep explanatory power. It was essential to include everyday science experiences in the life of the young learner that would transfer back to home or school. Since kinesthetic investigations with water, light, simple machines, and animals serve as the foundation for inquiry in young children's lives, these were selected as components for the tour. The title "Splash, Flash, Crank, Slide, Alive Tour" reflects the content standard and basis for interactive engagement at different learning stations throughout the museum:

(1) Splash at the Water Table: *Physical Science Standard B*. Water exists as a solid (snow and hail), liquid (rain) and gas (vapor) in the water cycle. The sun is the energy source. Liquid water has many physical characteristics. (Students engage to learn that water flows, creates pressure, has force, and pushes boats along a course.)

(2) Flash in the Light Room: *Physical Science Standard B*. Light travels in straight lines and where the light is blocked by your body, the phosphorescent wallpaper will not glow. (Students deduce that since the light energy causes the wallpaper to glow, the shadow is created by the body keeping this light energy from reaching the wallpaper.)

(3) Crank the Simple Machine: *Physical Science Standard B*. Simple machines can be used to do work easily. (Students lift and move the rolling bowling ball.)

(4) Slide the Super Slide: *Physical Science Standard B*. Objects are pulled down the slide by the force of gravity. (Students discover they go down the slide because gravity pulls them down and prevents them from sliding up.)

(5) Alive are the Animals: *Life Science Standard C* and (6) Fossils: *Earth Science Standard D*. Characteristics of organisms and organisms in their environment are displayed. (Students examine animals to determine they need food, water, and shelter. While examining the enormous aquarium, students learn that the fish need to stay in the water to breathe through their gills; the turtles need to come to the surface to breathe with their lungs. When examining fossilized organisms, students discover that the fossils are no longer alive, though the fossils are the preserved remains of something that was alive many, many years ago.)

To maximize the exploratory science experience, teachers are mailed a prepackage of investigative experiments and activities designed to prepare the students for their upcoming visit to the museum. The tour experience inside the museum is approximately 60–90 minutes, plus 30 minutes of freedom to "individually explore" on their own time. To offer another extension of the informal learning experience at the museum, teachers leave with a posttour package for wrap-up, review, or formative assessment of science concepts learned at the museum for use with their classes after they return to school.

More…Attention to Teaching Standards

The Teaching Standards are the guidelines followed for the informal inquiry-based tour developmental meetings for Discovery Center Staff and volunteer Docents (hereafter collectively referred to as Staff). Before implementation of best practices for teaching, everyone was simply shown how everything worked; as a result, novice Staff simply "told" students everything and left little to their imagination. Current sessions are conducted by skilled Staff who reinforce and model strategies to facilitate inquiry with student visitors. Since guiding student learning is not intuitive, outlines have been written for all tours to include strategies to engage student learners. In an effort to develop ease in facilitating the inquiry-based museum experience, most of the learning experiences for the new docents are conducted as an actual tour by Staff comfortably familiar with the hands-on, inquiry-based concepts and techniques. Science concepts are observed, communicated, analyzed, and experienced in context with the Staff standing in the shoes of the student. Looking at the world through the eyes of a child, the adult leader investigates, makes inquiries, reports, evaluates, and shares with others at the various tour stations. Sample questions directed to the group provide opportunities for learning to adapt subject content for each station: "What do you think we are going to do here? What does the Water Cycle mean to you? If you are going to 'dig' for a fossil, what are you looking for? Why can you not slide UP the slide?" Individual learning styles, strengths, and real-life experiences of the Staff are respected and utilized during the process. Collaboratively, experienced Staff leaders share their personal successful teaching techniques, information, examples of leading questions, and ideas throughout the sessions. The tour is often amended based on these "discovery" sessions because new insights are gained from new docents, and new tour experiences. Currently, because of the strong science and teacher educational background of Discovery Center Staff, most of this inquiry-based learning and tour development is done in-house. However, professors from Middle Tennessee University are invited, when needed, to conduct sessions to share additional background information related to science content.

More…Attention to Assessment Standards

Using the Assessment Standards, "Splash, Flash, Crank, Slide, Alive Tour" is designed for the Staff to be able to continually and actively focus on interacting and evaluating what the students have learned. Generally, students' listening vocabularies are larger than their speaking vocabularies, their reading vocabularies are larger than their writing vocabularies, and their oral language vocabularies are larger than their written language vocabularies. Pedagogically, this suggests instruction that fosters active listening and speaking activities. Student learning at Discovery Center is evaluated through probing questions and interactive dialogue. In formal classes, grades preK–2 students are not always evaluated through product assessments; using an interactive dialog with students models a formative assessment strategy for the teacher to try with science lessons in the classroom. Wrap-up questions directed to the students include: "What did you learn? What activity did you do differently from your classmate/friend? Were the results the same or different? Were you able to repeat your task?" During the summarization minutes, the evaluative question guiding the thoughts of the Staff facilitator is: "Did the students reinforce their past experiences, learn something new, develop new skills, and connect new ideas?"

Program Description

"Splash, Flash, Crank, Slide, Alive Tour" is Discovery Center's investigative general science tour for younger students. Groups are allowed extra discovery time in the museum following the guided portion of each tour. Even though they have access to the entire museum, students are usually observed returning to their favorite spot from the tour. The following paragraphs provide an overview of each hands-on station and guiding questions.

SPLASH! Water Cycle and the Water Table Investigations

The Water Table station highlights the water cycle and properties of fluids. Student questions shape water table inquiry; their questions are deferred back to them to enable them to make connections. Acting out or singing a water cycle song initiates a question-and-answer session about water. *Evaporation, condensation,* and *precipitation* are illustrated as participatory vocabulary words. As an assessment for the teacher, students are then given materials to draw and illustrate their own water cycle. Pollution problems and conservation are discussed through questioning the students, "What if the water becomes so dirty that it cannot be cleaned—what does that mean to you? How can you conserve and not use very much clean water while you are at home? At school?"

The Water Table has interactive stations all around the feature, including a thunderstorm simulation. Students have opportunities to manipulate levees, locks and dams, and water fountains; generate hydroelectric power; construct water tubes; experiment with boats; or create waves. Fluid

dynamics, water pressure, and physiographic components of the water cycle are underlying curriculum accomplishments that are experienced at the Water Table. Staff will use the last-minute
wrap-up times to review student observations, experimentation, results, and might ask questions
such as, "Did your boat always float down the river? Was anyone able to make the fish swim high
in the column? Were you able to make waves of different sizes?"

FLASH! Light and Shadows

The light and shadow room has phosphorescent wallpaper for experimentation with light and
shadows. Before stepping into the room, the Staff engages the children in a dialogue about the
importance of the Sun (heat and light energy), and the function of lightbulbs (light, but heat is
produced as well). Noting that light travels in straight lines, students are asked to stand against
the wallpaper and create a pose. Math is incorporated in differing ways to count the passage of 10
seconds (count by 5s or 10s, count backwards, etc.) and when the light is turned off, the wallpaper
glows, but a shadow remains where the body had been posing in front of the wallpaper. After a
short discussion of the glowing wallpaper (absorption of light energy causes the phosphorescent
wallpaper to continue to glow when the light is turned off), an assessment question is posed, "If
the light energy causes the wallpaper to glow, what makes the shadow?" Probing questions usually
lead some student to say, "You do!" (If a dear parent has not jumped in with the answer!) Evidence
leads the students to the conclusion that bodies are opaque and block the light from reaching the
wallpaper. Experimenting with "glowing handprints" left on the wall by warm hands (not by light
from within the hands) reinforces heat and light as being energy. Larger groups are allowed to
experiment with materials that are transparent, translucent, and opaque. A "class picture" with
all against the wallpaper waving their hands ends with a wrap-up assessment question of "Why
does waving your hand create a shadow without a hand?"

CRANK! An Experience With Simple Machines

Collaboration and experimentation are necessary for grades preK–2 students to move a bowling
ball successfully through the track within the enclosed exhibit. Staff begins the introduction to
the exhibit with questions about moving heavy objects, such as "Could you lift that ball over your
head by yourself? What are some other ways you can lift heavy objects and move them? Does a
wheelbarrow make moving heavy objects easier?" Along the course that the manipulated bowling ball must travel, simple machines (inclined plane, wheel and axle, and levers) propel the ball
forward. Four students work as a team to manipulate the bowling ball from the beginning position,
through the course to the end position of the track. Teams rotate through the exhibit. Wrap-up
questions might include assessment questions such as, "Did you use some energy to lift the bowling
ball high over your head? Was turning the wheel easier than lifting the ball might be? Did you
have to touch the ball to make it roll over the bridge? What made it go over the bridge?"

SLIDE! Gravity and Friction Are Explored With a Super Slide

The Super Slide is two-stories high and is a corkscrew configuration. Discussion centers on the
leading question: "Why do we go down a slide? Have you ever been able to slide *up* a slide?"

To engage the students about the invisible force of gravity, a challenge may be issued to the students: "Jump in the air and stay there!" An imaginary trip to outer space for a drop-the-apple experiment might be taken. The concept of "more or less" is used when comparing the size of the Earth to the Moon, and probing questions guide to students to discuss "more or less" gravity on these spatial bodies. The Earth is much bigger than people, so its gravity "pulls us" toward the center of the Earth; gravity "pulls us" down the slide. The introduction of "fast" and "slow" movement generates the discussion of creating friction to slow down the trip on the slide. Usually, groups are given the opportunity to go down the slide twice—once while sitting on a slick fabric and a second time without the fabric. Wrap-up questions evaluate their concept of the force of gravity on Earth.

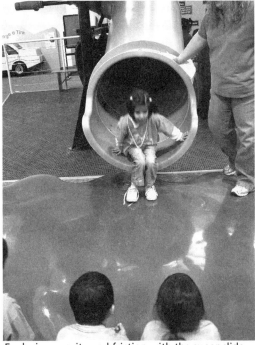
Exploring gravity and friction with the super slide.

Alive! Animal Diversity: Present and Past

Merely arriving in the Tennessee Live! area generates many questions from the students—before any discussion might be initiated. Students want to know, "Are those animals alive? What are those ropes doing in the rocks? Have those turtles drowned?" The prospects of digging for fossils and watching the swimming fish and turtles provide the necessary lead-in for participation in this station. The Staff asks students, "What about the animals that are mounted up on the shelves? What do you notice that leads you to think they are not alive?" Students observe the stuffed specimens and respond that they are not moving or blinking, not breathing, not eating or drinking, and Staff mention not going to the bathroom and not reproducing. An assessment question is then posed, "What

Young man peering into a container to look at a Green Frog. The container's top is a magnifying glass and makes the frog look huge to the children.

observations of the animals in the tank let you know that they are alive?" Further development of "alive/not alive" discussion leads to the topic of fossils, the development of fossilized remains, and the abundance of ocean fossils found in Tennessee. While half of the students are "digging" in the fossil pit, the other half are discussing their observations and characteristics of the animals being petted. Teams trade spots. Wrap-up questions include comparing and contrasting biology and habitats of fish to the aquatic turtles. A large aquarium divides the "dig pit" area from the petting area. The tank has many native aquatic animals (red-eared sliders, musk turtles, large mouth bass, catfish, green-eared sunfish, crayfish) in which students can observe animals swim or crawl. Classes are given the opportunity to draw what they see (as field biologists) and are asked to complete the drawing including all habitat necessities that would be needed to keep that animal alive. This formative assessment about habitats returns to school with the teacher for further discussion and posting in the classroom.

Assessment Practices at Discovery Center

Careful review of the National Science Education Standards has provided specific guidelines, along with the Tennessee Science Curriculum Framework, for the context and the content in the tour and the teacher pre- and postvisit packets. Since school groups have varied ages (grades preK–2), backgrounds (Title I public, private, and home school), and different purposes for participating in "Splash, Flash, Crank, Slide, Alive," the tour is designed to integrate science topics for early elementary learners using Content Standard A, Science as Inquiry. Each topic is introduced and then explored by the students. Museum staff guide student learning throughout the tour with questions that set the stage for student inquiry; students have the opportunity to find out answers on their own and "check them out" with the tour guide. The state of Tennessee does not assess student learning in science until grade 3, but grades K, 1, and 2 accomplishments in science that are components of "Splash, Flash, Crank, Slide, Alive Tour" are identified and included in teacher packets. Evaluations indicate that teachers use the tour and packets for introduction of new curriculum, as a review and extension of curriculum taught in the classroom, and some use the tour with the take-home packet of activities as closure to topics taught in the classroom.

Informal Assessment and Small Groups at Discovery Center

The informal assessments that return to school with children (grades K, 1, and 2) include a drawing of their interpretation of the water cycle on a durable paper plate, and groups also take home drawings of observed fish in a habitat that will sustain the animal. These informal assessments of student learning can be used as extensions to learning in the classroom, and suggested activities using these student products are included in the postvisit packet for the teacher. Questions that are included in the packet that relate to the student products are: How does water cycle through living and nonliving things? What does the fish in your drawing need to live? Staff of the informal science center is encouraged to have teachers report back in post surveys that they have used these student products as extensions to learning. Another powerful extension to student learning was reported from a group of kindergarten teachers, who commented that students from their school returned to class and used the science experiences from the tour to build a word bank of science terms. In class they had discussed *sink* and *float* and were able to see this in context and applied at the water table.

A class rotating as small groups through the different learning stations is a plus for the field trips because students are able to experience the exhibits truly and become involved in their own learning. One kindergarten teacher said, "They may not understand all of 'why' something happened, but they made it happen." A second-grade teacher visiting for the first time said, "I thought it would be more lecture and I'm glad it wasn't!" Another teacher comment related to the use of learning stations was, "The children are so involved and learn so much." Small group learning is a model with which the students are familiar, as evidenced by teacher comments in evaluations, which state that packet materials have been used in science center stations in the classroom, both before and after the field trip.

Teacher Pre- and Postactivity Packets Reinforce Student Learning

To address the curriculum standards better and "jump start" the inquiry-based tour while at school, a pretour packet was designed for preK and kindergarten and a separate one was created for first and second grades. Brief science explanations introduce the activities and suggested adaptive ideas are included. The teachers of the younger students receive copies of invented water cycle songs, sung to the tunes of "She'll be Coming 'Round the Mountain" and "The Wheels on the Bus." Investigations of the states of matter include experiments for evaporation (painting the sidewalk with water on a sunny day), condensation (observing a glass filled with ice water on a warm and sunny day), and precipitation (creating a graph of weather observations based on days of precipitation.) The fossilization process is explored manipulatively with homemade clay (recipe is included.) Students invent and create drawings of their own fossils, based on simple drawings of prehistoric animals and plants. The force of friction is introduced with "skating" over the floor in shoes as compared to socks; on carpet and on tile. Using the shoe soles as evidence, surfaces are examined, discussed, and grouped by "friction" types. Since literature connections are very important for the younger students, lists of appropriate books are included for teacher review.

The packet for the older students (first and second grades) has investigations about surface tension, friction, and fossils. Students manipulate droplets of water using their pencils, eyedroppers, pennies, and magnifying glasses. Science information and guiding questions are provided for teachers. In context at the museum, water tension is utilized in several locations on the Water Table. In preparation for the Super Slide, activities for friction reduction are included: semi-round rocks versus marbles to transport books across desks, hand lotion in contrast to water in hand-rubbing experiments; and fabric surface comparisons. (An important application question for the students is: "If you want to go FAST in the Super Slide, what should you wear?") Since fossils are incorporated into the tour, a page of fossil drawings is provided for students to infer a live animal through their own drawings. Writing or orally offering explanations of their animal introduces their ideas to the entire class.

The posttour packets, with follow-up activities are sent home with teachers. To continue the discussion of habitat requirements and animal adaptations, teachers are given drawings of various modern-day animals. Students are asked to pick an animal and focus on species-specific adaptations to habitat. Guiding questions for the teacher are included to reinforce the idea of inquiry and not just memorization of facts. Sample questions include: What does this frog in the picture need to live? What does a butterfly need to live? What is the same? What is different? To reinforce the concepts of light energy (light travels in straight lines; light is energy) that were demonstrated in the shadow room, an activity involving the Sun's light energy is included in the packet. Students create a Sun Clock using an upright post from a drinking straw or pencil, clay, and paper. Students simply trace shadows created by the post at various times of the day. During the tour, students are given an Ultraviolet (UV) color-changing bead necklace. Additional investigation at school is encouraged. Experimental questions for the students are provided: What color do you think the bead will be on a cloudy day? Is it possible for UV light to be present on a rainy day? Do lightbulbs give off UV light? Does UV light travel through window glass? To extend their informal learning experience and play from the Water Table, an experimental activity about aluminum foil boats in bowls of water is provided. Questions for students are: How many beans can you put in your aluminum boat have and it still float? Why does the aluminum boat float at all? Does the boat get higher or lower in the water? What happens to the level of the water in the bowl? Using the students' water cycle paper plates, previously created at the museum, the water cycle is revisited as students use a straw and a few drops of water to demonstrate the simple pathway that some drops of water may follow (their paper plate has been covered with transparent plastic film). If teachers desire to follow up with more learning about toads, frogs, and birds, websites that have pictures and song recordings of the animals are listed.

Evaluations of the Program and Staff Reveal Success

To determine if "Splash, Flash, Crank, Slide, Alive Tour" is effective in meeting the science needs of visiting groups, teacher packets include a postvisit evaluation (see page 164). Selected items from the surveys returned (the return rate averages about 65%) are included in Table 1. Teachers have rated the program and staff 4.8 on a 5.0-point scale (5.0 is the best, 1.0 is poor), which provides strong evidence that teachers perceive that the Discovery Center has been successful in program planning, presenting, and staff educational development. More than 30% of the visiting schools have returned for three years consecutively and 50% have returned two out of three years to participate in the "Splash, Flash, Crank, Slide, Alive Tour." The total number of student and adult participants since 2003 is 13,385 from 149 schools, with multiple grades from the same school choosing this specific program out of 20 that are offered. The "Splash, Flash, Crank, Slide, Alive Tour" in the 2005–2006 school year had the greatest number of participants in March, one month prior to standardized assessments in schools. Although kindergarten students are not assessed in science in Tennessee, first and second graders are assessed in all subjects. Since the program tour is highly interactive and engaging, perhaps teachers bringing classes prior to standardized testing see great benefits for their students.

Table 1. Teacher Postvisit Evaluation Results Returned by Mail or Email

	2003–2004[a]		2004–2005[b]		2005–2006[c]	
	# of Responses		# of Responses		# of Responses	
(1) Was the overall experience what you expected?	53	96% Favorable	43	98% Favorable	33	91% Favorable
(2) Amount of time for exhibit appropriate for age?	48	96% Yes	38	97% Yes	38	95% Yes
(3) Hands-on activities age-appropriate and relevant to curriculum?	49	96% Affirmative	43	100% Affirmative	33	100% Affirmative
(4) Was the staff knowledgeable, personal, and effective?	45	96% Affirmative	39	100% Affirmative	31	100% Affirmative

Note: [a] 57 schools; 4,269 students and adults
       [b] 47 schools; 4,171 students and adults
       [c] 45 schools; 4,945 students and adults

Future Plans and Partnerships

Discovery Center's objectives to provide daily, high-quality, unique programs and exhibits on science and technology, the environment and conservation, arts and culture, and health and safety will continue to guide the future direction of the nonprofit 501C-3 Center. The museum is currently focused on life science and physical science topics and a second expansion of 7,500 square feet will provide a gallery on transportation, with exhibits that address the NSES related to space, engineering, and environmental impact. In addition to the hands-on components, signage will offer suggestions of inquiry-based activities guiding visitors to the science background explanation for the exhibit. Assistance for several new exhibits will be provided in partnership with NASA Marshall Space Flight Center. Discovery Center works with the city of Murfreesboro and several Foundations (General Mills, Hospital Corporation of America and Nissan) as partners supporting Discovery Center initiatives. Close partnerships that involve educational research with regional schools and Middle Tennessee State University will continue to expand through a National Science Foundation Academy for Young Scientists award to establish out-of-school-time experiences for middle school students. Through active learning programs, partnerships, and outreach efforts, Discovery Center is highly invested in the principles comprising the National Science Education Standards to help develop scientifically literate citizens.

Dear Teacher,

Thank you for the opportunity to share our program with you and your class. Your feedback is a valuable tool in the evaluation of our programs, helping us continue to improve your tour experience. *We ask that you please complete this evaluation and return it to the museum, either by mail or by requesting an e-mail.*

Please circle the number that best fits your experience, with 5 being the best:

Please answer these questions:	Best				Poorest
Was the amount of time for each exhibit area appropriate for your age group? Comments: _____	5	4	3	2	1
Did the hands-on activities enhance the learning of the children? Comments and specific examples: _____ _____	5	4	3	2	1
Were the teacher packets (pre and post) of any value? Comments: _____	5	4	3	2	1
Was the additional e-mail or letter outlining the program of value to you and your team of teachers? Comments: ____	5	4	3	2	1
Do the objectives of the tour match and meet your grade's curriculum standards? Comments: _____	5	4	3	2	1
Does the tour specifically match any points of mastery on any tests? Comments: _____ _____ What needs to be added to meet your needs? _____ _____	5	4	3	2	1
Was the staff knowledgeable, personable, and effective? Comments: _____	5	4	3	2	1

How many years have you chosen this tour for your class? _____
Comments: _____
Was the information of the tour used as
_____ Introduction to new material?
_____ Review of materials taught in the classroom?
_____ Closure to materials taught in the classroom?
Additional questions are on the back.
Do you have examples of measurable gains as a result of your class participating in the tour?
_____

Have you taken the hands-on activities from the tour and expanded them into your regular teaching style?_____
_____

If you were able to use the free admissions for children on the free and reduced-lunch program, (thanks to Nissan Foundation) please comment. _____
_____

If your bus trip (one way) is more than 45 minutes, would you like to be able to request additional free exploration time in the museum? _____
_____

Additional Comments or Ideas _____
_____
_____

We really do use your information and feedback to improve the tours. Thank you for your time, comments, and your visit!

Mail to: Bonnie Ervin, Education Department
         Discovery Center at Murfree Spring
         502 Southeast Broad Street
         Murfreesboro, TN 37130
OR If you would like an E-Mail form, send request with your school name, and date of tour to: *bervindisccenter@comcast.net*

If you would like to participate in brainstorming sessions for tour improvements or new tour ideas, please send a message to the above address, with your name, grade level, and interests.

Splash, Flash, Crank, and Slide_____ Date of program: _____
Name of docent(s): _____
School: _____ Grade: _____

Grands Are Grand:

A Cross-Generational Learning Experience at the North Museum of Natural History & Science

Esther D. Wahlberg
The North Museum of Natural History & Science

G*rands Are Grand* is a monthly program for children ages 3–5 and their grandparents offered by the North Museum of Natural History & Science in Lancaster, Pennsylvania. This program reflects the Museum's commitment to providing engaging informal science experiences for all ages.

The North Museum's mission is to "promote lifelong learning throughout the community by generating excitement and curiosity in the natural and physical sciences and technology." This community museum has provided personal educational experiences to adults and children for more than 50 years and its heritage collection goes back hundreds of years. In the late 19th century, Lancaster County was home to an active group of naturalist-collectors called the Linnaean Society. In time, this organization's rich and varied collections were entrusted to Franklin and Marshall College, who built the Museum in 1953. In 1992, the museum was reorganized and incorporated as an independent nonprofit institution.

Today, the museum serves the region as its only natural history and science museum and planetarium. It preserves and protects over 350,000 objects organized into major collections of regional archeology, botany, geology, mineralogy, mammalogy, ornithology, and paleontology. A recently refurbished planetarium is Central Pennsylvania's largest, and is the centerpiece of the museum. The North Museum is conveniently located within the City of Lancaster and is fully accessible. Excellent programs, generous admission policies, and a comfortable and inviting environment—all of these qualities contribute to the museum being named Lancaster's favorite museum for the fourth year in a row.

Grands Are Grand programs utilize both the Museum's authentic objects and touchable specimens, including pelts, skeletons, casts, and models for hands-on exploration.

National Science Standards Blueprint for Change

The *Grands Are Grand* program has placed specific emphasis on the following components of the NSES:

- Teaching Standard: Guiding students in active and extended scientific inquiry.
- Content and Inquiry Standards:
  (1) Understanding scientific concepts and developing abilities of inquiry;
  (2) Studying a few fundamental science concepts (relationships in nature);
  (3) Creating activities that investigate and analyze science questions; and
  (4) Using multiple process skills—manipulation, cognitive, procedural.

Three lessons are included to illustrate this emphasis. They are titled *Susie-Q, Snakes and Spirals*, and *Frogs*.

Guiding Students in Active and Extended Scientific Inquiry

Grands Are Grand lessons include a wide variety of touchable, visual, and audible materials that present opportunities for active exploration and learning. Children are able to touch live animals (*Snakes and Spirals*), feel their skins and skeletons, and watch how they move. The literature selections used to introduce children to topics actively involve listeners in new worlds. Puppets enable young children to relate to animals and create concrete experiences otherwise unavailable to them, such as the comparison of frog and toad skins (*Frogs*). Active learning may also be presented in the form of a self-correcting puzzle (*Frogs*) or using a chocolate chip cookie to pretend you are a paleontologist (*Susie-Q*). By mixing formal presentation with active engagement, the program focuses on the needs of preschool children.

Extended scientific inquiry has always been an important aspect of *Grands Are Grand*. Since the program's inception, take-home activities (such as puzzles, games, baking experiences, poetry) have been included with each lesson to reinforce the lesson objectives and provide additional sharing opportunities for grandparent and grandchild. The museum, particularly in its Discovery Room, offers many opportunities for extended learning for young children. Grandparents are given suggestions on how the experience can be extended using museum exhibits and resources.

Grands Are Grand maintains a consistent focus on the concept of relationships in nature. Lessons pertaining to animal life emphasize predator/prey relationships, the connections between anatomy and survival, as well as habitat and life-ways. Botany lessons have a strong life cycle component. Understanding that fossils are a part of the terrain (*Susie-Q*) further develops the connection between living things and their habitats. Examples of these connections are woven throughout the included sample lesson plans. Our focus on relationships in nature emphasizes structure and function, variation, and diversity.

Although *Grands Are Grand* content varies, relationships in nature are consistently explored. Since grade preK children are actively learning about themselves and their world, learning about the relationships of other living things is an age-appropriate theme. The National Center for Science Education recommends nine scientific concepts for elementary school curricula. Our focus is on three of these: structure and function, variation, and diversity.

With some guidance, preschool children make effective comparisons to investigate and analyze science questions. For example, they are able to compare the size of the front and hind legs of frogs (*Frogs*) and determine why the strong hind legs are important. Grandparents effectively prompt this thinking process and work within their grandchild's particular abilities.

Hands-on learning is a critical component of *Grands Are Grand* programs. Children benefit from the Museum's extensive materials that they can handle and explore. Problem-solving activities begin with the literature component of each lesson because children are asked to predict outcomes. This continues through science activities that require comparisons and conclusions. *Grands Are Grand* introduces children to classification by considering species when looking at groups of similar living things. For example, frogs are introduced as amphibians and snakes as reptiles.

Program Description

Goals

Grands Are Grand is a monthly program for children ages 3 to 5 and their grandparents designed to develop curiosity and excitement about the natural world while providing multigenerational sharing and problem solving opportunities. Instruction is aimed primarily at the children. The program is based, in part, on Vygotsky's social cognition learning model and zone of proximal development. "The zone of proximal development bridges the gap between what is known and what can be known." Vygotsky claimed that learning occurred

Grandparents and grandchildren examine a bull skeleton following a reading of a grandparent favorite, *Ferdinand the Bull*.

in this zone" (Riddle and Dabbagh 1999). Grandparents' understanding of their grandchildren's abilities and guidance through the zone of proximal development is key. *Grands Are Grand* recognizes varied learning styles and provides concrete materials and movement opportunities that reflect the needs of young learners.

Grands Are Grand also aims to rekindle or supplement grandparent interest in the natural world and the museum. The informal atmosphere lends itself to questions and discussion between the adults and the instructor. Grandparents have commented on their own learning experiences during the programs.

Relying, in part, on the writings of psychologist Mihaly Csikszentmihalyi, Caryl Marsh writes in *Visitors as Learners: the Role of Emotions* (1996), "There is strong evidence that visitors go to museums seeking enjoyment and understanding. These two factors seem to interact in a reciprocal fashion. The more enjoyment, the more likely there will be learning. The increased learning and understanding lead to more enjoyment." The relationship between grandparent and grandchild brings a high level of enjoyment and pleasure to *Grands Are Grand* classes.

In addition to the museum's educational goals, *Grands Are Grand* addresses three of the museum's strategic objectives. First, the museum was attracting substantial interest among active seniors of Lancaster County and additional programs were needed to meet the demand. Second, the museum's literature-based programs for preschoolers had been successful and *Grands* responded to current emphasis in formal education. Third, by providing programming during off-peak hours, the museum more fully utilized its limited space.

Setting, Environment, and Schedule

Grands Are Grand is offered in the North Museum's Kinsey Community Room, a multipurpose meeting room located on the second floor of the museum. The room is carpeted, comfortable, and inviting. An effort is made to create a warm and intimate setting.

To encourage multigenerational sharing and a friendly atmosphere, children and grandparents are seated next to each other at rectangular tables. The small group size (maximum 28 grandparents and grandchildren) contributes to the nonthreatening environment. Puppets are often used to welcome children or may be incorporated into the lesson.

Consideration is given to the needs of working parents. *Grands Are Grand* programs are presented Friday afternoons at 4:00 pm. While grandparents spend quality time with their grandchildren, busy parents can get a little time to themselves at the end of a stressful week. The late afternoon classes follow afternoon or whole-day school programs. A consistent schedule, every third Friday, enables families to plan *Grands Are Grand* attendance well in advance.

Varied Curriculum

To date, more than 40 individual *Grands Are Grand* programs have been offered. Age-appropriate topics have been selected to incorporate museum collections and coordinate with museum exhibitions. For example, during our 2005–2006 yearlong celebration of spirals in nature, the programs *Spirals: Whirls Without End*, *Snakes and Spirals* and *Along Came a Spider* were added.

In addition to topics relating to animals—their characteristics, adaptations, habitats and relationships to each other—the following subjects have also been offered: botany, astronomy and meteorology, paleontology, physical sciences, math in nature, and natural history museums.

Grands Are Grand Lessons: July 2003–November 2007

2003	July	*Meet the Snakes*
	July	*Hoot, Hoot*
	October	*Hoppin' Into Science: Frogs and Toads*
	November	*Growl-l-l! Grand Bears for Grand Kids*
2004	January	*Weasily Weasels*
	March	*Moth or Butterfly*
	April	*Springtime is Planting Time*
	May	*Puffy or Spikey: Pufferfish*
	June	*Imagine: Mollusks*
	July	*Clouds: Pictures in the Sky*
	September	*Be Your Grandparents' Tour Guide*
	October	*Bats and More*
	November	*Swooping Down From the Sky: Raptors*
	December	*Wintry Menu*
	December	*Party Sounds*
2005	January	*Megasharks*
	February	*Be An Astronomer*
	March	*Susie-Q: Fossils to Museums*
	April	*Dinosaur Families*
	May	*Blue Feet, Blue Tongues, and Other Oddities*
	June	*Nature's Apartment: Trees*
	July	*Hives and Ant Hills*
	August	*Beach Homes*
	September	*Snakes and Spirals*
	October	*Along Came a Spider*
	November	*Penguin Families*
	December	*Trees: Alike & Different, Conifer & Deciduous*
2006	January	*Backyard Winter Birds*
	February	*Snuggles*
	March	*Eggs, Eggs, and More Eggs*
	April	*Springtime is Planting Time*
	May	*Hoppin' Into Science: Frogs & Toads*
	June	*Hide & Seek: Animals Under Rocks*
	July	*Incredible Insects!*
	August	*Let's Celebrate Winter in the Antarctic!*
	September	*Squirrels and Nuts*
	October	*While You're Sleeping: Nocturnal Animals*
	November	*The Otter's Susquehanna River Feast*
	December	*Pine Cones: On the Tree, on the Ground, and in our Hands*
2007	January	*Wintry Menu Along the Susquehanna River*
	February	*Ferdinand and His Big, Big Bones*
	March	*Turtles, Turtles and More Turtles*
	April	*Fossils Found in Pennsylvania*
	May	*Flowers and Bees; Helping Each Other*
	June	*Crunchy Critters in the Susquehanna River*
	July	*Maize; Then and Now*
	August	*Pictures in the Sky: Clouds*
	September	*Animals With Pouches: Near and Far*
	October	*Magnets Everywhere*
	November	*Petroglyphs*

Lesson Components

Each *Grands Are Grand* lesson is divided into three major components: children's literature, a science activity/lesson, and a craft. Take-home activities and suggested reading lists are provided at the conclusion of each class.

After learning about pinecones, grandmother and grandson collaborate on a creative project.

(1) *Children's literature.* Following introductions, the chosen literature selection focuses everyone's attention on the topic. The story is presented with children seated on the floor in a circle. Questions and active participation are encouraged and, occasionally, puppets are used. Books are selected based on the presentation of accurate scientific content combined with an imaginative story.

Grandparents provide encouragement to children who may be reluctant to join the circle. At the conclusion of the story, children return to their seats and comments are often exchanged between grandparents and grandchildren, reflecting on content, illustrations or other aspects of the literature selection.

(2) *Science activity/lesson.* Real specimens, hand-held magnifiers, replicas, puppets, photographs, and audio equipment are used to present science concepts. Songs and finger plays may be included. Children and grandparents are encouraged to handle touchable objects while fragile specimens are made available for up-close observation. Concrete experiences, such as petting a live snake, sitting on a polar bear pelt, and examining owl wings and fossils enable children to compare and analyze adaptations. Children and grandparents may participate in experiments that facilitate greater understanding of adaptations. Varied topics, vocabulary, and experiences encourage thinking about broad themes pertaining to relationships in the natural world such as predator and prey, life cycles, and the relationship between wildlife and human beings. We introduce children to natural history vocabulary such as "specimen" and "replica."

Sitting close to each other, grandparents and grandchildren share by handling objects together. Grandparents intuitively individualize their instruction according to their grandchildren's level of knowledge and provide them with the appropriate level of assistance.

(3) *Craft.* Using a craft as a concluding activity enables grandparents and children to be creative together while reinforcing science knowledge. Puzzles, matching activities, and books are available for those young children who may have less interest in crafts.

Sample Lesson Overviews

Susie-Q for Grands: Fossils to Museums

As they arrive and sit down, each child is provided with a chocolate chip cookie and toothpicks and is challenged to dig out chocolate chips without breaking them. Children are asked not to eat the cookies until later. Visitors respond excitedly to working with something familiar and tasty and begin a collaborative project, with grandparents frequently functioning as coaches, suggesting a slow and patient effort. When children are asked if they were able to dig any chips out without breakage, they respond eagerly and may count the chips. Sometimes the chips mysteriously vanish, creating a light touch to the start of this lesson. Children are eventually allowed to eat their cookies. This activity offers an opportunity to connect the delicate work of paleontologists to the child's own experience.

Reading *The Field Mouse and the Dinosaur Named Sue* leads to discussion of fossilization, specimens, and models. Looking at a partially fossilized porcupine skull helps children understand the fossilization process and also illustrates the fact that the animals that formed the fossils of today were, at one time, alive. Grandparents' fascination with the porcupine skull adds to its impact.

While additional objects are being handled, future visits to our own Dinosaur Hall are encouraged for extended learning. The Discovery Room, with its fossils discovery box, is suggested for additional hands-on exploration.

Skulls and footprints and their connection to herbivore and carnivore classifications are used to represent knowledge gained from fossils. Grandparents and grandchildren use herbivore and carnivore dinosaur footprint shapes to create stories. Children may step into an authentic *Allosaurus* footprint and compare actual sizes.

The clay and shell fossils made in class are taken home and serve as prompts for discussion, reading, additional museum visits and, of course, memories of a happy time at the museum.

Snakes and Spirals for Grands

The life-sized boa constrictor puppet welcomes children. Manipulating the puppet can immediately introduce children to spirals. Curiosity is indicated by the children's questions relating to the size and color of snakes.

Children's literature is used to introduce key concepts of this lesson. The setting for the children's story *Crictor* is Paris in the early 20th century. Characters are fictional and illustrations look like cartoons. The title character is a pet boa constrictor whose agile spine enables him to help children learn as he forms letters and numbers and who saves the day by wrapping itself around a burglar. Children participate in the story by saying letters and numbers, giggle when they see Crictor's very long bed, frown and show concern when the burglar appears, and sigh with relief when they learn of the snake's ability to defend its owner's home. The word *constrictor* takes on meaning visually and also reflects this important ability. Using visuals at the conclusion of the story easily connects the constrictor's shape to spirals.

After children rejoin their grandparents, constrictors are differentiated from venomous snakes and everyone is allowed to get a close look at a preserved rattlesnake while shaking a snake rattle. Predator and prey relationships are a natural part of the comparison between constrictors and venomous snakes.

Children are assured that there are no live venomous snakes at the museum and are introduced to a living ball python. Visitors watch intently as the snake curls and uncurls while the instructor holds it and describes the animal's anatomy and survival techniques. Everyone handles shed snakeskin and has the opportunity to touch the python in order to feel its skin and its long spine. Some people are reluctant, others are eager, and children and grandparents benefit from each other's curiosity and bravery.

While distributing materials for the spiral snake craft, the instructor may ask questions to determine if children understand that spirals are similar to circles within each other and that constrictors form spirals to catch their prey. As they provide support with cutting projects and feedback regarding coloring efforts, grandparents frequently repeat the vocabulary. Children and grandparents may also go to the table where skins, skeletons, and specimens are displayed and may make a snake skeleton rubbing.

Take-home materials include a Slithering Snake Cookie Recipe, a baking activity that encourages conversation about snakes and perhaps another visit to the Museum's live animal collection.

Frogs for Grands

Frog and toad puppets welcome children and quickly illustrate differences in size and skin texture. Seated at tables while waiting for others to arrive, children and grandparents work collaboratively on a self-correcting frog life cycle puzzle. They may also use magnifiers to look at the plastomounts on each table. "Is this real?" and "Why did you kill it?" are frequently asked questions when children are first exposed to plastomounts. They are assured that museum staff like to have animals live in their natural habitats and that we do not kill animals. Sometimes the children's questions lead to a discussion of how animals die.

Bullfrog at Magnolia Circle, a Smithsonian's Backyard book, illustrates the beauty and danger of life in a bayou. As the plot unfolds, predator and prey concepts are easily emphasized.

After returning to tables, the frog and toad puppets are reintroduced and touched. Differences in size and skin texture are discussed. Lyrics to "The Skin Song" are distributed to grandparents, and the adults smile broadly while they sing to the tune of "London Bridge" as follows:

The skin of a frog is moist and smooth,
Moist and smooth,
Moist and smooth.
The skin of a frog is moist and smooth,
My fair froggie.
The skin of a toad has warts and bumps,
Warts and bumps,
Warts and bumps.
The skin of a toad has warts and bumps,
My fair toady.

Children join in for the repeat performance, a fun-filled, shared learning experience that can be repeated at home.

As children look at the toad skeleton and various plastomount specimens, they are asked to compare front and hind legs and consider why this difference in size exists. With the help of grandparent prompts, children often arrive at the conclusion that frogs and toads need large and strong hind legs to jump and spring.

Life cycle plastomounts, plastic manipulatives, and the puzzles handed out at the start of class illustrate frog development. Comprehension of this process is assessed when children are asked to use their bodies to show how a frog might grow. They are asked to curl up in a ball to represent the egg and, when asked what happens next, they lay down and swim like tadpoles and, eventually, jump like frogs. Like "The Skin Song," this activity may be repeated at home.

The grandparents' capable one-on-one guidance is important to the successful completion of the paper bag frog puppet. As grandparents' play with their grandchildren, their imaginations and knowledge prompt dialogue with the puppet that reinforces vocabulary and concepts.

Assessment

Monthly *Grands Are Grand* programs are independent of each other and, therefore, attendance varies. Teachers observe behavior throughout the lesson and especially during concluding activities to assess comprehension, such as, at the end of the *Frogs* lesson when children are asked to dramatize the frog life cycle.

Over a third of grandparents who come to *Grands Are Grand* return for another program and 11% bring grandchildren to five or more programs. Some grandparents have brought consecutive grandchildren to *Grands* after their first grandchild has reached age six. Observations show that returning children happily walk into the Kinsey Room and are increasingly more willing to join the story circle, handle animals and specimens, and more frequently speak of showing craft projects to their parents. Returning children are also increasingly willing to participate in discussion, and their questions and responses indicate awareness of relationships in nature. For example, returning children ask how a specific animal defends itself or what it eats. Smiles and verbal indication of interest in attending subsequent programs show that *Grands Are Grand* is an enjoyable experience for grandparents and grandchildren.

The North Museum is currently looking at all of its educational offerings to ensure that programs are meeting audience needs. To that end, a comprehensive member survey has just been created and a specific summative evaluation has been distributed to participants of *Grands*. Participants ranked program features as "not valuable," "somewhat valuable," and "very valuable." Storytelling, handling real objects, take-home activities, and facilitator/leader are features that were all ranked "very valuable." A majority of grandparents indicated that the 45-minute class is an appropriate length for their grandchildren. Typical comments reflected grandparents' interest in sharing experiences with their grandchildren, fostering their grandchildren's learning, and continuing their own learning. Comments included "Excellent learning-bonding experience," "Fabulous. I always learn something," and "Very interesting, valuable, hopefully will foster an interest in science."

The museum offers an opportunity to purchase a Grand family membership that families greatly appreciate. We believe that *Grands Are Grand* has had a positive impact on the purchase of such memberships and has brought older residents of Lancaster County to the museum for repeat visits.

Future Plans

Grands Are Grand programs will continue to provide diversification of topics and coordinate with the Museum's new permanent exhibition *Natives of the Susquehanna*. Future programs will expand our offerings in anthropology, botany, meteorology, paleontology, and physical science.

Grands Are Grand programs have been done in cooperation with the Lancaster County Public Library and this will continue. Suggested reading lists are being included in take-home materials.

Future plans also include teacher training which will incorporate continued emphasis on guiding students in active and extended scientific inquiry.

Summary

As noted earlier, the North Museum's mission is to "promote lifelong learning throughout the community by generating excitement and curiosity in the natural and physical sciences and technology." *Grands Are Grand* presents an informal learning environment that benefits the very young as well as adults continuing to learn.

Grandparents support their grandchildren's learning in two significant ways: They help create a supportive and encouraging environment and they individualize instruction by guiding and helping children through specific tasks, as needed. Since "child-teacher interaction is a primary mechanism through which classroom experiences have effects on development" (Pianta 2003), this grandparent-assisted instruction positively affects learning.

Grandparents also benefit from the program in two distinct ways. First, they have an opportunity to share, influence, and continue a unique learning experience with their grandchildren. Second, their own knowledge and appreciation of the natural world is enhanced or reaffirmed. Research has indicated that instruction of older adults "should take place in stimulating environments; e.g., hands-on settings, group learning, high interactivity with the curriculum, many and varied visuals, tailored feedback, intergenerational situations" (SPRY Foundation 1999). *Grands Are Grand* lessons will continue to fill several of these criteria.

Sharing a hands-on science experience.

References

Riddle, E. M., and N. Dabbagh. 1999. Lev Vygotsky's social development theory. http://chd.gse.gmu.edu/immersion/knwledgebase/theorists/constructivism/ vygotsky.htm (Note: link is now inactive.)

Marsh, C., 1996. Visitors as learners: The role of emotions. *ASTC Newsletter.*

Pianta, R. C. 2003. *Standardized classroom observations from preK to 3rd grade: A mechanism for improving classroom quality and practices, consistency of P–3 experiences, and child outcomes.* New York: Foundation for Child Development.

SPRY Foundation. 1999. *Bridging principles of older adult learning: Reconnaissance phase final report.* Washington, DC: Author.

Children's Literature Referenced in This Chapter

Dennard, D. *Bullfrog at Magnolia Circle.* Norwalk, CT: Soundprints.

Ungerer, T. 1983. *Crictor.* New York: Harper.

Wahl, J. *The Field Mouse and the Dinosaur Named Sue.* New York: Cartwheel Books.

A Sea of Possibilities:

Inspiring Scientific Thinking in Teachers and Students Through the Charismatic Research Organisms at Mote Marine Laboratory

David H. Niebuhr, Elizabeth K. Metz, and James M. Wharton
Mote Marine Laboratory Education Division

Founded in 1955 on the southwest coast of Florida, Mote Marine Laboratory is an independent, nonprofit organization dedicated to the advancement of marine and environmental sciences through scientific research, education, and public outreach, leading to new discoveries, revitalization, and sustainability of our oceans and greater public understanding of our marine resources. The Laboratory has a staff of approximately 230 employees; a volunteer corps of over 1,400; an annual operating budget of $20 million; and four facilities sites on City Island in Sarasota (main campus), east Sarasota County (Mote Aquaculture), a field station on Demerey Key in Charlotte Harbor, and two locations in the lower Florida Keys (Mote Tropical Research Laboratory). The Mote Research Division comprises seven centers of excellence including the Center for Shark Research, a national center designated by the U.S. Congress in 1991 and the world's largest research center dedicated to the scientific study of sharks, skates, and rays, the Center for Marine Mammal and Sea Turtle Research, as well as centers of research in toxicology, coastal ecology, tropical ecology, fisheries, and aquaculture research and development.

Through the Centers for School and Public Programs, Distance Learning, and Volunteer and Intern Resources, the Mote Education Division (MED) offers a full complement of programs at Mote facilities, through mobile exhibits and via distance learning videoconferences. MED audiences include K–12 children and their families, undergraduate and graduate school interns, preservice and inservice teachers, and the resource management community. In addition to these formal educational programs, the Mote Aquarium hosts approximately 400,000 visitors each year in a free-choice learning environment.

The Mote Marine Laboratory and Aquarium attracts volunteers, interns, and students to the study of ocean sciences,.

The National Science Education Standards and Mote Educational Programs

Informal education venues, by their very definition, are predisposed to the successful implementation of the *More Emphasis* conditions of the National Science Education Standards (NSES), and Mote Marine Laboratory is no exception to this trend. The movement away from content-focused learning strategies to process-focused learning strategies has empowered free-choice education venues to play to their particular strengths. At Mote, we have embraced the new standards and bring students (and their teachers) into the world of scientific thinking and inquiring—not by requiring their attention to details and definitions—but through exploring, developing, and testing questions of interest to the students. While our situation is different from most classroom applications, we strategically address the following NSES areas.

- *Teaching:* We strive to focus student understanding on the use of scientific knowledge, ideas, and inquiry process by linking all education activities at Mote to genuine scientific research being conducted at the Lab. Students are immersed in a world of scientific investigation, interview or observe scientists as they conduct their research, and are challenged to develop scientific questions and mechanisms to test their hypotheses.

  Inherent in the informal setting is the need to integrate and adapt our topics into the home curriculum of each class that visits the Lab. Furthermore, because the students are immersed (sometimes up to their necks) in the environment as they explore answers, they are intimately involved in the learning process, they must articulate and defend arguments and conclusions, and are the leaders in their own learning.

- *Assessment:* While our partner teachers must concern themselves with standardized state testing, our informal setting alleviates this concern in our programs. Yet, despite our removal from the testing process, preliminary evidence suggests that students engaged in our programs read more (in the content area) and perform better than similar ability students on standardized tests (Niebuhr and Metz, forthcoming).

  On a student level, our programs also emphasize self-assessment in the learning process. Many programs involve continuous testing in the form of game-show quizzes, evaluating levels of requisite understanding before being able to continue on with an activity or experiment, and other forms of informal assessment.

- *Content and Inquiry:* All of our programs are embedded in the context of inquiry, technology, and science in the community. All exhibits, interviews, and human interactions are integrated within the programs and focused on the seven areas of marine research conducted at Mote.
- *Staff Development Standards:* We are presently implementing the recommendations (based upon the NSES goals) of a Blue Ribbon Education Panel that all teacher and preservice teacher programs emphasize the community of scientists and explorers over their individual content areas.

The goals of the NSES have been fully integrated into our educational programs for both students and teachers. Mote education programs strive to involve classroom teachers in inquiry as a part of the greater community of scientific learners. We are continuing this effort and are creating additional programs for preservice teachers who have limited experience and expertise in the sciences (especially elementary teachers).

The Mote Education Division

Mote scientists study sharks, dolphins, sea turtles, coral reefs, manatees, and other organisms and ecosystems; therefore, our education programs concentrate on the research being conducted by our scientists in our geographical area. We use these organisms and topics as the foundation for our classes. By concentrating our efforts, we can deliver meaningful experiences using dramatic examples and focusing the participants' exploration in ways that can provide the greatest extension of learning into other science topic

Mote students are actively engaged in the exploration of the world around them.

areas. Given our focus on local research, we specifically target audiences across the spectrum of learners (from preK to senior adults) and provide educational experiences that range from individual instruction and mentoring to broadcast media programs. To meet the needs of our audiences and to effectively distribute our resources, the Mote Education Division is organized in three Centers for education.

Center for School & Public Programs

The Center for School & Public Programs (CSP) brings Mote science and educational programming to visitors to the Mote Marine Laboratory campuses and communities by translating Mote's current marine science research into hands-on opportunities for students of all ages, backgrounds and abilities. Using discovery-oriented teaching methods and technologies, CSP staff strives to mentor learners in science-based critical-thinking and creativity skills. The ultimate goal of these efforts is to inspire learners to fully explore environmental and conservation issues and become informed decision makers regarding our coastal resources.

From the beginning of the laboratory, Mote research and education programs have been linked through public fascination with the Laboratory and local environment. Residents and visitors alike consistently come to Mote with questions about what they found on the beach, saw in the water, or smelled in the air. To meet these needs, on-site education programs began more than 15 years ago with summer opportunities for children and presentation of the JASON project. After years of evolution, onsite programs now range from daily field trips to yearlong school partnerships, overnight programs for schools and community groups to teacher workshops, and family programs. Each program combines current findings of Mote research and appropriate scientific and creative thinking skills.

Center for Volunteer & Intern Resources

The Center for Volunteer & Intern Resources (CVI) provides direct educational experiences for adult learners and provides support for Mote research, aquarium, and education programs. Additionally, interns and volunteers fulfill career or life interest aspirations through active participation in Mote's programs.

Throughout the years, volunteers and interns have played a critical role in the development of Mote Marine Laboratory and Aquarium. Like many other programs, the volunteer and intern program evolved informally. During the years when Mote was located on Siesta Key, a few college students conducted research projects at Mote and a few volunteers helped the researchers and gave informal tours of the lab. As the Laboratory expanded and the Aquarium opened in 1980, the need for well-trained volunteers and interns intensified. The demand for additional support was met by the volunteers themselves as they created the original organization and training guidelines

Mote education programs focus on the individual learner, such as this volunteer in the ecotoxicoloy program

for the program. The earliest written documentation indicates that five docents provided tours of the Siesta Key facility as early as the 1960s and the earliest formal intern program saw three college interns assisting in research projects in 1986. Today, over 1,400 volunteers provide more than 200,000 volunteer hours to the Lab each year while more than 120 student interns provide academic enthusiasm and youthful experience in support of Mote's research, education, and aquarium programs.

Center for Distance Learning

The Center for Distance Learning (CDL) brings Mote science and educational programming to a wide variety of audiences throughout Florida, the nation, and the world through interactive videoconferencing and other distance learning technologies. The SeaTrek program targets

K–12 audiences and their teachers. Audience development efforts include programming for preservice teachers, marine resource managers, and public visitors to other aquariums, science centers, museums, and libraries.

Inspired and initiated by Mote's longstanding involvement with the JASON Project, the SeaTrek program was begun in 1996. The SeaTrek model is based upon two dynamic components: (1) high-interest, live, interactive programming over videoconference systems, and (2) high-caliber, online support materials and curricula.

The SeaTrek distance education program uses interactive video conference technology.

The SeaTrek program is currently delivered widely in Florida and has expanded from the original seven Sarasota schools in 1998, to 43 schools across the state. Mote also delivers programs to schools across the nation, and last year presented over 260 videoconferences in 35 different states and three nations. This growth has been achieved through three consecutive Florida Department of Education Technology Literacy Challenge Fund grant awards, in partnership with Sarasota County Schools, and legislative appropriations from the state and federal government. These funds provided equipment, training, and programming to over 40 mostly underserved schools throughout the state of Florida. The funds also provided the infrastructure for completing the technological components of the Keating presentation and studio spaces, making improvements to the general electronic capabilities of the lab, and improving internet support and infrastructure for Mote's Tropical Research Center in the Florida Keys.

The Keating Marine Education Center houses two state-of-the-art interactive videoconference (IVC) studios, thereby increasing the efficiency and capacity for greater delivery of videoconferences to schools, museums, libraries and science centers.

SeaTrek presently offers 15 different IVC programs for students (preK–12) and their teachers. Each SeaTrek program features highly charismatic organisms and environments, along with interviews and video segments featuring scientists describing their work and career paths and conducting research.

Each live, interactive videoconference (IVC) meets the need for a truly interactive experience and measurably enhances student learning and enjoyment by using charismatic organisms and environments of south Florida. This project is supported by the vision stated in the IMLS publication *The 21st Century Learner,* by Beverly Sheppard (2001). This report states that, "The bold vision for the future must be a new kind of network, an infrastructure or system of complementary resources, tools and connections that serve the varied paths of today's learners." The report also states, "By erasing the boundaries between institutions, technology offers… unlimited potential for combining resources and the ideas inherent in them."

In addition to the IVC programs, each program topic is supported by educational materials that focus on student-driven inquiry and investigation. Processes that are emphasized include reasoning skills (Paul 1992) and research skills that advance independent learning (Boyce 1997).

Students are inspired to wonder about marine organisms and explore the world using scientific inquiry.

Content focuses on the themes addressed previously and is directly related to the NSES for elementary, middle, and high school science. Yet, the true potential of the SeaTrek model springs from fun and engaging interactivity with a live person, who presents the content in an enthusiastic multimedia format, using humor, surprise, music, sound effects, video, animation, models, and artifacts. Videoconferencing has been shown to be as effective as on-site presentations when specific care is taken to promote interactive discussion and participation (Galvin 1987; Stout 2004). The value of interacting with a live person is further emphasized by Falk and Dierking (1992) in *The Museum Experience*: "We would strongly endorse integrating people in the exhibit design whenever possible. Some of the most striking museum exhibits have been those in which people played an integral role in the exhibit as live artisans, musicians, scientists, and interpreters. When real people are integrated in an exhibit, [students] can appreciate the scale of an object and its relationship to the world beyond the museum."

The SeaTrek program is an innovation, a new model for creating a more interactive, personal, natural and fun environment for learning. As stated in *The 21st Century Learner*, "Lifelong learning is by nature learner-centered, personalized, inquiry-driven and activity-based. An infrastructure to support such needs must include broad and varied content, a commitment to physical and intellectual access and a delivery system that can support urban, suburban and rural needs." The SeaTrek program's premise is that the student's experience will be enhanced by (1) the added value of content they would not otherwise access in their area, (2) the dynamic, participatory nature of the interactive videoconference, and (3) specific discussion, with the MML science educator, of related activities, themes, and classroom topics at their school. The interactive nature of the model creates dialogue on themes of universal scientific relevance across geographic distances.

Changing Emphasis: Evaluating Mote's Education Programs in Terms of Learning

Mote is committed to demonstrating real science in real ways to visitors, students, and volunteers. Participants in the programs experience the scientific process from isolating questions, to testing hypotheses, to inferring and interpreting conclusions. Mote strives to include inquiry and exploration in all programs, letting students interact with their environment and letting their emotions guide their interest. Information itself becomes the afterthought of the experience rather than the purpose of the experience, because learning is initiated by providing opportunities to ask questions, collect data, and formulate testable hypotheses. By providing powerful experiences, coupled with immersion in an atmosphere of scientific research, participants leave with an increased desire to generate scientific questions and explore scientific answers.

Evidence for SeaTrek Success in Science Education

Seatrek has received local, state, national, and international acclaim as a highly respected education endeavor. In addition to 19 Florida counties, Mote currently serves over 30,000 students across the United States (Texas, Ohio, Arkansas, and Michigan being some of the leading user states) as well as Canada and England. Mote programs have recently been recognized by the US Institute for Museum and Library Services through the award of a competitive National Leadership Grant to produce IVC-based traveling exhibits for use in museums, libraries, aquariums, and zoos across the country.

SeaTrek was originally funded through a series of competitive awards from the Florida Technology Literacy Challenge Fund (TLCF) as a cooperative project of the Sarasota County Schools and Mote Marine Laboratory. SeaTrek received the TLCF awards from 1999 through 2001, when efforts were concentrated on schools with struggling or failing school performance. In 2002, SeaTrek then received a legislative appropriation to train teachers in the effective use of IVC, provide essential internet connectivity for the participant schools, develop five programs designed to motivate science learning in underperform-

Preliminary test results suggest that students in SeaTrek programs perform better on science content tests.

ing middle school students, and to collect preliminary data on the effectiveness of this program on student performance. Test data and teacher responses indicate that students participating in SeaTrek programs improved performance on both reading and science assessments. Performance was measured using qualitative (teachers surveys) and quantitative (pre- and posttests of science content and processes). In the pre- and posttests, 98% of the middle school student participants (n = 437) exhibited improved scores, with score increases ranging from 24–40% (Niebuhr and Metz, forthcoming). Mote will repeat this evaluation to compare these results with performance on the recently instituted science FCAT (Florida Comprehensive Assessment Test) exam.

In addition to improved performance on examinations, several of the teacher surveys of student performance indicated an increased interest in scientific investigation, the scientific process, and increased desire for individual reading after participation in the SeaTrek programs. One teacher wrote, "In the fall, only 33% of our total fifth graders met grade-level expectations with 0% in the high-performing category; this spring 63% met grade-level expectations with 13% in the high-performing range. I attribute their success to the large amount of nonfiction reading they did preparing for the teleconferences as well as the reading they did because of their interest in these science subjects…."

Mote Marine Laboratory has demonstrated success and the educational infrastructure is in place to deliver SeaTrek programs to schools throughout the nation. The next step is to rigorously test SeaTrek schools to determine the level of effectiveness in improving reading and science scores on standardized tests. They will also continue to work with underserved and resource-limited schools to ascertain the most efficient way to provide their students with the same level of excellence available to their more affluent neighbors in other areas of the nation.

The last few years have witnessed an explosion in the availability and use of IVC technology, not only in classrooms, but also in libraries, museums, zoos, and more, across the country. This expanding infrastructure has much greater potential for creative, collaborative, and learner-centered programming than is currently being reached. As networking connectivity becomes even more robust in the next few years, technology will allow for virtually seamless full video and audio interactivity between sites. The resource sharing that can occur will make it possible for any interested school or informal learning institution to access quality informal learning experiences for their audiences. Additionally, there are innumerable ways that on-site, hands-on learning can be combined with IVC learning in a mutually enriching experience. The creative applications of combined educational resources will be virtually unlimited as collaboration between schools, museums, and libraries accelerate through communications technologies in the coming years.

References

Boyce, L. N. 1997. *A guide to teaching research skills and strategies for grades 4–12*. Williamsburg, VA: College of William and Mary, Center for Gifted Education.

Falk, J. H., and L. D. Dierking. 1992. *The museum experience*. Washington, DC: Whalesback Books.

Galvin, P. 1987. *Telelearning and audiographics: Four case studies*. Ithaca, NY: Cornell University.

Paul, R. 1992. *Critical thinking: What every person needs to survive in a rapidly changing world*. Dillon Beach, CA: Foundation for Critical Thinking.

Sheppard, B. 2001. *The 21st century learner*. Washington, DC: Institute of Museum and Library Services.

Stout, K. L. 2004. Effect of multimedia instruction on parent knowledge of special education and participation in the individualized educational program conference. Doctoral Dissertation, University of Utah.

FAMILY MATH and Science Education:

A Natural Attraction

Grace Davila Coates and Harold Asturias
Lawrence Hall of Science

M any Americans understand the personal and national necessity of being more scientifically literate. Yet, the swift advances in science today are leaving many of us not understanding these advances and more importantly, not understanding the social and immediate consequences they produce. It is not just the science education (or lack of it) we receive in schools that causes these gaps in understanding or knowledge. The National Science Education Standards (NSES) offer tools and a cohesive vision of what it means to achieve scientific literacy for all regardless of background or circumstance. These standards specifically address the importance of coordinating efforts by all who have a responsibility for science education reform. Among them are families, parents, grandparents, and other caregivers. Without tools and or knowledge, however, many families find themselves wanting to help but not knowing how to help their children better understand science, mathematics, or new technology. FAMILY MATH, located at the Lawrence Hall of Science, has been working with families for over 23 years to spread the word that we are all capable of learning mathematics, and that mathematics plays a critical role in science education.

The Lawrence Hall of Science

The Lawrence Hall of Science (LHS) is the Science Center of the University of California at Berkeley, created for the purpose of making science accessible to the public. In this capacity, the Lawrence Hall of Science has developed expertise and experience in communicating science to the public through exhibits, school programs, instructional materials, professional development and public programs for more than 35 years. LHS is a singular resource center for science and mathematics education, and a public science center with exciting hands-on experiences for learners of all ages. Established in 1968 at the University of California, Berkeley, in honor of Ernest O. Lawrence, the University of California's first Nobel laureate, Lawrence Hall of Science is a national leader in the development of innovative materials and programs for students, teachers, families, and the public at large. By designing every activity around its mission: *To inspire and foster lifelong learning of science and mathematics for all,* LHS fosters understanding and enjoyment of science and mathematics for audiences of all ages. Similarly, it has expertise in delivering mathematics instruction and professional development to students, teachers, mathematics coaches, district administrators, community leaders, and parents. The body of work in informal and formal education includes development of exhibitions, published curricula used by more than 20% of the nation's K–12 students, and hundreds of programs for students and teachers. LHS programs capitalize on a multifaceted, rigorous approach to public understanding of science and mathematics. These programs include the Full Option Science System (FOSS), Great Explorations in Math and Science (GEMS), Marine Activities and Resources Education (MARE), EQUALS (dedicated to increase access and equity in mathematics and science for students and adults, especially for traditionally underrepresented students in math-based fields of study), Alliance for Collaborative Change in School Systems (ACCESS), and our most exciting program for parents: FAMILY MATH (FM) and Matemática Para La Familia.

FAMILY MATH: Program History and Description

The origins of FAMILY MATH are deeply rooted in the work of the EQUALS program. For many years EQUALS has worked with teachers to improve mathematics teaching and learning in their classrooms and schools. The EQUALS staff noticed that there were few girls enrolled in the museum's after-school classes. As a response to remedy this problem, they developed the book, *Math for Girls.* Based on research that addressed learning, mathematics, and gender, the book emphasized cooperative work, problem solving, graduate student role models, active learning, and working with manipulatives. EQUALS followed that by providing teachers with opportunities to learn these teaching strategies and to increase confidence by increasing competence.

As the teacher participants learned new strategies for teaching, they found some resistance from parents who were looking for the standard drill sheets they were used to seeing in mathematics. During this time, an EQUALS participant, and assistant principal who was responsible for working with classroom paraprofessionals, most of them parents, requested materials and strategies he could use to help them understand this new way of approaching mathematics. The EQUALS staff responded by creating a separate program designed to focus entirely on parents and children learning mathematics together (Stenmark, Thompson, and Cossey 1986).

Grants from the Fund for the Improvement of Postsecondary Education (FIPSE) and the Carnegie-Mellon Foundation provided the initial funding so that the staff could develop their ideas and test them out in diverse communities, with families from inner cities, suburbs, and rural areas. Since then, over five million families have experienced FAMILY MATH throughout the world. The program has been presented in over 30 languages, including English, Spanish, Chinese, and Swedish. Parents and caregivers ages range from 16 to 84.

FAMILY MATH in Action

To get a better picture of the program, imagine a lively, chatty group of 20 or so families with children of varying ages shaking beans in cup and throwing them on the table, counting and tallying them as their children make tallies on a chart on the blackboard. They are arguing about how many they think will land red-side-up or white-side-up. Some count, some tally, others watch and join in on the conversations. A class leader asks questions about the outcomes: What are the probabilities? How many beans do we have to toss to be assured our projected outcomes? What other experiences have we had that examined probability?

Families answer some of the leader's questions, shy children tell their parents some possible answers and the parents repeat them to the group. Some parents hold back and don't speak, while others boldly step share their thinking about how probability works. There's a woman and her partner laughing because they disagree about the possible outcomes, but realize that both their thinking about it makes sense. "Are we saying the same thing differently?" they ask.

The class leader asks them to talk with one another in groups and come up with three observations (or true statements) about their results. Then she asks them to make up three questions they still have about the activity. The families get involved in talking with each other, while dinner is brought in. The class leader invites them to discuss their questions while they eat. "After dinner, we will discuss the big math ideas," she says. As the families eat, they discuss what they perceive to be the important ideas in the tasks they completed or the games they tried.

Program Goals

FAMILY MATH is built on the belief that all children can learn and enjoy mathematics and focuses entirely on families learning mathematics together. Its goals include:

- Provide positive mathematics experiences for students and their parents together.
- Engage children and their families in mathematical thinking.
- Give children an opportunity to see that their parents value mathematics.
- Help develop a view of mathematics as more than a set of algorithms.
- Provide resources to families so they may continue to think about mathematics at home.

The strands of FAMILY MATH include building awareness, confidence, competence, and encouragement. Teachers and students are made aware of the need for understanding mathematics and its role in our lives. Confidence is built by providing strategies for success in mathematics that lead to improved competence in mathematics, and encouragement involves motivating students to continue studying mathematics and to consider a wide variety of careers.

Awareness, confidence, and motivation are the building blocks of learning and retention. In FAMILY MATH, this focus plays a major role in creating safe places to learn and take risks when learning with adults and children. One effective characteristic of the program is promoting the understanding of mathematics in a nurturing environment, while maintaining a focus on organization and rigor.

In many current educational contexts where high-stakes, standards-based decisions and measures of success external to the classroom are overemphasized, it is difficult to talk about "nurturing" learning. However, as we place more emphasis on these basic learning blocks of understanding mathematics in a comfortable—safe, yet challenging—environment, families return to sessions, they become more involved in their children's schooling, and in some cases, make different choices for their own lives.

Equity as a Guiding Principle

Equity requires that we understand that everyone is different, learns in a different manner, and more importantly, may require differing points of reference for establishing contexts for learning. Exemplary programs acknowledge and honor these differences by adapting to meet regional needs. The models collected in these adaptations are formalized and shared through a network of directors, educators, and families.

One excellent example of this idea is the misunderstanding of fractions by Native American students in the Le Grande Ronde nation in Oregon. Students kept insisting that they were one-third local Indians, one-third Hupa, and a combination of other Indian blood.

When the tribe's Elders hosted a series of classes and presented the *Fraction Kits,* families experienced a deeper understanding of fractions. When prompted to come up with other ways to show familial connection, families illustrated the ancestral family trees and could explain to one another why their original ideas about being one-third of a various combination of tribes, were not complete. These revelations were shared among the participants, and parents and students came to understand how fractions applied to their everyday knowledge. Knowing how much of any particular tribe one belongs to has strong political, personal, and sometimes financial implications. In this particular case the class facilitators addressed the dual issues of adapting curriculum for regional purposes and responding to individual community needs and interests.

The informal nature of the class meetings, the activities, and the content delivery structures allows the community to experience mathematics in ways that builds on parents' knowledge base in a manner that is rarely available to them in this culture (Shields and Ramage 1994). It is through these active processes that families share information with one another and come to deeper understanding of the mathematics concepts and their relevance to their lives.

A mother and daughter explore fractions.

Careers in Mathematics and Science

Including career education as part of family-learning classes helps families understand the role of mathematics and how it can affect a person's goals. Students often ask, "Why do I have to learn this?" Parents often ask, "What does math have to do with our everyday lives?" Although families may not think of the mathematics in their daily lives, they see the need to know some mathematics in their jobs. It also allows families opportunities to see what skills or knowledge various careers or jobs require. The informal nature of the FAMILY MATH classes allows for different ways to present career information. Often this session might include a person who has a "secret" (their career). They bring tools of the trade as clues and the audiences ask them questions until someone guesses the career. Guests talk about how mathematics and science play a role in their work. One parent, an x-ray technician, demonstrated connections between a game titled *Rainbow Logic* and the process of reading MRIs at the hospital where he worked. The careers are as diverse as the guests; from alligator farmers in Louisiana, to astronomers in Central America, the career guests play an important role in helping families see how mathematics and science impact our lives, our jobs, and our families.

Content Standards and Principles for Teaching Mathematics and Science

Inquiry in Mathematics

When families are encouraged to develop problem-solving skills, they are learning to think about a problem using strategies such a looking for patterns, creating illustrations, working with a partner or with a group, working backward, or eliminating possibilities. This relieves the frustration of not knowing how or where to begin. By placing more emphasis on developing strategies, abilities, and ideas to be learned, we move both students and their parents closer to developing an understanding of the role of inquiry in the classroom. Parents also develop an understanding of the importance of inquiry as a process in learning, and students are given opportunities to practice skills in meaning-ful contexts. Although mathematics is structured differently than science, the processes of posing overarching questions, forming hypotheses, investigating possibilities, and determining outcomes are common to both fields and lead to deeper mathematical and scientific understanding.

Mathematics and Science as Active and Interactive Learning

FAMILY MATH has a tradition of using "hands-on" materials. These often include items such as blocks, beans, pennies, string, toothpicks, or other things that may be easily found in a home. These are used to help us understand what numbers and space mean, and they help all of us solve problems. Traditionally these materials are used in the early elementary years, and are replaced with paper and pencil by the latter half of elementary school. This is unfortunate, as most of math-ematics and science can best be explained and understood using models and concrete materials. Many research and applied mathematicians do just that. Here are some ways in which FAMILY MATH connects to the National Science Education Standards.

Making Connections to Science in FAMILY MATH

NSES Standard (Grade Level)	FAMILY MATH Activity
Objects have many observable properties, including size, weight, shape, color, temperature, and the ability to react with other substances. Those properties can be measured using tools such as rulers, balances, and thermometers. (K–4)	Chapter 4 in the FM book titled *Measurement* is devoted to measuring activities. *Comparing and Ordering, The Magnified Inch, Making Balance Scales, Activities With Area, Capacity and Volume*, among others, are designed to help families understand the concepts of measurement, weight, and the conservation of area and volume.
Earth Materials are solid rocks and soils, water, and the gases of the atmosphere. The varied materials have different physical and chemical properties, which make them useful in different ways, for example, as building materials, as sources of fuel, or for growing the plants we use as food. Earth materials provide many of the resources humans use. (K–4)	Leaf Treasures, Seashells, and Rocks, ask families to sort and classify objects based on their physical characteristics.
The Sun, moon, stars, clouds, birds, and airplanes, all have properties, locations, and movements, which can be observed and described. (K–4)	Moon and Stars, and Shadows, from the FM for Young Children book, invite families to observe, describe, and record the phases of the moon and their shadows at different hours of the day.
A substance has characteristic properties such as density, a boiling point, and solubility, all of which are independent of the amount of sample. A mixture of substances often can be separated into the original substances using one or more of the characteristic properties. (5–8)	A deep understanding of the proportionality and the related ideas about ratio and proportion are essential to this standard. Several activities, such as Three Bean Salads, and Gorp help families develop these mathematical ideas.

Mathematics and Science as Public Discourse

While hands-on activities are important, they are not sufficient in fully developing an under-standing of an idea or concept. Families often meet their neighbors as they discuss, agree or disagree, and share ideas with one another about mathematics outcomes, strategies, or events. As families create models, they are asked to think about how they might justify their solutions or strategies so they can explain, and sometimes defend, their outcome with another group's solution. Justifying solutions or strategies is a different experience for many parents. Most recall mathematics as mostly numbers and symbols. Many recall going to the blackboard to write a solution to a problem, but not necessarily to talk about what they wrote. As families explain their strategies, solutions, or ideas, others are forming questions, changing their own thinking about the work at hand, and deepening their understanding.

Public discourse is an important part of the mathematics process. This shift in emphasis from only one person communicating ideas or knowledge to the class leader or teacher results in more ideas being generated and shared as common understandings and public knowledge. The discussions make learning more meaningful and allow the individual to retain new understanding.

Addressing the Teaching Standards

Creating Contexts for Learning Mathematics and Science

Like the science standards moving away from rigidly following a curriculum, FAMILY MATH encourages class leaders to respond to family interests, cultural relevance, and meaningful applications of the ideas at hand. They bring mathematics ideas to families through investigations, activities, and games. To do this and to be relevant in various communities, a program must be dedicated to cultural inclusion.

If fractions are the topic, class leaders step away from the book to allow for the examination of how fractions impact Native American youth as they explore their ancestral roots. If patterns are the topic, it makes perfect sense to note and describe the patterns of local South African art, Maori icons, or the everyday materials of the Navajo. Moving away from the book and encouraging class leaders to make these changes allows the program to respond to community interests, strengths, and experiences. Sharing new learning across cultures helps families make connections between ideas and concepts.

Sharing Responsibility for Teaching and Learning: Collaboration

Who teaches out-of-school classes? Many individuals can lead a class. However, they must be enthusiastic, kind, and not afraid. They do need to have a curiosity for learning and be willing to "look things up" or to ask someone else for needed information. In some of the most successful sites, parents have taken the lead and presented the classes. At university sites, teacher educators present the work in their communities. A strong team can consist of a teacher and a parent or other community member. We do know that people working together enhances the program. Each team member contributes their knowledge and skills to create richer learning experiences.

Supporting a dynamic learning community requires collaboration, shared responsibility, and respect for all team members. This cooperation also creates a strong base for successful long-term program implementation.

Extending Learning to the Home: Questions That Promote Mathematical Thinking

Class leaders of informal classes do not have to be experts or authority figures. Asking thoughtful and relevant questions, posing suppositions, and presenting justifications are all skills that class leaders get better at as they work in their communities. The exercises invite questions, the games encourage economical strategies, and the problems have various ways of hinting at solutions. As a result, families extend this learning and create environments for problem solving in the home (Sloane-Weisbaum 1990).

There is a wealth of information to be gained in asking open-ended questions (Stenmark 1989). It is important to provide models of potential questions for class facilitators and parents to support them as they lead the classes or to use at home. The following is a

A father and son collaborate on a project.

collection of questions for class leaders to share with parents or other class leaders.

- Are there other possibilities? If so, what might they be?
- What other ideas do you have about how we might begin?
- How do we know when we have reached the limit?
- How can we be sure?
- How can we do this differently?
- How did you figure that out?
- Is there a pattern here? Describe it.
- Tell me about your design.
- What do you suppose would happen if...?
- What other things can we find shaped like a square/circle/triangle...?
- What will you do next?
- Why do you think that?
- Can we make a model of it? Describe it or build it.
- What other problem that you have done does this remind you of?
- Hmm-mm, I had not thought of that. Tell me more about it.
- How can we check to see how close your guess is?
- How did you decide which objects go in the circle?
- I wonder...?
- How do we know there is something missing?
- That is interesting. Tell me about how you did that.
- What is most (least) likely?
- What other ways can we show that?
- What would you do with this?
- Why does this work?

Families are reminded to be careful not to ask too many questions all at once. One or two well-placed questions go a long way toward encouraging thinking and creating deeper understanding.

Addressing the Staff Development Standards

Who are the Experts?

Too often teachers attending staff development are treated like some students are treated, as empty vessels waiting for the expert or authority to fill their intellectual glass with new and improved knowledge. FAMILY MATH acknowledges that teachers, like their students, have their own life experiences, their own knowledge, cultural perspectives, and areas of expertise. The program strives to create an environment where these experiences are not only acknowledged, but also respected and shared. It is this informal sharing that makes the program relevant in many settings. More importantly, class leaders come to understand that when families and students are treated in a similar fashion, learning thrives.

Collegial and Collaborative Learning

Collegial and collaborative learning extends beyond a workshop or class attended. Creating opportunities for future meetings, informally or formally, creates communities of teachers and learners. Some may return for leadership sessions, while others return for sessions dedicated to their grade levels, or to learn about topic-specific ideas. Creating a listserv for site directors, parents, and interested others allows for an exchange of ideas within networks of long-term relationships that have evolved into a dynamic and fluid international learning communities. Many educators have experienced increased mathematics learning and understanding resulting from working with their network partners. Programs at the Lawrence Hall of Science know this. There is an extensive network of FOSS, MARE, EQUALS, GEMS, and FAMILY MATH sites throughout the world.

Teacher as Leader and Facilitator of Change

Education leaders are often harbingers of change in their communities. Those attending professional development at the Lawrence Hall of Science have chosen to attend sessions that require that they actively engage in mathematics and science investigations even though they may not feel that confident in their own mathematics abilities or their knowledge of science. Yet, they are willing to extend their learning and thinking. Many learn more mathematics and science as they learn how to implement the programs in their classrooms or at their school sites. They share what they have learned with other school staff. They share ideas that worked well and tell what they wish they had done differently (Devaney 1986). Leaders continue to ask questions about how to make their programs better. These are the behaviors of teachers that excel. They are reflective, they share learning, they are not teaching faddists, and they produce knowledge about teaching and learning.

Assessment: Analysis and Communication

The informal nature of family learning is the reason for FAMILY MATH's success. Although there is no test administered to participants or the leaders of the program, assessment of students and their parents understanding of mathematics is carefully considered in the discussions, which are the heart of the program. Assessment in this informal setting takes many shapes and the evaluation studies have demonstrated the benefits of the families' experience.

FAMILY MATH participants increase their awareness of the role of analysis in mathematics and in their daily lives. They learn to analyze data on charts, they make product comparisons at the supermarket, and they learn to analyze what they read in the newspapers. Initially, families do not connect analysis with mathematics, mostly because they consider mathematics to be mostly about numbers. As they work with Venn diagrams and make observations of patterns and events, their reasoning skills improve and their explanations become more sequential, more articulate, and more mathematical. The NSES indicate that assessment should include opportunities for individuals to evaluate and reflect on their own understanding and ability. When families talk with others about what they are learning, and when they compare responses and discuss differing outcomes, deeper understanding is achieved.

Involving "Difficult to Reach" Families

Research indicates that most educators want to involve families in the schools but do not know how to build positive and productive programs (Epstein et al. 1997). FAMILY MATH has a reputation as a forerunner of reform and advocacy in the area of mathematics teaching and learning. It connects families who may have never come to school events otherwise, in positive and safe environments for purposeful learning.

When is a parent an "involved parent?" Involved parents are supportive of education and their children through various means and in different ways (Kellison McLaughlin 1993). What makes a family "difficult to reach?" Many families who speak languages other than English often find themselves on the perimeter of school activities. This language barrier has many implications; families are identified as not being interested in their children's education, they are tagged as "hard to reach" or as not having the same values as the dominant culture. However, participants in effective programs come from many parts of the country and classes are typically taught in the languages of the communities being served. They stay involved because they all want the same thing—a better education for their children than they had. The most obvious impact has been the empowerment of minority parents (Ramage and Shields 1994). Parents offer classes in their homes when teachers or classrooms are not available. In one example, parents formed a group to address the issue of Hispanic children not being represented in the school's Gifted and Talented programs. They also actively recruited other parents to join advisory boards and to attend meetings.

Program Effectiveness

We know from research that there is a correlation between parent involvement and increased student achievement (Henderson and Berla 1997). The central goal of FAMILY MATH is to bring families together for the purpose of learning mathematics and understanding the role of math in school, work, and in their daily lives. Studies and program evaluations support the following results for participants in FAMILY MATH programs:

- Enhances self-concept and confidence in parents, to better help their children with mathematics homework (Draper 1992).
- Involves "hard to reach" parents in their children's education and in the school (Shields and David 1988).
- Improves parent/teacher communication regarding student learning (Sloan-Weisbaum 1990).
- Changes the way participants view mathematics and their relationship to it (Shields and Ramage 1994).
- Provides classroom teachers with models for changing their own mathematics teaching (Devaney 1986).
- Improves student attitudes toward mathematics (Sloane-Weisbaum 1990).
- Reduces anxiety (in adults and children) about mathematics (Sloane-Weisbaum 1994).
- Increases the understanding of mathematics usefulness and role in society (Kreinberg and Thompson 1986).

Program evaluators found that sessions lasting less than six weeks (one session per week) were not enough to produce the positive changes noted here. Sessions lasting "too long," or over eight weeks, resulted in lower attendance. Although not a formal part of these studies, mothers, fathers, teachers, and other caregivers have been affected in profound ways. Many have returned to complete their high school diploma; others have started or returned to college, and others changed careers. In the Matemática classes, some have enrolled classes to learn English. Overall, parents indicate that they want to help their families rise and that they wish to be good role models in education for their children.

Future Visions

FAMILY MATH continues to serve as a model for numerous projects across the country interested in developing family learning programs, such as the Family Science Program developed in conjunction with the Oregon Museum of Science and Industry. Gallaudet University's Laurent Clerc National Deaf Education Center is developing Families Count! Program kits. They are adapting activities to meet the learning needs of deaf and hard of hearing audiences.

The Spanish Language Media Project, based at the Lawrence Hall of Science is publishing math activities in three regions of the country. The activities are expanded upon and presented locally in community-based organizations and festivals. In addition, the project is designing a website to disseminate the math and science activities.

As family-centered and student-directed online programs grow, there is continued and increased interest in repurposing and updating the materials. Both nonprofit organizations and private companies seek creative collaborations to animate the mathematics activities and to create learning DVDs to reach a new generation of families seeking support in mathematics.

Conclusion

The lessons learned in this program serve informal learning well. As exemplary informal learning programs are developed, they include models of collaboration between educators and parents, public discourse about mathematics, cooperative learning between children and adults, engaging yet challenging academic content, culturally relevant curriculum, and assessment that informs the teacher and serves the learner. All are carried out in safe environments for teaching and learning.

Informal learning times provide families with the luxury of time to investigate, talk, share discoveries, to make mistakes, and correct them. Informal learning allows families to play with ideas and potential solutions in ways that connect them to their own experiences and previous knowledge. Families can take the time to explore mathematics and science in the arts, in literature, through movement, or other forms of learning. What is important to note is that both science and mathematics require conditions for the mind to be challenged, encouraged, and engaged. One often leads to the other, and this natural attraction can occur with any group that is motivated and curious.

References

Devaney, K. 1986. Interviews with nine teachers. Lawrence Hall of Science for EQUALS.

Draper, D. 1992. A phonomenological investigation of the impact of a FAMILY MATH program on elementary students, their parents, and teachers. Doctoral dissertation submitted to the University of New Mexico. Albuquerque, New Mexico.

Epstein, J. L., L. Coates, K. C. Salinas, M. G. Sanders, and B. S. Simon. 1997. *School, family, and community partnerships: Your handbook for action*. Thousand Oaks, CA: Corwin Press.

Henderson, A. T., and N. Berla, eds. 1997. *A new generation of evidence: The family is critical to student achievement*. Washington, DC: Center for Law and Education.

Kreinberg, N., and V. Thompson. 1986. FAMILY MATH: a report of an intervention program that involves parents in their children's mathematics education. Paper presented at the annual meeting of the American Association for the Advancement of Science, Philadelphia, PA.

McLaughlin, C. K. 1993. *The do's and don'ts of parent involvement: How to build a positive school-home partnership*. Torrance, CA: Innerchoice.

National Research Council (NRC). 1996. *National science education standards*. Washington, DC: National Academy Press.

Schauble, L., and R. Glaser, eds. 1996. *Innovations in learning: New environments for education*. Mahwah, NJ: Lawrence Erlbaum Associates.

Shields, P. M., and K. Ramage. 1994. *Matemática para la familia, San Diego county: An evaluation report*. Menlo Park, CA: SRI International.

Sloane-Weisbaum, K. 1990. Families in FAMILY MATH: A qualitative study of parents' role in their children's formal and informal mathematics education before and after working with FAMILY MATH. Unpublished.

Stenmark, J. K. 1989. *Assessment alternatives in mathematics: An overview of assessment techniques that promote learning*. Berkeley, CA: Regents of the University of California.

Stenmark, J. K., V. Thompson, and R. Cossey. 1986. *Family Math*. Berkeley, CA: University of California.

The Body of Evidence:

COSI's *In Depth: Autopsy* Videoconference Program

Gail Wheatley and Jen Snively
COSI: Center of Science and Industry Columbus

COSI Columbus is a hands-on science and technology center in Ohio's capital city that for the past 40 years has helped children, families, and educators understand their world and inspired them to learn more about it. COSI, the Center of Science and Industry, provides engaging, informal learning experiences within its innovative facility and through traveling exhibits and electronic and traveling outreach programs that serve students and teachers across Ohio, nationally, and internationally. COSI inspires children to become the scientists, astronauts, and inventors of future generations. The museum's interweaving of hands-on science learning, exhibitions, demonstrations, and films has delighted "children of all ages" and helped make science literacy a family activity.

Throughout its history, COSI has cherished its responsibility to impact education both in the classroom and beyond. COSI's education programs align with national and statewide science, math, and technology curricula and standards. School activities include daytime and overnight field trips, outreach into the classroom, after-school programs, electronic education programs, and teacher professional development.

In 1999, COSI relocated to a state-of-the-art facility on the Scioto Riverfront on the west side of downtown Columbus. At the same time, the Electronic Education program was launched with an interactive surgery program called *Surgical Suite*. This very successful program was just the beginning for Electronic Education. During the last seven years the program has grown to include four styles of programming, all built on the premise of providing students access to experiences that are unique and normally difficult or impossible for classroom teachers to obtain. Since 1999, Electronic Education programs have reached more than 100,000 participants in 41 states and three foreign countries.

COSI's Electronic Education program launched *Surgical Suite: Open Heart* and *Surgical Suite: Total Knee Replacement* in 2000 and 2003, respectively. Students could watch a live surgery from their own school or at COSI and ask questions of the surgeon or operating room team as the surgery progressed. Teachers quickly began to ask for more and more of this type of program—the ability to see something "real" and ask questions of a professional in the field. The majority of the teachers requested that COSI develop such a program around an autopsy. After looking into the situation extensively, we determined that, for legal reasons, it would not be possible to develop a program around a real-time autopsy procedure. Instead, we turned to the possibility of taping an autopsy and developing a program around that videotape. This move away from a live experience toward taped programming gave us the opportunity we needed to create a more "real-world" experience for students. This would seem to be paradoxical, since nothing can be more real than a live surgery! But the very nature of the live surgery and the fact that the procedure changes slightly, or sometimes extensively, for every patient is a limiting factor in developing truly powerful pre- and postvisit activities. Using a taped production with live narration for the autopsy program would allow the COSI team to fully explore pre- and postvisit opportunities, because the team would be controlling all aspects of what the students experienced during the videoconference. That level of control allowed us to feed students information, just as a real pathologist or coroner would receive it for a real case. Even though the patient in this program is fictional, and a conglomeration of several different bodies and their organs, the case unfolds just like a real case would for the professionals in a morgue or coroner's office.

In Depth: Autopsy allows students to see and participate in an autopsy as much as possible, given the limits of videoconference technologies. The program puts anatomy, physiology, and pathology lessons in a context where they are used extensively. Memorization of organ names or locations does not help students determine the cause of death for the fictional patient. However, knowledge of the function and appearance of each organ is critical. The pathologist covers most of this information, so students that do not have this knowledge can still fully participate. However, those students with prior knowledge of healthy organs are better able to ask questions of the pathologist during the program. Student guides to the autopsy procedure are provided for all students participating. As with any real scientific endeavor, we encourage good note taking and emphasize the fact that once the procedure is over, there is no going back and trying to recapture what has been missed

Science-process skills, including observation, recordkeeping, measurement, collecting and interpreting data, and drawing conclusions and defending them with data are emphasized throughout the program. Students begin the program by learning about the pathology of various organs and presenting this information to their classmates during the previsit activities. Each group of students has a different organ to research, so must learn from the other groups in order to establish a more complete picture of the common pathologies that might occur in the fictional patient. Students must then research and develop an autopsy plan after reading the "case history and medical information" about the specific patient they will be seeing. These plans are presented to the forensic pathologist that is narrating the videoconference program. This experimental design gives the students the answers they want from the autopsy with a minimum of time and money expended. Thus, students are asked to follow the same process as real coroners and medical examiners would during this planning stage, balancing the needs of society, the need to save taxpayer money, and the wishes of the deceased's family.

The videoconference program requires students to use both cognitive and procedural skills. The pathologist talks about the autopsy procedure and what constitutes the correct order of steps within the procedure. For example, certain small organs can be lost if not taken out at the proper time. Other organs can contaminate the entire abdomen or tissue samples taken, if not removed at the proper time and in the proper way. Toxicologic and histologic samples must be removed carefully and at the appropriate time and from the appropriate location, again to make sure results are accurate. Cognitive skills are used throughout the program, as more information becomes available about the various organs. Students are able to ask questions about a collapsed lung or a myocardial infarction that is seen on the heart. Basic information is given about any abnormalities during the procedure, but students must elicit further information from the pathologist during the times set aside for questions.

After the videoconference program, students are asked to conduct an experiment and study the toxicology and histology reports generated for the fictional patient. Students must manage and synthesize the data they received from the videoconference program and pre- and postvisit activities in order to reach a conclusion about the cause of death. No "right" answer is given to the students. They must defend their answers with data and evidence, just as a real pathologist would. Finally, the students generate a "final report" for the autopsy, cataloging all information found and defending their conclusions. Many teachers require the students to present these papers in class, so their conclusions can be challenged by other students, who might disagree or who have interpreted the data differently.

The vision for this program was to mirror the process of an autopsy as closely as possible. In achieving this vision, the COSI team created a real-world science experience that contains many of the aspects that the NSES would like to see emphasized for students. The program also puts the teacher in the role these standards recommend, that of a guide or leader of inquiry, rather than as the center of the classroom or a lecturer. Lastly, if the program is done in its entirety by the participating teachers, the sum total of pre- and postvisit activities and the videoconference take over five hours of time, allowing students to explore a topic for a longer period of time, work collegially, and, to a great extent, control their own learning. Teachers are also encouraged to allow students to assess their own and each other's learning through the use of the built-in assessment tools, such as class presentations and reports.

In Depth: Autopsy Program Description

Teachers that make a reservation for the *In Depth: Autopsy* program receive a set of materials approximately four weeks in advance of their program. The Teacher's Guide outlines the program and describes the pre- and postvisit activities. The program proceeds as follows:
- Previsit activities: Autopsy Images, Pathology, Autopsy Plan
- Videoconference program
- Postvisit Activities: Toxicology, Histology, Autopsy Report, Forensic Pathology, External Findings

Previsit Activities

Because this is a videoconference program, COSI team does not go to the school. Consequently, COSI has no control over the teachers, the amount of time they spend on this program, or how they implement it in their classrooms. In order to prevent the students from being shocked by the graphic nature of an autopsy, it is strongly recommended that teachers show their students still images of an actual autopsy prior to having them attend the videoconference program. These images are provided on a CD that is included with the materials. Teachers are expected to accomplish at least this step of pre-preparation.

It is also recommended, though not required, that students do the other two previsit activities. The second activity involves students working in groups of three or four to learn about the pathology of a particular organ. The organs assigned to the class as a whole include: heart, kidney, lungs, coronary arteries, and brain. The COSI team struggled with how to limit this information so that students would not get lost in researching all the diseases known to mankind. Eventually, the decision was made to limit the pathology to disease processes that are clearly visible during an autopsy and are fairly common in the general population. Once the student groups have researched their organs and the assigned pathologies, they report their results to the class. Each organ is assigned to two groups so if one group does a poor job, the class can still benefit from the knowledge gained from the second group. Photos of the assigned organs and pathologies, as well as open-ended questions, are included on the CD, so PowerPoint presentations can be easily created. Classes are asked to build a master vocabulary list of words the pathologist might be expected to use as they conduct research and as presentations are given. However, vocabulary is not stressed simply for the sake of vocabulary.

Class discussions about the assigned pathologies are recommended because at this point, the students have no idea what they will see during the autopsy. If students do not know what a myocardial infarction looks like, they are likely to miss something similar during the autopsy that will be shown during the videoconference. As part of piloting this program, COSI team members went to three local schools and observed roughly 150 students developing their reports and presentations for the class. The biggest challenge that existed was that the majority of students observed did *not* want to be limited to the pathologies assigned. The level of curiosity about diseases and disease process was truly surprising to the COSI team making observations. However, the presentations that were made indicated that the students gained a very wide, but very shallow, knowledge of the diseases that they were assigned. For example, the students assigned the heart covered several diseases that were not included in the recommended list, but neglected to mention that myocardial infarctions are dead heart tissue caused by lack of blood flow to the heart muscle itself. Most, but not all, of these groups assigned the heart did manage to include in their presentations that heart attacks are caused by blocked arteries.

After gaining a very basic knowledge of pathology, students are then asked to research autopsies and determine what the procedure typically includes. From this research they are asked to write an autopsy plan that will be submitted to the pathologist at COSI prior to the start of the videoconference program. In planning the autopsy, students are asked to strongly tie all desired outcomes to a step in the autopsy plan. For instance, if urine and blood samples should be analyzed for drugs, when and how the samples are to be collected should be included in the plan. Students are provided the medical history of the patient, as far as it is known, at this step of the procedure. Included with the history are the desires of the family and/or permissions required for the autopsy. In planning the autopsy, students are asked to consider not only the desired results, but also the considerations of the family and the budgetary limitations of the average coroner's office. Expensive tests cannot be ordered unless there is a very clear cut reason for them and no cheaper, equally effective alternative test is available. The majority of students are very, very thorough with their plans. In fact, the majority inserted many steps and tests not included in the average hospital or forensic autopsy. It is probably no coincidence that the majority of these expensive steps and tests are things that are seen on television crime shows.

The Videoconference

The students' autopsy plans are given to Dr. Larry Tate, the forensic pathologist who narrates the *In Depth: Autopsy* program. The videoconference program opens with Dr. Tate going through the plans submitted, asking the students questions, and making comments. This step occurs in real autopsies where medical residents are in training. It allows the supervising or attending pathologist to understand what is planned and to have the opportunity to change those plans before the first incision is made. Dr. Tate brings a real-world perspective to this part of the program by letting students know that while many tests and technologies are great for television mysteries, in most instances they are too expensive or time consuming for the average coroner's office.

Dr. Tate applies logic and humor to the plans submitted to him and significantly expands the students' knowledge. For example, many students have in their plans that stomach contents must be examined to determine what the person ate last and then this information can be used to determine time of death. The time of death is already known for our patient, who died in the hospital. If it is not necessary to examine stomach contents to determine what the person last ate, then this test is not ordered. Dr. Tate also points out that stomach contents cannot determine time of death, since everyone digests food differently and even the same individual would have variable rates of digestion according to the meal eaten, state of stress, temperature, state of health, and other factors. It is a myth perpetuated by crime shows that stomach contents are important. In most instances, unless the person is suspected of dying from poison, stomach and intestinal contents are not examined, although samples are taken, just in case.

After completing the discussion of the students' autopsy plans, the program proceeds to the external examination. In order to preserve patient confidentiality, only part of the body is shown. Dr. Tate runs through his "findings" from the external examination and asks students to take notes on a diagram in their student guide. The external exam form (p. 204) shows the page that allows students to take notes quickly without slowing the tape or the program down substantially to clarify details. This form is based on the one used by the pathologists at The Ohio State University Medical Center. Should students really get lost during this section, teachers have the information in their guides and can let students know what they missed.

After the external examination, the program proceeds to the Y-incision, removal of the chest plate, tying off and removing the intestines and removal of the organs in a single block. Because

CASE NO. ——————————— NAME——————————————

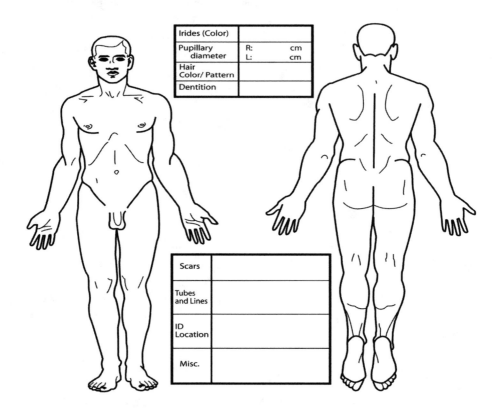

Irides (Color)	
Pupillary diameter	R: cm L: cm
Hair Color/ Pattern	
Dentition	

Scars	
Tubes and Lines	
ID Location	
Misc.	

most students are taught anatomy and organ placement from the front of the body, COSI includes a diagram of the back of the organ block. That diagram is shown in on page 205.

After the organ block is removed, dissection of the block begins followed by dissection of each individual organ. The pathologist is careful to note any abnormalities and inform students what to look for with each organ. Where possible, arrows and markers are added to the tape to make certain students know what is being discussed. Additionally, the pathologist covers the steps of the procedure and why the order is important, as contamination of certain organs or fluids could change results and impact the determination of cause of death for the patient. Students are given the opportunity to ask questions at regular intervals throughout this portion of the program.

Once all the abdominal organs have been weighed, dissected, and thoroughly examined, the program shows a section on careers associated with morgues, coroner's offices, and pathology. These interviews with professionals in the field allow students to explore possible careers they might not have known about and take a mental break from the rigors of the procedure. The interviews focus on what the individuals like or find challenging about their careers, also giving students an idea of what types of personalities might do well in those careers.

Dr. Tate returns with an examination of the thoracic organs. These are also weighed, dis-

          National Science Teachers Association

sected, thoroughly examined, and discussed with students. The heart in particular is examined very carefully, with all arteries, valves and chambers being checked for both form and functionality. Photographs of the examination of heart and brain can be seen in below and on page 206.

After the thoracic organs are examined, there are more career interviews. The program then moves on to the removal of the brain. This is typically a very intense part of the program for students and they have many questions. After the brain is removed from the skull, it is processed for three weeks in formaldehyde to preserve it and also to stiffen the tissue to the point

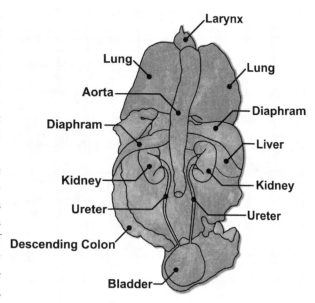

Diagram of the back of the orgain block.

where it can be easily sliced. The examination of a brain other than our patient's is shown and the procedure is discussed. Then our patient's brain is shown and the abnormalities discussed. A few more career interviews follow and the program moves to the postautopsy procedures and requirements. Dr. Tate shows a Toxicology request form, discusses the implications of the various tests that can be ordered and spends a few minutes on the chain of evidence requirements for all autopsies performed. He also discusses the histology slides that will be "prepared" for the students and how they will use them to help determine cause of death. He stresses the importance of having data and evidence to support any claims or statements made in the final autopsy report. Any autopsy can be challenged in court, and the pathologist that performed the autopsy should be prepared to answer questions and defend conclusions, particularly if the death is a result of criminal activity.

At that point, the program is open to questions from the

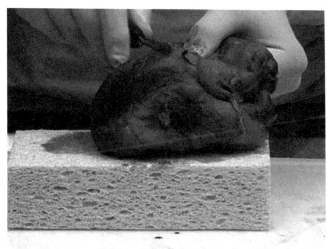

Examination of the heart.

Slicing the brain into sections for examination.

students. Questions are taken in a round-robin fashion from up to six groups, five audiences connected via videoconference and one audience attending the program at COSI. Questions typically range from findings on the autopsy and their implications for the patient, to how accurate the crime shows the students have seen on television are, to what happens to bodies after transportation to funeral homes. Dr. Tate is also asked for personal cases, such as most gruesome, the oddest, or the most interesting case he has worked on. The program usually ends before students are finished asking questions, so COSI allows students and teachers to ask additional questions via e-mail.

Postvisit Activities

After the program is over, students are left with a lot of notes and a desire to determine cause of death for the patient. While there were two findings on the autopsy that could have led to death (a myocardial infarction and a hemorrhage in the brain), there is no indication what might have caused either condition. Students are challenged to examine the histology slides provided by COSI on the CD and compare the tissue samples taken from the patient with those considered to be normal. They will also conduct a test of "urine and blood" samples provided by COSI and examine a toxicology report of the fluids that were removed from the patient when he was admitted to the emergency room. At this point, the students have the information they need to construct both the cause and manner of death. The cause would be the immediate cause, such as infarction or hemorrhage, as well as the underlying cause for the abnormality. For example, did the patient have severe atherosclerosis, which in turn caused a heart attack? In addition, the manner of death needs to be determined. Did the patient die of natural causes, suicide, murder, accident, or undetermined causes? Students are asked to write a report and defend the report after collecting all the data available. One teacher reported that she had tried to skip the postvisit activities but her students would not let her. She decided to assign the determination of cause of death as a homework assignment in order to maintain her class schedule, but even then students requested a class period to discuss their results with each other.

The final postvisit activity allows students to use vinyl cling film to simulate skin and ballistics gel to simulate muscle. Teachers are asked to stab the vinyl/ballistics gel combination with a variety of instruments such as Phillips and straight screwdrivers, single- and double-edged knives, hammer, fish hooks, awls, etc. Students are then asked to identify what caused the "wounds" and to determine how much of what they hear on television regarding wounds is accurate. Students should be able to narrow down the cause of the wound fairly quickly. The vinyl cling film shows details much like skin does. Identifying the type of instrument is as far as pathologists can narrow things down. The TV coroner that proclaims the wound was made by a 6-inch kitchen knife made by Chicago Cutlery is indeed fictional. There is no way to determine this level of detail from the wounds made, given how the body compresses, and changes position and shape (if muscles are flexed or not). Students should be able to determine this for themselves based on the vinyl cling/ballistics gel substitutes provided in the materials. To a great extent, the teacher has to facilitate this activity for students to get the maximum learning from it. COSI provides questions to be answered such as, "How can you determine the length of a knife blade from the wound?" However, in observations of this activity in local classrooms, it was noted that the activity is either over in less than five minutes with fairly poor outcomes, or it is still going on by the end of the class period with students asking many additional questions of their own. This particular activity, more so than the rest of the program, is dependent on the teacher's comfort level with inquiry methodologies and facilitation.

In-Class Assessments

There are four assessment tools that are built into the program for teachers to use. These are: (1) class presentations on the assigned organs and pathologies, (2) student autopsy plans, (3) student note-taking in booklets provided, and (4) final autopsy reports with supporting data. As reported above, COSI observed these assessment tools in use with 10 local classrooms. The presentations on organs and pathology often indicated a shallow level of knowledge gained. Student autopsy plans, on the other hand, are typically very thorough and unrealistically detailed. However, watching the autopsy procedure and asking questions of Dr. Tate seemed to clear up many of these misconceptions. Observations of student note taking indicate there are often three to four avid note takers per class, with many of the other students getting the information needed from those few that take notes. It may be, however, that students simply feel overwhelmed by the procedure, to the point where they do not ask questions or take notes. We have not yet been able to determine what percentage of students feel too overwhelmed by the autopsy to take notes. This phenomenon was noted during the first *Surgical Suite* programs. Students were too fascinated or too engaged in what they were seeing to ask questions of the surgeons. Steps were taken to minimize this feeling by creating interactive websites that allowed students to perform the procedure themselves prior to attending the surgery program (see *www.cosi.org*, Visitors tab, online activities for virtual knee and heart surgeries). These websites effectively prepared students for the experience and gave them additional information around which to frame their questions. For *In Depth: Autopsy*, funding has not yet been secured to develop an interactive web site. For this reason, teachers and the COSI team have decided, at least for the moment, that student note taking in the booklets provided is not a clear indicator of either learning or engagement in the program.

The last assessment tool built in to the program is the final autopsy report. In observations of classrooms, this is where learning was conclusively demonstrated. Students who presented their findings most often did a very good job of summing up the evidence for their conclusions, demonstrating knowledge of organs and how they function, and the effect of various ingested substances.

Also, student groups that had done a relatively poor job of presenting the assigned organs and pathology demonstrated that, in most cases, they had gone back and done more research about pathologies that applied to this particular case. This indicates a self-assessment that knowledge was not sufficient to proceed, so additional information is sought. This is also a typical learning pattern demonstrated by many adults learning new information for the work place.

Students who arrived at the correct cause of death demonstrated the ability to synthesize information from a variety of sources on a variety of subjects. In the classroom observation sessions, COSI went in with a list of facts and data that could be used to support conclusions. There were very few groups presenting their conclusions that hit all items on COSI's list. However, the majority of advanced or AP student groups were able to get almost all of the supporting data. With more average classes, students were still able to arrive at the correct answer, but less data were used to support the conclusions. There was only one class of students participating in the testing and observation that were considered lower level or below average. This class of students struggled more with their conclusions and about 30% arrived at the wrong answer. "Supporting evidence" for this class consisted as much of television myths as of true data provided or discovered through the program activities. Follow-up research has not yet been conducted to determine if the poor outcome from this one class was caused by the program being too advanced for the students, poor implementation by the teacher (not all activities were observed), or lack of prior knowledge of anatomy and physiology. For all classes, the level of engagement was high and discussion occurred after every presentation, with students evaluating additional data presented or arguing points made.

A few teachers report developing their own assessment tools in addition to those provided. Two-thirds of teachers who said they had developed their own assessments also indicated they spent larger amounts of time on the program and used all pre- and postvisit activities.

Teachers report that student motivation is high for this program and that the level of interest demonstrated provides a number of positive results. In a written survey, conducted by COSI of the 150 teachers that had participated in the program by late fall, 2006, teachers were asked how the program stimulated their students' interest in science. This open-ended question was answered a variety of ways, but the answer that was given 50% of the time was that the increased student interest was caused by the "mystery" that needed to be solved and resulted in greater time and attention being paid to applying knowledge that had been gained during normal class activities toward reaching a solution. Students corroborated this on surveys conducted last school year. Over 75% indicated that solving for the cause of death is what made the science fun. On that same student survey, 62% indicated that they would participate in the program again, if given the opportunity. There were no follow-up questions, but two students wrote in the margins of the survey that they wanted to participate a second time so that they could look for more details to support their conclusions regarding cause of death.

In the same survey, COSI asked teachers what they wanted their students to learn by participating in the program. There are a wide variety of classes participating in the program including anatomy/physiology, health sciences (vocational) programs, microbiology, AP biology, and general science classes; there are also a few of the newer forensic science classes. Given the variety of subject areas participating, it is not surprising that teachers had a wide variety of goals for their students, including such things as understanding the procedure, seeing "real" anatomy, and participating in a "real-world" science experience. All teachers, with the exception of the forensic teachers, indicated that the program met their goals for their students, and most indicated that the program strongly fit their curriculum. The two forensics teachers indicated that the program did not meet their goals of exploring a crime scene and determining who the criminal was. This result is interesting because these teachers seem to be accepting what they see on television above the information given to them by Dr. Tate, a professional who has 30 years of experience in the field of forensic pathology and who has never examined a crime scene.

Another interesting result of the survey was in the interpretation of science-process skills. Teachers were asked if they thought students had gained knowledge of science process skills and if so, to describe. There seems to be a very wide interpretation as to what science process skills actually are. Forty-four percent of teachers mentioned problem-solving, logic, or following a specific procedure as being the skills students learned and demonstrated. Only 6% of teachers mentioned designing the autopsy plan to achieve the desired results, recordkeeping, organizing data in understandable formats, or drawing or defending conclusions as being skills scientists use. It is possible that teachers simply did not want to take the time to list these other skills, or they may have many other ways of teaching them and therefore are not interested in this program achieving those results for their students. However, in personal conversations with a teacher who participated in the program, the phrase "experimental design" was used to describe the autopsy planning process. The high school anatomy teacher did not and, even after conversation, could not associate the planning process with experimental design. This would tend to indicate that teachers themselves have a very imperfect body of knowledge regarding scientific processes and ways of thinking. Further research is needed to determine if this is the case.

It has been over three years since COSI conducted a survey regarding the two videoconference surgery programs. The last time a survey was conducted, teachers indicated that they spent roughly one to two hours in pre- and post-visit activities for these programs. The results of the feedback forms included in the kits indicated that for the 2005–2006 school year, teachers used 43% of the available hands-on activities for the open heart surgery program and 51% of the available activities for the total knee replacement surgery. These activities are stand-alone experiences that explore a particular aspect of surgery, such as suturing or aligning a knee. They do not create a comprehensive view of surgery as the activities do for *In Depth: Autopsy*, because the surgeries change enough each time to prevent this sort of cohesiveness. For the *In Depth: Autopsy* program for the same school year, 76% of the available activities were performed by teachers, with the majority of teachers indicating that they spent five or more hours of class time on the pre- and postvisit activities. By far, the activity performed least by teachers and students is the forensic stabbing activity, which is not directly tied into solving for the cause of death. This indicates that when there is a compelling reason for, or experiences to be gained that are not easily obtainable in other ways, teachers will perform the pre- and postvisit activities, even in this "teach to the test" educational climate.

There is further evidence to support this contention. During the first six months of the *In Depth: Autopsy* program, launched in January 2006, Dr. Tate received very few autopsy plans to discuss with students at the beginning of the program. However, as schools and teachers repeated the program, the percentage of participating classes turning in autopsy plans increased dramatically. A complete lack of autopsy plans was a production problem that cropped up frequently during the first months of running the program. Currently, the opposite problem occurs more often—there are so many plans submitted that Dr. Tate does not have time to discuss them all before being forced by time limitations to begin the taped autopsy procedure. Teachers are not required to turn in plans for their students. They are welcome to participate in the program without undertaking this step. However, the majority of them now feel that this step is of sufficient value that they are requiring these plans from their students.

Future Plans

Teachers are already clamoring for additional causes of death for the *In Depth: Autopsy* program. Many of their classes are comprised of students in grades 10–12. Apparently, the lower-grade students share the "answer" with other students before they participate in the program. Teachers have asked for two other alternate endings besides the one currently offered. COSI is currently seeking funding to develop these alternate causes of death.

COSI is also seeking funding to conduct a full assessment of student learning for the program. Prior surveys and interviews focused on teacher opinions and implementation of the program. It is hoped that funding can be secured for longitudinal assessment of retention of knowledge gained during the program. Further research questions that we would like to have answers for include, but are not limited to:

- *What effect does the teacher have on student learning for the videoconference programs?* Since no COSI team member is there to facilitate, this question has many implications for future program development.
- *What factors result in some classes of students asking many questions of the pathologist, and some asking very few?* The Electronic Education team tracks which classes ask questions and which do not. At one point, it was thought that those classes that perform more of the previsit activities ask more questions during the program. However, further research indicates there is no correlation between these two things. So what does create the significant differences between classes in number of questions asked?
- *How does solving for cause of death as a motivating factor impact student learning?* If alternate causes of death are developed, it would be possible to mix and match the activities. For example, the histology activity for the current cause of death could be combined with the toxicological results from an alternate cause of death. Learning could be assessed using disjointed activities versus those activities that lead to a conclusion. The same amount of learning could potentially take place with both methods, but the student desire to solve the mystery would be absent with the disjointed activities. This could be one way to determine how student motivation to determine cause of death impacts the amount of learning that takes place.

In addition to alternate program endings and further research, COSI would like to explore the program concept further. There was real trepidation during the planning of the *In Depth: Autopsy* program because the live, real-time Surgical Suite programs were so powerful and had such a positive impact on both teachers and students. The COSI team wondered if a videotaped autopsy would have the same impact. Given the rapidity with which all three programs sell out every year, and the high marks received on the teacher feedback forms, the *In Depth: Autopsy* program is every bit as powerful and satisfying to teachers and students as the live surgery programs are. COSI would like to further explore this program concept by developing other programs using a taped experience narrated by a professional in the field. Other ideas on the table include heart transplant or heart pump surgery, large building construction or destruction, gene therapy, genetic engineering, or crash scene reconstruction.

COSI will continue to develop and study its videoconference programs to determine their effectiveness and to determine how this type of programming differs from those offered at museums or those offered at schools where a COSI demonstrator or program leader is present. The information gained from these efforts will help shape programming efforts at COSI and could potentially have a much greater impact on the broader field of informal education.

Program Developers are Gail Wheatley, Myra Peffer, Jill Rosenfeld, and Jen Snively.

Citizen Science at the Cornell Lab of Ornithology

Rick Bonney
Cornell Lab of Ornithology

The Cornell Lab of Ornithology is an international center for the study, appreciation, and conservation of birds located on a 200-acre wildlife sanctuary in Ithaca, New York. Founded in 1915 by Arthur A. Allen, the world's first professor of ornithology, the Lab originally became known for its pioneering work in bird photography and natural sound recording. Today the Lab is home to more than 200 staff, faculty, postdoctoral associates, and graduate and undergraduate students engaged in "interpreting and conserving the Earth's biodiversity through research, education, and citizen science focused on birds." Administratively the Lab is located within the College of Agriculture and Life Sciences at Cornell University, with financial support coming from 30,000 members, as well as grants, contracts, and gifts.

The Lab has been involved in public education ever since Dr. Allen first began using the phrase "Lab of Ornithology" to distinguish his work from that of his colleagues in his original academic home, Cornell's department of entomology. In fact, Allen's desire to embrace the public by involving bird watchers in field research launched the Lab on an important path that it continues to this day—that of breaking down barriers between "science" and "public" by actively engaging citizens in the process of scientific inquiry. What Allen started by asking local birdwatchers to keep track of bird populations around Ithaca has become the Lab's Citizen Science Program, for which thousands of individuals contribute important bird data to a variety of projects each year.

Of course citizen science is not the only work in which the Lab is involved; numerous other programs focus on additional areas of bird research and conservation. For example, the Lab's Macaulay Library contains the largest collection of natural sound recordings and animal behavior videos in the world. Its Bioacoustics Research Program studies how and why animals communicate using sound. Its Evolutionary Biology Program studies the interrelationships among bird species; its Bird Population Studies Program examines how and why bird populations are changing throughout North America; its Conservation Science Program develops plans for bird conservation throughout the western hemisphere; and its Information Science Program develops and implements web-based technologies to manage and visualize data.

Citizen science has, however, become the cornerstone of the Lab's educational efforts, and the institution's various citizen science projects provide much of the data and information that Lab scientists, particularly in its Bird Population Studies and Conservation Science programs, use to study birds. What exactly is citizen science, and why has the Lab invested so much time and effort into developing this technique of scientific investigation?

To understand the answers to these questions, first consider the early days of scientific discovery in North America, from the 1600s through the 1800s and even into the early 20th century. During this period, almost any inquisitive person could be a scientist. All it took was a desire for systematically unraveling the ways in which the world works. Indeed many of our early scientific discoveries, particularly in the natural sciences, were made by individuals with no specific scientific training. Natural history pioneers such as Charles Darwin, Henry David Thoreau, and John Burroughs had to be self-directed, because their lives predated most of the formal science programs that sprung up at schools and colleges during the 20th century.

Even into the 20th century, the idea that laypeople could contribute to scientific understanding persisted in certain fields, particularly in the natural sciences, and especially in ornithology. For example, the only person ever to have been president of all three of North America's major ornithological societies, Harold Mayfield, had no formal training in ornithology. Although he published more than 200 scientific papers, by profession he was a personnel manager at Owens-Illinois Inc. He died in 2007 at the age of 94.

More commonly, however, 20th-century science became specialized to the point where knowledge became challenging to assimilate. Many students began to fear science because the subject was so often presented as a confusing accumulation of random facts. As a result, the general public became so estranged from science that many, perhaps most, people no longer understand how scientific knowledge is developed.

The need to increase such understanding is well documented. While some studies have shown that more than half of adults can correctly answer questions about science that are concrete and which relate to their own experiences (Durant, Evans, and Thomas 1989; Wynne 1995), only 33% of adults understand how a subject is studied scientifically (NSB 2002). One reason for this discrepancy may be that science education has typically employed a "deficit model," in which the public is viewed as an empty bucket to be filled with facts prescribed by scientists (Gregory and Miller 1998; Roth and Lee 2002; Brown, Reveles, and Kelly 2005; Falk, Storksdieck, and Dierking, forthcoming). Unfortunately, simply providing facts has shown little influence on scientific understanding (Greenberg 2001, Sturgis and Allum 2004).

This problem is clearly understood by the "Science as Inquiry" section of the National Science Education Standards (NSES), which state that engaging students in inquiry helps them to develop an understanding of scientific concepts; an appreciation of "how we know" what we know in science; an understanding of the nature of science; and the skills necessary to become independent inquirers about the natural world (NRC 1996, p. 105). Although the Standards were developed for classrooms, the concepts they espouse are applicable to learners in essentially all situations, including informal or free-choice settings.

One question, then, is what techniques can be used to involve free-choice learners in inquiry? One answer, which occurred to a handful of Lab educators in the late 1980s, is to engage the public in professionally developed research projects designed to answer important scientific questions. When Lab staff came up with this idea the Standards were still a decade away from publication, but a few individuals already were considering how they could help people understand many important concepts: How questions are framed for research; how comparable data can be gathered by multiple researchers; how large quantities of data can reveal trends; and why results of small-scale observations might not be representative of overall patterns. Lab staff speculated that if they provided standardized procedures for public data collection; developed a method to accept, vet, and archive data; organized and analyzed the data; and finally provided results of their analyses for the public to read and contemplate, then individuals who collected the information and reflected upon its implications would begin to understand something of the process by which scientific discoveries are made and publicized.

In truth, the idea of developing organized, large-scale, volunteer-conducted research projects was not new. Many important projects that relied on volunteer data already had been developed, including the National Audubon Society's Christmas Bird Count, which started in 1900; the US Fish and Wildlife Service's Breeding Bird Survey, begun in 1965; and several projects developed in Europe, such as bird study programs operated by the British Trust for Ornithology. And the Lab itself had started a nest record card program in 1965, which involved several dozen volunteers who contributed data from across North America.

What Lab staff proposed to add to such efforts was a complete "Research Kit" that would orient participants to the project and help them learn about birds and scientific investigation as they engaged in data collection and submission. They envisioned detailed instructions and resource guides that would explain to project participants how and why they were helping to advance scientific knowledge. The Lab also planned to provide extensive project results as quickly and completely as possible, so that participants could learn how their local data collection informed knowledge on a much larger scale.

The experiment started with the development of Project FeederWatch in 1987. FeederWatch was rapidly followed by other projects such as Project Tanager, Project PigeonWatch, and The Birdhouse Network. In the mid 1990s the Lab coined the term "citizen science" to refer to its expanding concept of public-conducted research, and by 2007, the Lab's Citizen Science Program (*www.birds.cornell.edu/LabPrograms/CitSci*) included multiple projects designed to answer a range of scientific questions and to facilitate participation by individuals of varying levels of expertise, in all locations, at all times of year (See Table 1). The projects have engaged many thousands of individuals in observing birds, collecting and submitting bird data, reading about project findings, and sometimes analyzing and interpreting project data for themselves.

Table 1. Ornithology Projects

chapter 16

Table 1. Ornithology Projects

- Project FeederWatch (1987)
- Project PigeonWatch (1993)
- Project Tanager (1993)
- House Finch Disease Survey (1995)
- The Birdhouse Network (1997)
- Birds In Forested Landscapes (1997)
- Cerulean Warbler Atlas (1997)
- Great Backyard Bird Count (1998)
- Golden-Winged Warbler Atlas (1999)
- eBird (2002)
- Urban Bird Studies (2002)
- Project NestWatch (2006)

Despite their different foci, each project is guided by a common format. It starts with project participants who, following specific protocols, collect data about birds and their environments and send the information to the Lab. The protocols are provided in field-tested instruction booklets or on web pages and are enhanced by educational support materials such as posters, identification guides, and CDs or online streams of bird sounds. Project data forms, also field tested, are as simple and straightforward as possible and are submitted either online or on computer-scannable sheets.

Once data arrive at the Lab, scientists edit, organize, and analyze the information and publish the results, not only in scientific journals but also, with the help of Lab education and publications staff, in a variety of popular venues ranging from project websites to newsletters. For example, the Lab's newsletter, *BirdScope,* features highlights of citizen-based research and is mailed to more than 50,000 addresses each quarter. And each of the project websites, on which results are posted and updated regularly, reaches hundreds of thousands of viewers every month. Project participants are thus able to see how their observations compare with those of other observers across the continent, and to learn how their data are used for purposes of both science and conservation.

Serendipitously, the emergence of citizen science as a discipline has coincided with the development and expansion of the internet and its incredible capabilities for interaction and community building. Indeed, the internet has expanded the possibilities for citizen science in ways that were scarcely imagined just a few years back. For example, in most of the Lab's projects, data submitted online are now edited in real time. Thus if a participant enters a bird count that seems suspicious for his or her reporting location, a message asks for verification. Such online data vetting allows errors to be caught before the information enters the database. In addition, online data submission enables project participants to visualize project data as quickly as they are submitted.

Participants in most of the Lab's citizen science projects also can manipulate online data to conduct their own analyses, pursuing research questions both simple and complex, independently of the Lab's professional scientists. Thus our online software helps to guide participants in active and extended scientific inquiry. We feel that this functionality is especially important, because only when participants have asked and answered their own questions using original data have they truly become scientists as opposed to citizen data collectors.

Citizen science serves both education and science and appears successful in both arenas.

Considering the scientific impacts of Lab projects, staff proudly point to the growing body of peer-reviewed journal articles that make extensive use of citizen-generated data. In fact, many questions about North American bird populations could not be answered by any other investigative method. In the past 10 years publications have examined how bird populations change in distribution over time and space (Wells et al. 1998, Hochachka et al. 1999); how the breeding success of certain species is affected by environmental change (Rosenberg, Lowe, and Dhondt 1999, Hames et al. 2002a); how acid rain affects bird populations (Hames et al. 2002b); how emerging infectious diseases spread through wild animal populations (Hochachka et al. 2004, Dhondt et al. 2005); and how seasonal clutch-size variation is influenced by latitude (Cooper, Hochachka, and Dhondt 2005; Cooper et al. 2006). These and other publications demonstrate the proven ability of citizen science to help understand large-scale biological patterns and processes.

Citizen science also appears effective at increasing public understanding of both the content and process of science. To investigate this claim, this chapter will focus on the development and impact of three Lab projects: Project FeederWatch, the Great Backyard Bird Count, and eBird.

Project FeederWatch

While the roots of the Lab's citizen science program can be traced to the origins of the institution, "modern" citizen science at the Lab arguably began with the 1987 development of Project FeederWatch (*www.birds.cornell.edu/pfw*). Conceived as a joint project of the Lab and Ontario's Long Point Bird Observatory (now Bird Studies Canada), FeederWatch was designed as an annual survey of winter bird populations for which participants periodically count the kinds and numbers of birds that visit their backyard feeders from November through early April.

The FeederWatch "Research Kit" included a written project rationale, complete instructions for setting up an observation area and collecting data, computer-scannable data forms, and a subscription to a newsletter providing detailed FeederWatch data analyses. Originally all materials were mailed to and from participants, but in the late 1990s the project was migrated to the internet (although some participants still prefer to mail in computer-scannable forms).

The FeederWatch website is a treasure trove of information on backyard birds and bird feeding. In addition to instructions and "smart" data forms, participants can view summaries of their own counts; see summaries of all birds reported by state, province, or region; view confirmed reports and photos of rare birds; and create a nearly limitless number of maps and trend graphs based on millions of bird sightings made across the continent. These features were explicitly included in the site to allow participants to manipulate and explore data to answer their own musings about bird populations, both locally and continentwide, thus facilitating original inquiry experiences based on personal interest. Providing such opportunities relates to the NSES Teaching Standards that call for being able to understand and respond to the interests, strengths, experiences, and needs of individual participants. The site also includes authoritative information on identifying, feeding, and learning about backyard bird biology, and a large "News" section contains stories and articles based on FeederWatch data analyses.

During its first 20 years of operation approximately 44,000 participants from across Canada and the United States contributed more than 1.1 million feeder bird checklists (about 15,000 in-

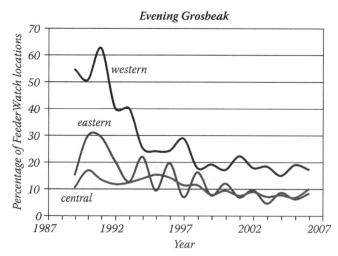

Graph of Evening Grosbeak data.

dividuals currently participate each year with a renewal rate of about 70%). The wealth of contributed data has helped Lab scientists document the irruptions of species such as Common Redpolls; watch as Carolina Wrens, Red-bellied Woodpeckers, and other species expand their ranges to the north; monitor a dramatic reduction in sightings of Evening Grosbeaks; and learn an enormous amount about more than 100 other species that regularly visit feeders somewhere on the continent (See graph of Evening Grosbeak data). Detailed project results are published in an annual report called *Winter Bird Highlights* (*www.birds.cornell.edu/pfw/News/AnnualReports.htm*). Since its inception, this project has been supported largely by its participants, who currently pay an annual fee of $15 for the opportunity to be part of the FeederWatch network.

FeederWatch has unquestionably helped many participants learn more about birds, bird biology, and bird behavior. FeederWatch staff receive hundreds of notes and e-mails each year stating how much participants enjoy the project and how much it has contributed to their enjoyment and understanding of nature. "Project FeederWatch taught me so much in such a short time," said a participant from North Carolina. "I loved feeding and watching the birds before, but now it is so much more interesting and useful." A participant from Massachusetts wrote, "Thank you for providing us with a motivation to really pay attention to our local bird populations. Winter weekends, especially snowy ones, go by very quickly when watching birds!" A watcher from New Mexico wrote "After participating in Project FeederWatch for several seasons, my bird identification skills have improved immensely. This winter I found myself identifying birds by their behavior: how they fly into the feeding site, where they land, if they sit or take right off again, and which feeder they choose." And a participant from Pennsylvania said, "When I became seriously injured in a car accident, I thought I would be unable to do FeederWatch. But I managed to maneuver my wheelchair to my 'bird watching window' to do my counts. It meant the world to me to be able to participate." Such quotes certainly suggest that FeederWatch participants are experiencing the richness and excitement of knowing about and understanding the natural world as they participate in the project.

Lab staff periodically survey FeederWatch participants to understand more about their demographics, knowledge, interests, and abilities. In April 2006, at the end of the 2005–06 FeederWatch season, a survey was placed on the website and all participants who had previously subscribed to an electronic newsletter received a message encouraging them to fill it in. About 15% of all registered FeederWatchers, 2,157 individuals, responded within two weeks.

The survey revealed that FeederWatchers are older individuals: 75% of them are over 50, and 26% are over 65. They are predominately Caucasian (96.8%), two-thirds female (70%), and very well educated—76% have a college degree, and 35% have a post-graduate degree. Most FeederWatchers (85%) have been watching and feeding birds for more than five years, but the majority (54%) consider themselves only intermediate birders, with 34% self identifying as advanced in their birding skills.

Thus FeederWatch provides what some call "lifelong education" for an appreciative audience. And many of them do seem to be "studying" birds: 62% read the Rare Bird Reports; 62% use the Map Room; 67% peruse the Top 25 lists; 86% use the Personal Count Summaries; 78% use the State/Province Summaries; and 56% have created trend graphs for particular species.

Most respondents believe that they have learned about birds as a result of their participation. Fifty percent said that they discovered a greater diversity of species than they knew before; 64% said that they learned how to identify more species; 70% stated that they learned how the bird community changes through the seasons; and 74% said that they observed interesting behaviors. Only 6% said that they didn't learn anything in particular through their FeederWatch participation.

These assessments suggest to us that participants are understanding scientific concepts and developing abilities of inquiry. We also feel that they are learning about birds and ecology in the context of inquiry and technology in a personally meaningful way.

Over the years the Lab has designed additional projects to offer FeederWatch participants opportunities to engage in deeper inquiry. For example, 1992 marked a milestone for citizen science when the Lab received a grant from the Informal Science Education Program at the National Science Foundation to develop a project called "Public Participation in Ornithology: An Introduction to Environmental Research." Through this landmark grant, Lab scientists and educators developed three "National Science Experiments" including a Seed Preference Test designed to determine which of three types of seeds ground-feeding birds like best: sunflower, millet, or milo. At the time the project was developed, conventional wisdom stated that most birds preferred sunflower, that few ate millet, and that all avoided red milo. Many FeederWatch participants, however, especially from the Southwest, had told us that their birds loved milo, also known as sorghum. We wanted to find out whether the seed had been getting a bad rap.

During the winter of 1993–94 the project enrolled more than 17,000 participants. Recruitment was boosted when the project was featured on "Good Morning America." FeederWatchers who requested the Research Kit received one free of charge; other participants paid a $7 fee, which included a one-year's subscription to *Birdscope*. The kit included instructions, a booklet describing the scientific process, and a beautiful color poster of common feeder birds. Each participant followed a simple experimental protocol in which they provided each type of seed in rotating locations and counted the numbers of birds that came to each seed type. Although some people had trouble attracting birds to their experimental setups (and some never tried), about 5,000 individuals returned completed data forms describing nearly half a million bird visits and showing seed preferences for more than 30 species.

Analyses showed that birds that usually feed in trees, such as chickadees, nuthatches, and finches, did prefer sunflower seeds, but that the seed of choice for most birds that normally feed at ground level was millet. Furthermore, five ground-feeding species ate lots of milo, and three—the Steller's Jay, Curve Billed Thrasher, and Gambel's Quail—actually seemed to prefer it. What's more, all of the species that ate substantial amounts of milo were birds that lived only in the Southwest or West Coast regions. So, the anecdotal claims of FeederWatchers—that birds in the Southwest ate more red milo than birds in the East—were confirmed.

Developers of this project tried hard to integrate all aspects of science content, to implement inquiry as ideas and strategies to be learned, and to develop activities that specifically investigated and analyzed scientific questions. As a result, participants seemed to enjoy the project and to learn about the challenges of scientific experimentation as they attempted to follow the project protocol. We know this because many participants wrote to project staff about their trials and tribulations in attracting and counting their subjects. As part of project evaluation, Lab staff coded the comments from 750 participants into several "categories of inquiry" based on the Biological Sciences Curriculum Study (BSCS 1970, pp. 27–37) and the National Science Education Standards (NRC 1996, pp. 175–176). The categories were "Nothing," "Observation," "Observation Plus," "Took Action," "Hypothesis," "Hypothesis Plus," and "Hypothesis and Improvement." Of all letters, 30% fell into the latter three categories. This finding suggested to us that participants were actively engaged in the experimental process. For instance, to be included in the Hypothesis category (which made up 23% of letters), a writer would need to explicitly state possible reasons for her bird observations or explain her actions in modifying the project design. To be placed in the Hypothesis Plus category (3%), a writer would need to contribute more than one hypothesis to explain her observations. And to fall into the Hypothesis and Improvement category (4%), a writer would need to form a hypothesis to explain her results and also use her hypotheses to devise another way to investigate the question.

The fact that nearly one-third of the letters fell into the hypothesis categories suggested that participants generally did not follow the project protocol in a mindless manner. When they encountered problems they took the project seriously enough to make it work, using their knowledge of birds and bird behavior to adapt the procedures. Many participants also made additional observations about the microecology of their feeding sites or about animal behavior. Therefore, for many people, the process of participating in this citizen science project appeared to contribute to their thinking about biology and the scientific process. These results suggest that project participants were, as the developers hoped they would, using appropriate scientific processes and principles in making personal decisions (Trumbull et al. 2000). They were applying the scientific method and learning science within the context of real research.

Another project designed for the FeederWatch network is the House Finch Eye Disease Survey (*www.birds.cornell.edu/hofi*). In fact, the idea for this project came from a handful of FeederWatchers who reported seeing House Finches with crusty, puffy eyes during the winter of 1993–94. Since that time, this project has shown explicitly how this disease has spread through the House Finch population throughout North America, causing House Finch numbers to decline in many areas. It is the first study ever to document how disease spreads in a wild animal population. Even better, the project gives FeederWatchers the opportunity to engage in even more careful observation as they examine House Finches for signs of conjunctivitis and, in many cases, provide detailed descriptions about diseased birds and their behaviors. The citizen scientists involved in this study know that their findings could have implications for understanding other disease outbreaks such as West Nile Virus.

The Great Backyard Bird Count

1998 marked another milestone for citizen science when the Lab and the National Audubon Society codeveloped The Great Backyard Bird Count (GBBC) (*www.birdsource.org/gbbc*), the first citizen science project to operate solely online. Originally designed as a test of the internet's ability to facilitate citizen science, GBBC is now the most popular of the Lab's programs and introduces thousands of individuals to the citizen science concept each year.

GBBC takes place over four days (Thursday to Sunday) during the third week of February. During that time, participants across North America tally birds for as few as 15 minutes or as long as they like, recording the highest number of individuals of each bird species that they see together at one time. Bird watchers of all ages and abilities are encouraged to report birds not only from their backyards but also from public lands and local parks. Participants enter their counts online and

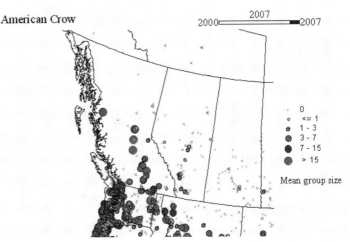

Mean group size of American Crows in the Pacific Northwest from February 16–19, 2007 as reported by participants in the annual Great Backyard Bird Count.

can explore lists, charts, and maps of sightings as the count progresses. Project data are viewable within moments of submission, and all data from all years remain accessible at *http://gbbc.bird-source.org/gbbcApps/results*. Both raw and summary data can be viewed and mapped by location or by species (See example above). Participants also may submit photographs of the birds they see; a selection of images is posted in the GBBC online photo gallery.

The GBBC website includes links across the top of the home page that walk a participant through the project: (1) What is the GBBC?; (2) Learn About Birds; (3) How to Participate; (4) Submit Your Checklist; and (5) Explore the Results. The "Learn About Birds" section includes links to articles about identifying birds, to articles on selecting binoculars and bird feeders, and to the CLO Online Bird Guide. "How to Participate" includes complete instructions, and "Submit Your Checklist" provides a form for online data submission. The checklist form can be arranged either in alphabetical or in taxonomic order, and each species shown on the form is hyperlinked to the appropriate entry in the CLO Online Bird Guide. After each year's count, project staff examine the results and post summaries highlighting the year's trends and findings in the "Science

Stories" section of the project website at *www.birdsource.org/gbbc/science-stories*.

GBBC has several specific educational goals. These include increasing participant interest in birds and bird-watching; helping participants identify unfamiliar species; encouraging participants to explore data on the GBBC website to learn more about birds in their own communities and to compare local bird populations to those in other areas; helping participants understand that counting birds can be challenging; and helping participants learn that bird populations frequently change over time and space.

While these may seem lofty goals for a project that spans just one weekend each year, we believe that the excitement of collecting original data, and understanding that the data are being combined with those of thousands of other birders across the continent, helps participants use multiple process skills in a personally meaningful context, allowing them to conduct investigations to develop individualized understanding and knowledge of science content.

GBBC is a popular project. In 2006, participants submitted more than 60,000 checklists documenting 623 species and 7,587,054 individual birds. In 2007, participants submitted more than 80,000 checklists documenting 616 species and a record-breaking 11,082,048 individual birds. The event also attracts a great deal of media attention, with dozens of stories reported on the event each year.

GBBC has been collecting information about its participants through an online survey since the project began. In the early years, the survey focused primarily on demographic information such as a visitor's sex, age, occupation, and the types of birding equipment owned. In 2004 the survey was enhanced to include information about visitors' bird-watching habits and the perceived impact of GBBC participation on bird-watching interest and knowledge.

Visitors learn about the General Survey through a link at the top of the GBBC home page. Roughly 13% of project participants fill out the survey in any given year. Therefore, the data may not mirror the exact population of GBBC participants. However, they are remarkably consistent from year to year.

Participants in GBBC are slightly younger than those in FeederWatch, with 63% over age 50 and only 18% over 65. Like FeederWatchers, GBBC participants are approximately two-thirds female and one-third male. They are slightly less educated, as only 71% are college graduates. Nearly 40% are in professional/management positions or are self-employed, and 30% are retired. Nearly half participated alone, although 45% participated with some member of their family (including grandchildren).

Participants in GBBC consider themselves to be slightly more advanced in their birding skills than those who participate in FeederWatch. This fact is particularly interesting to Lab staff, who originally conceived of the GBBC as a simplified version of FeederWatch that could entice beginning birders to sign up for FeederWatch after the GBBC was over. Perhaps the fact that the project operates entirely online has attracted a younger and more advanced group of birders into participation.

About 20% of GBBC participants identified at least one species that was new to them, with the number of new species seen ranging from 1 to 54. As might be expected, participants with lower self-reported bird identification skill were more likely to see a new species: 37% of those who rated their birding skills as "1" or "2" saw at least one new species, while only 15% of those rating their skill as "4" or "5" saw a new species. Thus participants are not just counting the birds they already know. They also are identifying unfamiliar species to ensure that the data they submit are accurate and complete.

Project designers very much want participants to view and learn from the millions of data collected each year, and happily, nearly two-thirds of respondents indicated that they viewed data on the GBBC website in 2005. Of these viewers, 90% looked to see what birds had been reported in their local area. Nearly 60% examined data for a particular species of interest, and about one-quarter looked at data comparing populations in different areas, or changes in population over time. Thus participants are not simply counting and reporting birds. They also are exploring the online database to "manage" their personal ideas and information.

In 2005, project staff collaborated with Seavoss Associates, Inc. and eduweb to conduct an extensive survey of first-time GBBC participants. Like the general survey, the first-time survey included questions about visitor demographics and their bird-watching habits. Unlike the general survey, participants filled out the first-time survey both before and after conducting their counts, allowing evaluators to look for changes in habits and behavior that might have occurred in tandem with project participation.

The first-time survey also included a three-part Personal Birding Narrative (PBN) modeled on the Personal Meaning Mapping (PMM) protocol developed by John Falk and his colleagues at the Institute for Learning Innovation (Falk, Moussouri, and Coulson 1998; Adelman, Falk, and James 2000). The PBN respondents were asked what words, thoughts, images, or ideas came to mind when they read each of three prompts: (1) Bird-watching; (2) Conservation; and (3) The GBBC is about…. For each prompt, they typed their thoughts into a large text box. Respondents also were able to upload an image to accompany each response, either from their own files or from CLO's "All About Birds" website. Thus the PBN was a guided interview that allowed respondents to construct their own narrative about their birding and conservation experiences and how they connect to larger concepts such as attitudes and understandings about conservation.

Six weeks later, all respondents received an e-mail inviting them to fill out the second part of the survey and to update, if desired, their responses to the PBN. Amazingly, 1,181 individuals returned the Time 2 survey. Of these, 899 actually had participated in the GBBC. The 282 individuals who did not participate thus served as a serendipitous control, allowing evaluators to compare outcomes for first-time participants (hereafter, data collectors) with outcomes for individuals who had planned to participate but, for various reasons, did not (hereafter, noncollectors).

Data collectors and non-collectors did not differ significantly in terms of sex, age, education, self-reported bird identification skills, or motivation for participating. However, they did differ in several other statistically significant ways. In the six weeks following the project, collectors were more likely than noncollectors to have joined conservation-related organizations. They increased the number of days on which they watched birds. They recorded data on an increased percentage of days, and showed a greater tendency to acquire new birding equipment. These are rewarding findings for a project that involves only a few days of active participation (Thompson, Allison-Bunnell, and Bonney 2006).

Unfortunately the sample of changed PBN responses was too small to detect changes in participant behavior or understanding. Only 18% of respondents made changes to their PBN responses and, of those, only about half were substantive (e.g., changes to content rather than corrections of grammar or typographical errors). Furthermore, substantive changes were often minor or were simply narratives explaining why an individual was unable to participate in the count. Nonetheless, carefully examining all of the responses, whether or not they had been changed, provided significant insight into the ways that both data collectors and noncollectors view the GBBC and about their attitudes toward conservation.

For example, a majority of respondents clearly understand that bird populations change over space and time. However, their perceptions of GBBC extend beyond simply viewing the event as a bird-counting activity. Participants also see the GBBC as an enjoyable activity that offers opportunities for personal learning as well as a chance to spend time observing nature and the world around them. In addition, respondents expressed particular concern for birds and their habitat (Thompson, Allison-Bunnell, and Bonney 2006). Through the PBNs, we are able to discern that citizen scientists engaged in the Great Backyard Bird Count are engaging intelligently in public discourse and debate about matters of scientific concern. Furthermore they are communicating science explanations and their ideas to others.

eBird

In 2001, when the GBBC was three years old and clearly showing the potential of the internet to revolutionize the citizen science movement, the National Science Foundation awarded the Lab another major grant called "Citizen Science Online." The focus of this award was development of a bird checklist project for which anybody could report any bird they saw, from any location in North America, at any time they desired. The project launched in 2002 as eBird (*http://ebird.org*) and has grown rapidly ever since. Participants can report birds as often as they like from as many locations as they like. Some participants report birds only occasionally. Others submit complete checklists of all the species they see each day, often from several locations—home, office, vacation spot, favorite birding location. In 2006, participants submitted more than 323,500 checklists including more than 4.3 million observations (i.e., a bird at a location on a specific date). These data provide an extremely accurate representation of the distribution and abundance of bird populations at both the backyard and continental levels.

To report sightings, participants choose a location from dropdown menus of birding "hotspots," such as nature reserves, which have been entered into the database by project staff and other eBirders. Observers also can use eBird's online mapping software to select any number of new reporting locations. For instance, many participants pinpoint their home. That location is then stored in the database so that participants can report the birds they see there anytime they choose. Participants also can enter locations using latitude and longitude.

Once a participant chooses a location, the eBird website displays a checklist showing birds that could be seen in that state or region. The participant then fills in the number of individuals of each species seen and submits that information to the eBird database where it can be sorted and viewed by anyone with access to the internet. ("Suspect" sightings are flagged by project software, and participants are often contacted for further details on rare or unusual birds.)

To explore the database, participants first choose whether they wish to examine data for a certain species (for example, Yellow Warbler, Black-billed Magpie) or from a certain location (for example, county, state, or bird conservation region or their personal locations). Then the participant can create maps, histograms, and various types of graphs that combine all of the eBird data available for each species or location

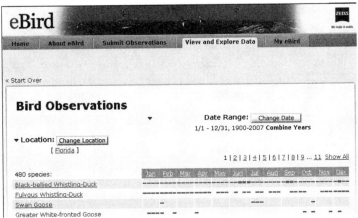

Example of histogram showing dates of bird occurrences in Florida as created by eBird data visualization software.

at any chosen time (See example above). Participants also can use the eBird site to keep track of their "life list," or all of the birds that they have seen, sorted by location—all at no charge. Anyone can manipulate and visualize eBird data whether or not they enter data of their own.

At the eBird website, CLO educators and scientists post weekly updates and features of bird population dynamics based on eBird data. The site also includes links to many regional eBird projects, such as Vermont eBird, Gulf Coast Bird Observatory eBird, and eBird Puerto Rico.

eBird has several educational objectives. These include teaching participants various methods for gathering scientifically useful data (point counts, transects, area searches). The project also seeks to help participants explore eBird data to learn more about birds in their own communities and to compare local bird populations to those in other areas; to understand that bird populations change over time and space; and to understand the value of eBird data for informing bird conservation efforts. More so than any other project, eBird attempts to provide opportunities for participants to use multiple skills—manipulative, cognitive, procedural—while helping participants use evidence and strategies to develop explanations for their birding observations.

eBird is among the most thoroughly evaluated of our projects to date. In 2005, again in partnership with Seavoss Associates and eduweb, we examined the impacts of eBird participation on new participants by employing a pre- and postproject assessment (Thompson and Bonney 2007). For this research we combined standard survey questions with a simplified version of the Personal Birding Narrative that we had developed to evaluate the GBBC. We also asked participants to answer several questions whose answers required understanding of eBird's various data visualizations.

eBird has the youngest audience of the three projects described in this chapter, with 48% over 50 and just 11% over age 65. The project is also more evenly gender balanced with a nearly 50-50 split. Participants are highly educated, as a whopping 91% have a college degree. However, only 23% consider themselves to be advanced birders, while 26% feel that they are beginners.

Like participants in the GBBC, respondents to the eBird survey were divided into two groups: individuals who collected and submitted data (data collectors, n = 37) and those who planned to but did not (noncollectors, n = 45). From examining the surveys we learned that collectors and noncollectors did not differ significantly in terms of age, sex, education, birding skill, or motivation for participation. However, engaging in data collection and submission did appear to broaden the scope of birding activity in ways directly related to eBird's mission. eBird data collectors recorded data from more of their birding sessions, visited new locations, and identified new-to-them species after they began participating. Collectors also began recording data on the time they spent observing and the number of birds seen per species; both of these data types are among those requested on (but not required for) eBird's checklists.

We also learned that most survey respondents made use of eBird's "View" and "Explore Data" tools, including the non-collectors. Respondents used the data tools to answer a variety of questions about bird distribution and abundance, such as when certain species were present in their area; where rare birds were seen; and how populations change over time. They also used the data to compare birds at different locations and to plan birding trips. However, when asked to examine live data to answer some basic questions about bird populations, fewer than half were able to identify the most appropriate data visualization to use (e.g., map, abundance estimate, or frequency estimate). This information suggests that we need better online tutorials explaining how to use the various eBird data visualization features. This kind of assessment helps us to focus on understanding not so much the knowledge gains of our participants, but their ability to use knowledge to engage in inquiry.

For the final part of our eBird evaluation, we coded responses to the online Personal Meaning Mapping exercise, for which we had asked participants to write what words, thoughts, images, or ideas came to mind when they read the phrase "Conservation." We coded these responses into 10 categories: Emotional content; nature; specific issues and resources; involvement or action; urgency; specific people, places, and organizations; future orientation; spiritual or religious references; need for education/awareness; and other. Most respondents offered comments on specific conservation issues, such as habitat preservation or pollution. Many also mentioned specific actions, such as recycling, reducing consumption, and planting trees, along with government policies related to conservation. Gathering information about participant knowledge and attitudes is crucial so that educational support materials can be tailored to audience needs, rather than developed with an attitude of "one size fits all."

Like respondents to the GBBC Personal Birding Narrative, very few participants in the eBird Personal Meaning Mapping exercise changed their responses during the postproject survey. However, the responses that they did give suggested that eBird attracts participants who are knowledgeable about and invested in conservation. We are pleased that we are able to offer this audience a meaningful opportunity to learn while collecting data that can be used to better understand bird population distribution and conservation needs.

Conclusion

We believe that citizen science can provide a powerful mechanism for involving the public in the process of meaningful scientific investigation. We don't expect every project participant to conduct cutting-edge scientific explorations in their backyards or local parks. But we do hope that participants will immerse themselves in citizen science data, using online tools to muse about bird population changes. By manipulating a few simple variables, individuals can see how bird populations change over time; how the birds in their neighborhood compare with birds in other areas; and how the data they collect are helping to paint an overall picture of bird numbers and distributions. We also hope that personal explorations will, over time, cause participants to observe nature in a more systematic way, and to understand that scientific investigation consists in large part of making careful observations and examining resultant data to search for patterns. People who understand this will be well on their way to becoming lifelong learners who can access, analyze, and synthesize information and apply it to a diverse range of new situations and problems (NRC 1996, p. 31).

When designing citizen science projects for free-choice audiences, particularly when audience members are working on their own—far from the sight of project developers—the biggest challenge is guiding participants in asking and answering their own questions. One possible method is to use the internet to create fun and thoughtful exercises resembling computer games, which can engage the public in exploring original data to make sense of the world around them. Over the next few years we expect to spend significant time designing and testing several approaches to online data investigation. We can even imagine virtual "science fairs" for which participants use online bird data to create competitive data analysis projects.

In the meantime, we think that Lab founder Arthur Allen would be proud of the thousands of citizens who are currently observing birds, collecting data, and pooling their information—not only to help scientists understand the dynamics of bird populations, but also to personally appreciate the environment in which they live every day.

References

Adelman, L., J. Falk, and S. James. 2000. Impact of National Aquarium in Baltimore on visitor's conservation attitudes, behavior, and knowledge. *Curator* 43 (1): 33–60.

Biological Sciences Curriculum Study (BSCS). 1970. *Biology teachers handbook*. New York: John Wiley and Sons.

Brown, B. A., J. M. Reveles, and G. J. Kelly. 2005. Scientific literacy and discursive identity: A theoretical framework for understanding science learning. *Science Education* 89: 779–802.

Cooper, C. B., W. Hochachka, and A. A. Dhondt. 2005. Latitudinal trends in within-year reoccupation of nest boxes and their implications. *Journal of Avian Ecology* 36: 31–39.

Cooper, C. B., W. M. Hochachka, T. B. Phillips, and A. A. Dhondt. 2006. Geographic and seasonal gradients in hatching failure in Eastern Bluebirds reinforce clutch size trends. *Ibis* 148: 221–230.

Dhondt, A. A., S. Altizer, E. G. Cooch, A. K. Davis, A. Dobson, M. J. L. Driscoll, B. K. Hartup, D. M. Hawley, W. M. Hochachka, P. R. Hosseini, C. S. Jennelle, G. V. Kollias, D. H. Ley, E. C. H. Swarthout, and K. V. Sydenstricker. 2005. Dynamics of a novel pathogen in an avian host: Mycoplasmal conjunctivitis in House Finches. *Acta Tropica* 94 (1): 77–93.

Durant, J., G. Evans, and G. Thomas 1989. The public understanding of science. *Nature* 340 (6228):

11–14.

Falk, J., T. Moussouri, and D. Coulson. 1998. The effect of visitor's agendas on museum learning. *Curator* 41(2): 107–120.

Falk, J. H., M. Storksdieck, and L. Dierking. In press. Investigating public science interest and understanding: Evidence for the importance of free-choice learning. *Public Understanding of Science.*

Gregory, J. and S. Miller 1998. *Science in public: Communication, culture, and credibility.* New York: Plenum.

Greenberg, D.S. 2001. *Science, money, and politics: Political triumph and ethical erosion.* Chicago: University of Chicago Press.

Hames, R., K. Rosenberg, J. Lowe, S. Barker, and A. Dhondt. 2002a. Effects of forest fragmentation on tanager and thrush species in eastern and western North America. *Studies in Avian Biology* 25: 81–91.

Hames, R., K. Rosenberg, J. Lowe, S. Barker, and A. Dhondt. 2002b. Adverse effects of acid rain on the distribution of the Wood Thrush *Hylocichla mustelina* in North America. *Proceedings of the National Academy of Sciences* 99: 11235–11240.

Hochachka, W., J. Wells, K. Rosenberg, D. Tessaglia-Hymes, and A. Dhondt. 1999. Irruptive migration of common redpolls. *Condor* 101: 195–204.

Hochachka, W. M., A. A. Dhondt, K. J. McGowan, and L. Kramer. 2004. Impact of West Nile Virus on American Crows in the Northeastern United States, and its relevance to existing monitoring programs. *Ecohealth* 1: 60–68.

National Research Council (NRC). 1996. *National science education standards.* National Washington, DC: National Academy Press.

National Science Board (NSB). 2002. *Science and engineering indicators.* Arlington, VA: National Science Foundation (NSB-02-1).

Rosenberg, K., J. Lowe, and A. Dhondt. 1999. Effects of forest fragmentation on breeding tanagers: A continental perspective. *Conservation Biology* 13: 568–583.

Roth, W. M., and S. Lee. 2002. Scientific literacy as collective praxis. *Public Understanding of Science* 11 (1): 33–56.

Sturgis, P., and N. Allum. 2004. Science in society: Re-evaluating the deficit model of public attitudes. *Public Understanding of Science* 13 (1): 55–74.

Thompson, S., and R. Bonney. 2007. Evaluating the impacts of participation in an online citizen science project: A mixed-methods approach. In *Museums and the web 2007: Selected papers from an international conference,* eds. J. Trant and D. Bearman, 187–199. Toronto: Archives and Museum Informatics.

Thompson, S., S. Allison-Bunnell, and R. Bonney. 2006. Citizen science: Documenting the impact of participation on learning, behavior, and attitudes. Paper presented at the annual meeting of the Visitor Studies Association, Grand Rapids, MI.

Trumbull, D. J., R. Bonney, D. Bascom, and A. Cabral. 2000. Thinking scientifically during participation in a citizen-science project. *Science Education* 84: 265–275.

Wells, J., K. Rosenberg, E. Dunn, D. Tessaglia, and A. Dhondt. 1998. Feeder counts as indicators of spatial and temporal variation in winter abundance of resident birds. *Journal of Field Ornithology* 69: 577–586.

Wynne, B. 1995. Public understanding of science. In *Handbook of science and technology studies*, eds. S. Jasanoff, G. E. Markle, J. C. Petersen, and T. Pinch, 361–388. Thousand Oaks, CA: Sage.

Can an Informal Science Institution Really Play the Key Role in K–12 Science Education Reform?

Dennis Schatz
Pacific Science Center
and Washington State LASER

Most people think of science centers and other informal science education institutions as nice additions to the science education offerings in the community. They are great places to take the family on the weekend or for that end-of-the-year field trip for students to celebrate the end of the school year. But most people think "real" science education happens in schools, especially in the opinion of parents, educators, politicians, and community leaders.

With this adjunct opinion of the role informal science institutions play in society, is it possible for such an institution to play the pivotal role in statewide K–12 science education reform? If Pacific Science Center's successful leadership of Washington State LASER (Leadership and Assistance for Science Education Reform; *www.wastatelaser.org*) is any indication, the answer is a resounding yes!

Arches at the Pacific Science Center.

What Is Pacific Science Center?

Pacific Science Center, like many other science centers, is an independent, nonprofit institution dedicated to increasing the public's understanding and appreciation of science, mathematics, and technology through interactive exhibits and programs. From its origins as the U.S. Science Pavilion at the 1962 Seattle World's Fair, Pacific Science Center has become a highly regarded statewide resource for science education. Last year, Pacific Science Center served nearly one million people at its Seattle site and through traveling programs, which served all 39 counties in Washington State.

Onsite Instructional Programs, which include Science Demonstrations such as Super Cold and Combustion, are presented each day for groups of 15–250 visitors. Planetarium Demonstrations in the Willard Smith Planetarium are live, interactive presentations for groups of up to 40 people. Exhibits and IMAX films for school group visitors served more than 72,000 school children, teachers, and adults last year.

Our Camp-Ins address the science avoidance that female and minority students often experience. Summer Camps appeal to various interests and are offered in Seattle and at the Mercer Slough Environmental Education Center. Pacific Science Center received a grant from the Howard Hughes Medical Institute in 1992 to develop and operate educational programs at the Mercer Slough Nature Park, a 320-acre wetlands preserve in Bellevue, Washington. The mission of the Mercer Slough Environmental Education Center, a joint project of Pacific Science Center and Bellevue Parks and Community Services, is to promote an understanding and appreciation of wetland environments through direct observation and "hands-on" ecology activities and aquatic laboratory experiences. The Lake Washington Watershed Internship Program provides internships for high school students who carry out a water quality–monitoring program and educate elementary school students about watershed stewardship.

A hike through the Mercer Slough Nature Park.

Offsite, education outreach programs served more than 225,000 children (about 25% of our total attendance), teachers, and adults last year in Washington, as well as Idaho and Montana. The Science On Wheels program offers a choice of five curricula (astronomy, Earth science, engineering, mathematics, and physics) in vans that travel to elementary schools across the state. Science on the Go! utilizes the exhibits, science demonstrations, and workshops from the Science On Wheels program to serve audiences at nonschool settings such as fairs and malls. Storybook Science brings hands-on science workshops in a story time format to public libraries in western Washington. It is our extensive offerings statewide that have situated us to take a lead role in K–12 science education reform in Washington State.

Science On Wheels.

The Genesis of Washington State LASER

Washington State LASER started in 1999 as one of the eight regional sites for the NSF-funded Dissemination and Implementation project lead by the National Science Resources Center (NSRC; online at *www.nsrconline.org*). This NSRC project was titled Leadership and Assistance for Science Education Reform, thus giving Washington State LASER its name. The key elements of the services and products provided by NSRC during the first few years were:

- **Awareness Events:** One-day meetings for school district teams to better understand the elements they need to implement to establish a standards-based science program in their schools.
- **Instructional Materials Showcases:** One-day meetings for school district instructional materials selection teams to understand the nature of standards-based instructional material, to obtain review criteria for identifying standards-based instructional material, and to experience a selection of exemplary material with expert teachers of the material.
- **Strategic Planning Institutes:** Six-day residential institute, where school district leadership teams develop a five-year strategic plan for implementing a standards-based science program in their schools.

Team studies materials during showcase.

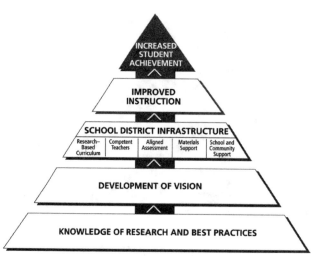

The NSRC developed this theory of action to guide school districts in the process of establishing research-based science education programs that result in improved instruction and increased achievement for all students.

Original material © 2003 National Science Resources Center.
Not for further reproduction or distribution.

The NSRC had offered Strategic Planning Institutes for more than a decade, so had a proven product that had been used by many school districts across the country to reform science education in their schools. The Institute is guided by a Theory of Action that helps school districts in establishing research-based science education programs that improve teaching and learning—thus increasing overall student achievement.

The unique feature of Washington State LASER is that we quickly saw the need to go beyond the development of strategic plans. We knew there needed to be a statewide infrastructure developed to support the selection and purchase of instructional materials, the ongoing science material refurbishment, and the ongoing professional development for teachers and administrators.

Pacific Science Center's statewide reputation and services, plus the institution being seen as neutral territory, was the combination needed to develop a leadership coalition that included

- The State Superintendent of Public Instruction's office in the state capitol;
- Battelle, a science-based business that operates the Pacific Northwest National Laboratories in Eastern Washington; and
- Pacific Science Center, the state's foremost informal science education institution.

The Mission and Vision of Washington State LASER

The four members of the Washington State LASER Leadership Group, working with a 25-person steering committee, developed a strategic plan for the infrastructure and services needed to serve all 296 Washington State school districts. Key elements of Washington State LASER's plan are:

The Vision: Have science education to be a critical part of children's education today, just as science is a critical part of today's world.

This vision drives all Washington State LASER activities and builds from the fundamental tenants in the National Science Education Standards (NSES). Washington State's standards (Essential Academic Learning Requirements, or EALRs) were based on the NSES. These standards call for a new way of teaching that reflects how science itself is done. The standards emphasized inquiry as a way of achieving knowledge and understanding about the world that requires changes in how science is taught. These changes—highlighted in the National Standards—require:

Less Emphasis on:	More Emphasis on:
* Memorizing answers	* Solving problems
* Focusing on facts	* Focusing on concepts
* Lecture and worksheets	* Experimentation and analysis
* Working alone	* Working in groups
* Providing answers to questions	* Communicating scientific explanations
* Recalling information	* Focusing on how to find information
* Teacher directed	* Student Directed

The Mission: Assist school districts with implementing an ongoing, K–12 inquiry-based science program, aligned with the Washington State science standards, including

- exemplary inquiry-centered instructional material;
- regular professional development for staff;
- effective strategies to use science as a vehicle to support reading, writing, communication, and mathematics learning;
- appropriate materials support;
- effective student assessment; and
- wide community and administrative support.

The Ultimate Objective: Have all 296 schools districts in the state implement a standards-based K–12 science program by 2017.

> LASER Regional Alliance meetings allow districts to share information and tackle tough problems such as materials management and teacher training together. LASER will make an important difference for teachers and students across the state as we continue to renew and enhance curriculum to meet state standards.
>
> *—Jean M. Lane*
> *Assistant Superintendent*
> *Richland School District*
> *Richland, WA*

The Services of Washington State LASER

In order to accomplish the missions, there are services that need to be provide on a statewide basis and other services that need to be offered on a regional basis.

Statewide Services

(1) Offer annual Instructional Material Showcases that show:
- What hands-on, inquiry-centered science teaching and learning look like
- What hands-on, inquiry-centered materials are available
- How one evaluates and compares instructional materials to ensure that a particular

program is the one best suited for a school district and its students
- How well these programs align with state and national standards
- How much professional development is required to implement inquiry-centered science

(2) Offer annual Strategic Planning Institutes that:
- Construct models for developing and sustaining a corps of leaders who will spearhead science education reform in their communities
- Assess the best use of state, regional, and national resources for implementing an inquiry-centered K–12 science program
- Develop five-year strategic plans in collaboration with nationally recognized experts and members of other teams to reform K–12 science education in their districts
- Understand how science enhances student skills in reading, writing, and mathematics

(3) Develop electronic networking and information sharing system via the internet to link school district personnel to resources relevant to effective teaching, assessment, and curriculum unit implementation. The main source of electronic connectivity at this time is via the LASER website (*www.wastatelaser.org*).

(4) Maintain and seek new public and private funding sources. The success of LASER would not be possible without the support of the legislature and the strong private-public partnership developed over the last six years, including the resources and investment of the State, Battelle, Boeing, Agilent Technologies, Intel, Washington Mutual, and the North Cascades and Olympic Science Partnership (NCOSP) at Western Washington University (WWU). The broad base of financial support includes:
- $6.2 million from the State
- $1.5 million from The Boeing Company
- $700,000 from Battelle, plus another $1 million in in-kind support from the Pacific Northwest National Laboratory
- $600,000 from Agilent Technologies/Agilent Technologies Foundation
- $360,000 from Intel
- $15 million from NSF for NCOSP at WWU
- Dollar-for-dollar matching from participating school districts and a commitment to maintain the program in the future

The success over the last six years have lead to a major initiative by the Governor that will increase funding for LASER's effort from $2.2 million per biennium to $14.3 million per biennium.

> The LASER workshop has "given" us a solid plan (developed by our team) for science reform in our district. This was accomplished through excellent sessions, guidance, background information, sharing, etc. One great aspect was the time provided for planning—we are leaving not only with mounds of information but also a VERY important piece—OUR strategic plan!
>
> —*Larry Byman, Teacher*
> *Mark Morris High School*
> *Longview School District*

As of the 2006 LASER Strategic Planning Institute, more than 150 school districts (serving approximately 75% of the students in the state) have attended a Strategic Planning Institute and are at some stage of implementing a standards-based science program (See stars on map below for location of Washington State LASER school districts).

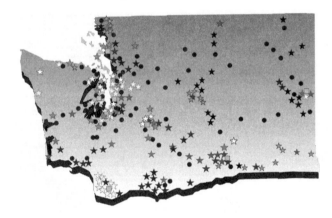

LASER School Districts
☐ **LASER Regional Alliances**
☆ **PreLASER** ● **LASER Outreach** ★ **1999**
★ **2000** ★ **2001** ★ **2002** ☆ **2003** ☆ **2004**
☆ **2005** ★ **2006**

Regional Services

The most important element of the regional services is the nine Washington State LASER Regional Alliances (see square icons on map) that provide the following key services:

(1) Purchase curriculum kits for use by participating school districts.

(2) Refurbish and distribute curriculum kits to participating school districts.

(3) Provide professional development for teachers from Alliance districts so that each teacher receives a minimum of 54 hours of professional development over three years. At the end of three years, teachers will:

- understand what is meant by inquiry-based science;
- have a basic understanding of the science content taught in the curriculum;
- know how to use the curriculum in the classroom, including classroom and materials management;
- understand how the curriculum aligns with the state's Grade Level Expectations (GLEs) associated with the EALRs and how to focus instruction on these Expectations; and
- understand how to connect the science curriculum with reading, writing, communications and mathematics.

(4) Develop a cadre of professional development providers who can offer the basic 54 hours of professional development.

(5) Work with Statewide LASER to develop and offer specialized symposia for school district leaders (e.g. central office administrators, principals, community leaders), so that they understand the importance of science education and know what quality classroom instruction looks like.

> The LASER Institute was a wonderful opportunity to create a district plan for improving science for students. The format, while demanding, enabled comprehensive thinking and planning to actually make something happen. I recommend the process—all six days of it, without reservation.
>
> —*Terry Nelson*
> *Assistant Superintendent*
> *Cheney School District*

Effectiveness of Washington State LASER

A simple comparison of LASER school districts vs. non-LASER school districts is not a reasonable comparison since some districts have just begun the process, while other have been involved for a number of years. In addition, the level of implementation can vary within a school district, depending on the emphasis and leadership provided by the principal and lead teachers in each school. Thus, the analysis of LASER's success has looked at key factors that influence success (e.g. hours of professional development received by teachers, number of instructional units taught, fidelity of teaching the instructional material as indicated in the teachers guide, and amount of class time devoted to science) to determine the impact on student achievement.

> LASER is a program that starts with a vision of science and it helps a team from a district come together and set a strategic vision for what they want to do, have access to research based curriculum that's hands on inquiry science, professional development for the teachers themselves and has very efficient delivery system so that you can do experiments in the classroom and you don't have to worry about plan B because you're going to have the equipment to actually implement your lesson for that day.
>
> —*Dr. Terry Bergerson*
> *Washington State Superintendent*
> *of Public Instruction*

RMC Corporation, the external evaluator of Washington State LASER, has conducted a number of studies of LASER's efforts. In 2004, RMC examined the relationship between the amount of professional development received by teachers in LASER schools and the number of fifth-grade students meeting standard on the state's science test (Washington Assessment of Student Learning, or WASL), which is designed to test how well students learned concepts identified in the GLEs. A strong positive correlation was seen (see graph):

Percent of Students in a School That Met Standard on 2004 Fifth-Grade WASL Compared to the Amount of Professional Development Received by Teachers in the School

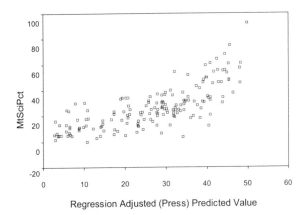

Regression Adjusted (Press) Predicted Value

PD Index for Teachers in Each School
(Note: Since we only had access to the percent of students who met standard in the entire school and because the success on the WASL should be related to the PD taken by teachers in earlier grades, we had to develop a PD index based on the PD taken by all teachers in the school and the WASL score of all fifth-grade students in the school.)

    Also in 2004, RMC Research explored the relationship between the levels of implementation of inquiry-based instructional materials and student success on a student assessment instrument designed for schools standards-based science programs. Forty-two classes across the state were selected for participation based on their level of implementation as measured using the science reform rubrics. Half of the classes were rated as being in high- or medium-implementation schools and the other half were rated as being in low- or nonimplementation schools. In addition, high- and medium-implementation schools were paired with demographically similar low- or nonimplementation schools.

    An analysis of the changes in student scores from the preassessment (fall 2003) to the postassessment (spring 2004) for the schools in each implementation-level group revealed that students in all groups except nonimplementation schools demonstrated significant gains from the preassessment to the postassessment. Furthermore, the high-implementation schools did better than the low-implementation schools at meeting the needs of students who qualified for free or reduced-price lunch. The graph below shows the change in mean scores from the preassessment to the postassessment for the FRL students and all other students. Students who qualified for free and reduced-price lunch demonstrated a greater growth than the other students and the difference was significantly ($p < 0.01$) greater for the students in the high-implementation classes.

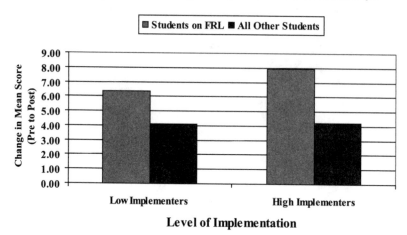

A 2005 case study in the West Valley School District near Yakima showed that fifth-grade students who experienced more LASER-endorsed modules scored better on the Science WASL than students in West Valley who experienced fewer modules (see graph below).

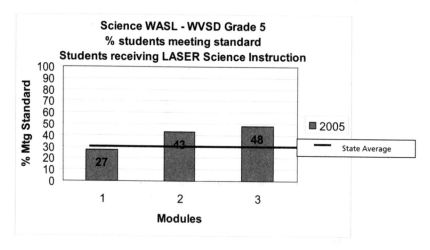

In a statewide study, RMC Corp examined the 2005 fifth-grade science WASL scores of 1,400 students in 54 classes in 36 schools across the state. The results of the study are summarized below:

- The more modules students experienced the better they did on the science WASL.
- Students did better on the science WASL when their teachers used the materials in the way they were intended.
- Students in classes of teachers with no training on inquiry-based science are less likely to perform as well on the science WASL as students in classes of teachers who have received any training.

- Lack of adequate training impedes student performance.
- The number of modules students used is a significant positive predictor of their performance on the WASL subscales for:
  • Properties of systems;
  • Changes in systems; and
  • Inquiry in science.
- The number of modules, fidelity of implementation, and whether the teacher has received training are all significant predictors of student performance on the open-ended items on the grade 5 science WASL.
- The more professional development the teacher has had on inquiry-based science the better his or her students did on the grade 5 science WASL.
- When aggregating to the class level, racial and ethnic differences were not a significant factor in the analysis model, thus supporting the notion that inquiry-based science
  • is effective with diverse populations; and
  • enables schools that serve high proportion of minorities and economically disadvantaged students to catch up.

In late 2006, the Seattle Times featured the success of Lake Washington and Issaquah school districts on the 2006 Science WASL (*http://seattletimes.nwsource.com/html/localnews/2003266789_science20e.html*). Both districts participated in a Washington State LASER Strategic Planning Institute, have adopted standards-based instructional material, and provided extensive professional development for their teachers. Both districts are active in one of the LASER Regional Alliances. The dramatic results of both school districts show what can be done when school districts:

- have a strategic plan,
- use effective science materials,
- have well-trained teachers that use the material with fidelity, and
- have sufficient time allocated in the school calendar to cover the material.

Although Washington State LASER is showing positive results, we still do not find enough students are reaching proficiency on the WASL. In late 2006 RMC undertook a study to determine what schools were doing that were highly successful on the fifth-grade science WASL. The study identified 40 top-performing elementary schools across the state on the science WASL. Since we are looking for schools that can demonstrate continuous improvement, the schools included in the study had to show a 17.5% increase over the last two years (2004–2006), with at least a 6% increase in each of those years. The results identified these key characteristics for the 40 schools:

- 100% are using inquiry-based curricula.
- 95% engaged students in some form of preparation for the Science WASL.
- 82% attributed success to having effective professional development for teachers.
- 78% are in LASER school districts, which means the district sent a leadership team to a LASER Strategic Planning Institute.
- 77% attributed success to one or two key advocates in the school or district.

- 51% attributed success to an increased emphasis on the alignment of the curriculum to the Science GLEs.
- 38% attributed success to increased science instructional time.

The Future for Washington State LASER

Our funding and efforts to date have focused on getting districts to develop a five-year strategic plan and then to implement standards-based curricula, including professional development for teachers. The new funding proposed by the Governor will not only increase the number of classrooms served by LASER, but will allow us to add additional services and emphasis in those other areas seen as essential to producing a successful science program. Especially important will be to develop teacher and principal leadership that can be the advocates in the school that will focus their efforts on science, including additional instructional time during the school day.

Most of the work done by Washington State LASER has been at the elementary level, with middle school added in the last few years. We will continue to serve more school districts at this level. We also operated a pilot program during the last three years at the high school level, with significant underwriting from the Agilent Technologies Foundation. We partnered with BSCS to hold a series of National Academy for Curriculum Leadership (NACL) workshops that served 16 Washington State school districts and two school districts from outside the state (See *www. bscs.org/page.asp?pageid=0|124|381|386&id=0|academy_overview* for more information about the NACL). A generous donation from Battelle will now allow us to offer the NACL to a second cadre of Washington State school districts.

Final Comments

Could another organization or institution have taken the lead to organize statewide science education reform in Washington State? Possibly. But none have the statewide emphasis and are seen as "neutral territory." The State Superintendents office is viewed as too closely connected to regulations and accountability. The universities tend to focus on their own areas of the state and many university faculty members express a need to "fix" K–12 education without a deeper understanding of the K–12 system. The Washington Science Teachers Association has a statewide focus, but it is led by a committed group of volunteers that doesn't allow for the time needed to lead such an effort.

Pacific Science Center not only has the statewide reach and is seen as neutral territory, but it has an administration that provides the time–and therefore the discretionary funds–for staff to pursue this effort. As a nonprofit organization we are well equipped to

- seek the private funding that is needed to leverage the state funding;
- build the coalition of people, organizations, institutions and businesses across the state required to be successful; and
- spend the time required to inform legislators and other community leaders about the importance of this effort.

We believe that in large measure the phenomenal success of the Washington state LASER Program can be directly attributed to the contributions of the Pacific Science Center. In this case, an informal science education organization was not only a contributor to formal education reform, it has played the pivotal role.

Advancing the NSES Vision through Informal Education

John H. Falk, Editor
Oregon State University
Institute for Learning Innovation

W hen they were created in 1996, the National Science Education Standards (NSES) were envisioned as applying exclusively to the formal school context. In fact, it is probably safe to assume that for many of the creators of the NSES, this single-minded attention on schooling was not based primarily on an effort to focus their task, but rather on the then prevalent notion that there was little benefit to considering the nonschool setting since most, if not all, science learning was assumed to occur in schools. We now know that this is not the case (Falk, Storksdieck, and Dierking 2007). A growing number of studies (Falk, 2001; Falk, Storksdieck, and Dierking 2007; Miller 1998; 2001; 2002; NSB 2000; 2002; 2004; Weiss et al. 2005) have shown that schooling is necessary but not sufficient to support lifelong science literacy. For example, 75% of Nobel Prize winners in the sciences report that their passion for science was first sparked in nonschool environments (Friedman and Quinn 2006). We also now appreciate that the public acquires science information continuously across their day and throughout their lives—even school-aged children utilize a wide range of nonschool sources for constructing their science understanding (Anderson et al. 2000; Bransford et al. Forthcoming). The fact that NSTA, still primarily a school-focused organization, has appreciated the important role that free-choice learning plays in science education is a sign of the growing awareness that public science education occurs not only in schools, but also museums, science centers, zoos, aquariums, on television and radio, on the internet, and in a wide range of other community settings and situations. The focus on informal settings in this volume of NSTA's *Exemplary Science* series represents an important milestone in the science education community's progress toward a more holistic view of lifelong science learning.

An important and exciting aspect of this book is that it provides a glimpse into the range and scope of science education efforts that are occurring around the country. Represented in this book are exemplars of efforts to support science education for school-aged learners from kindergarten through high school, but also efforts focused on preschool-aged children, and adults of all ages; often learners are in multigenerational groups. Learning opportunities are not limited to the nine-month school year and six-hour school day; learning occurs on weekdays and weekends, mornings, afternoons, and in the evening. Science learning is life-wide and lifelong, and the chapters in this book provide ample evidence of the important role played by the informal science education sector in supporting that learning.

Despite originally being almost exclusively focused on the school context, the NSES emerged as an amazingly relevant document for the informal context as well. All four of the Standards—Teaching Standards, Content and Inquiry Standards, Professional Development Standards and Assessment Standards—can, should, and as the chapters in this volume clearly attest, have been adapted for use in and by informal education institutions. As you read the chapters, you saw explicit discussion of how particular institutions, through specific programs, have attempted to implement a wide range of these standards. The importance of debate and discussion, collaborative and shared responsibility for learning and data-based inquiries, and an emphasis on process over content permeate the chapters. The encouragement of inquiry rather than mere information acquisition forms a leitmotif throughout these chapters and demonstrates the embodiment of the ideal that science education should be first and foremost about asking questions and striving to make meaning about natural phenomenon.

In fact, the first item in the Teaching Standards—*More Emphasis* on understanding and responding to individual learner's interests, strengths, experiences and needs—is one of the hallmarks of informal science education efforts, certainly most within this book. Informal settings have by and large always respected the importance of free-choice learning—learning that involves significant choice and control over the what, where, when, and with whom of learning; the result has been educational experiences that allow more personalization of experience. Free-choice learning is not a quality that is exclusive to the nonschool environment; good classroom teachers have long understood the importance of providing students choice and control over their learning. However, in this era of content-focused high-stakes testing, free-choice learning is in danger of disappearing entirely from America's classrooms, leaving informal settings as an important refuge for this key tenet of quality science education. Worthy of note, then, is the commitment to free-choice learning that emerges, sometimes explicitly and other times implicitly, as an important aspect of virtually all of the chapters in this book.

The authors of nearly all of the chapters make a strong case for how they have embodied the Content and Inquiry Standards. Examples abound of evidence-based investigations, learners engaged in debate and explanation, groups of learners actively involved in experimenting, collecting and analyzing data, and then synthesizing information for the purposes of communication to others.

The strength of most informal education programs then is their emphasis on free-choice learning, active engagement of learners in the scientific process, and promotion of inquiry; however, their weaknesses are often a lack of follow-through and commitment to long-term, extended investigations. Although there are a few notable exceptions amongst the exemplars included here, a clear deficiency within the informal setting are programs that allow learners to build continuously upon their learning over time. By this I mean not just within the confines of a specific institution, but across settings. Although there are programs that have attempted to build strong relationships and collaborations so that learners can have experiences in multiple settings, for example between the science center and school, most programs still do not fully embrace the ideals of lifelong learning to the point of actively building connections between what is learned as part of the program and what happens in the rest of the learner's life; arguably the citizen science programs of Cornell and the Florida Natural History Museum, the career ladder programs of the New York Hall of Science, and the program at Henry Doorly Zoo come closest to this reality. Too often, like so much of traditional schooling, informal education programs are content to situate science in the artificial confines of a lesson or experience rather than in the reality of the world; in particular the world of the learner.

Although most of the 17 chapters in this volume focus on teaching content and inquiry, professional development also emerges as an important theme in more than half. Collaboration tends to be at the core of the informal education ethos and thus it is not surprising that collaboration forms an important part of all professional development activities described in this book. Most informal science education institutions are amazingly unbureaucratic and supportive work environments. Accordingly, when placed in the role of professional developers, informal science educators tend to emphasize sharing and collegial learning; they are used to taking considerable responsibility for their own learning and development, and that ethos emerges in their efforts to facilitate the learning of other professionals. Although there are clearly some exemplary examples of professional development demonstrated in these pages, this is an area that could benefit by greater adherence to the NSES, in particular the greater emphasis on the teacher as an active part of the process rather than just the recipient of training.

Similarly, all of the chapters in this volume provide evidence of assessment, which as pointed out by my coeditor Robert Yager in the book's introduction, was a major criterion for being included in this book. However, far too many of the projects included here remain mired in traditional, relatively simple assessments that miss the higher targets defined by the NSES Assessment Standards. Too many of the authors reporting on their assessments were content to rely on either self-report data from participants or simple measures of student knowledge gains. On the positive side, an important characteristic of virtually all of the chapters in this volume was an equal emphasis on assessing attitudinal as well content knowledge. Although this is not surprising given the importance placed on awareness and attitude in the informal sector, it is a refreshing movement away from the overemphasis on content knowledge found in the formal sector. If the goal of science education is to promote and support lifelong science learning, then engendering a love of inquiry and science should be just as important an educational outcome as changes in information recalled. However, if we are going to achieve these outcomes, whether in the formal or informal sector, increased efforts at developing truly valid and reliable measures of attitude and interest need to be developed. And, it is hoped, that an increased emphasis on attitude change should be included as a co-equal assessment goal to content change in the next iteration of the standards.

Conclusion

The NSES provide a useful framework for re-envisioning science education in the 21st century, both in and out of school. These 17 chapters clearly demonstrate how the NSES can be explicitly used to inform and improve informal science education practice, and in the process enhance the lifelong science learning of millions of individuals both inside and outside of the classroom.

Hopefully, these chapters will serve to inspire a wide range of science educators across the myriad of informal contexts and provide concrete examples of how their own science educational practices could be improved. Specifically, we hope that some of the ideas shared will resonate with educators and encourage them to try new approaches, work with new audiences, and generally think outside of their traditional boxes of what is and should be possible. Certainly, we hope that these chapters will help raise awareness in the informal sector of the usefulness and value of the NSES and encourage informal educators to utilize the Standards as a guiding framework. Even those who currently do use the NSES at some level will hopefully appreciate that a fuller adherence to both the spirit and letter of the Standards will yield significant benefits.

In addition to serving the informal education community, though, we hope that the examples provided here will provide inspiration to those working within the formal education sector; there are many ideas presented that should challenge classroom educators to re-imagine their practice and encourage new approaches. We also hope, in some small way, that this book will continue to raise the profile of the informal education sector amongst science educators and policy makers currently focused solely on the formal sector, helping them appreciate the critically important role that free-choice learning plays in supporting a nation of lifelong science learners. We will not make real progress in furthering our shared goals of building a scientifically literate society until we fully embrace the reality that all parts of the educational infrastructure, formal and informal, are *equally* essential to the enterprise; neither is more nor less important. Only when we all work together toward a common set of share outcomes will we really make progress. The NSES, and hopefully the next iteration that equally embraces the realities of the nonschool world, provide the best current version of what that shared set of outcomes should look like.

References

Anderson, D., K. B. Lucas, I. S. Ginns, and L. D. Dierking. 2000. Development of knowledge about electricity and magnetism during a visit to a science museum and related post-visit activities. *Science Education* 84: 658–679.

Bransford, J., N. Vye, R. Stevens, P. Kuhl, D. Schwartz, P. Bell, A. Meltzoff, B. Barron, R. Pea, B. Reeves, J. Roschelle, and N. Sabelli. Forthcoming. Learning theories and education: Toward a decade of synergy. In *Handbook of Educational Psychology*. 2nd ed., eds. P. Alexander and P. Winne. Mahwah, NJ: Erlbaum.

Falk, J. H., ed. 2001. *Free-choice science education: How we learn science outside of school*. New York: Teachers College Press.

Falk, J. H., M. Storksdieck, and L. D. Dierking. 2007. Investigating public science interest and understanding: Evidence for the importance of free-choice learning. *Public Understanding of Science*.

Friedman, L. N., and J. Quinn. 2006. How after-school programs can nurture young scientists and boost the country's scientific literacy. *Education Week* (February 22).

Miller, J. D. 1998. The measurement of civic scientific literacy. *Public Understanding of Science* 7: 1–21.

Miller, J. D. 2001. The acquisition and retention of scientific information by American adults. In *Free-choice science education: How we learn science outside of school*, ed. J. H. Falk. 93–114. New York: Teachers College Press.

Miller, J. D. 2002. Civic scientific literacy: A necessity for the 21st century. *Public Interest Report: Journal of the Federation of American Scientists* 55 (1): 3–6.

National Science Board (NSB). 2000. *Science and engineering indicators: 2000*. Washington, DC: US Government Printing Office.

National Science Board (NSB). 2002. *Science and engineering indicators: 2002*. Washington, DC: US Government Printing Office.

National Science Board (NSB). 2004. *Science and engineering indicators: 2004*. Washington, DC: US Government Printing Office.

Weiss, H. B., J. Coffman, M. Post, S. Bouffard, and P. Little. 2005. Beyond the classroom: Complementary learning to improve achievement outcome. *The Evaluation Exchange* 11 (Spring): 1.

Appendixes

Less Emphasis/More Emphasis Conditions of the National Science Education Standards

The *National Science Education Standards* envision change throughout the system. The **teaching standards** encompass the following changes in emphases:

LESS EMPHASIS ON	MORE EMPHASIS ON
Treating all students alike and responding to the group as a whole	Understanding and responding to individual student's interests, strengths, experiences, and needs
Rigidly following curriculum	Selecting and adapting curriculum
Focusing on student acquisition of information	Focusing on student understanding and use of scientific knowledge, ideas, and inquiry processes
Presenting scientific knowledge through lecture, text, and demonstration	Guiding students in active and extended scientific inquiry
Asking for recitation of acquired knowledge	Providing opportunities for scientific discussion and debate among students
Testing students for factual information at the end of the unit or chapter	Continuously assessing student understanding
Maintaining responsibility and authority	Sharing responsibility for learning with students
Supporting competition	Supporting a classroom community with cooperation, shared responsibility, and respect
Working alone	Working with other teachers to enhance the science program

Source: National Research Council (NRC). 1996. *National science education standards.* Washington, DC: National Academy Press, p. 52. Reprinted with permission.

The *National Science Education Standards* envision change throughout the system. The **professional development standards** encompass the following changes in emphases:

LESS EMPHASIS ON	MORE EMPHASIS ON
Transmission of teaching knowledge and skills by lectures	Inquiry into teaching and learning
Learning science by lecture and reading	Learning science through investigation and inquiry
Separation of science and teaching knowledge	Integration of science and teaching knowledge
Separation of theory and practice	Integration of theory and practice in school settings
Individual learning	Collegial and collaborative learning
Fragmented, one-shot sessions	Long-term coherent plans
Courses and workshops	A variety of professional development activities
Reliance on external expertise	Mix of internal and external expertise
Staff developers as educators	Staff developers as facilitators, consultants, and planners
Teacher as technician	Teacher as intellectual, reflective practitioner
Teacher as consumer of knowledge about teaching	Teacher as producer of knowledge about teaching
Teacher as follower	Teacher as leader
Teacher as an individual based in a classroom	Teacher as a member of a collegial professional community
Teacher as target of change	Teacher as source and facilitator of change

The *National Science Education Standards* envision change throughout the system. The **assessment standards** encompass the following changes in emphases:

LESS EMPHASIS ON	MORE EMPHASIS ON
Assessing what is easily measured	Assessing what is most highly valued
Assessing discrete knowledge	Assessing rich, well-structured knowledge
Assessing scientific knowledge	Assessing scientific understanding and reasoning
Assessing to learn what students do not know	Assessing to learn what students do understand
Assessing only achievement	Assessing achievement and opportunity to learn
End of term assessments by teachers	Students engaged in ongoing assessment of their work and that of others
Development of external assessments by measurement experts alone	Teachers involved in the development of external assessments

The *National Science Education Standards* envision change throughout the system. The science **content and inquiry standards** encompass the following changes in emphases:

LESS EMPHASIS ON	MORE EMPHASIS ON
Knowing scientific facts and information	Understanding scientific concepts and developing abilities of inquiry
Studying subject matter disciplines (physical, life, earth sciences) for their own sake	Learning subject matter disciplines in the context of inquiry, technology, science in personal and social perspectives, and history and nature of science
Separating science knowledge and science process	Integrating all aspects of science content
Covering many science topics	Studying a few fundamental science concepts
Implementing inquiry as a set of processes	Implementing inquiry as instructional strategies, abilities, and ideas to be learned

CHANGING EMPHASES TO PROMOTE INQUIRY

LESS EMPHASIS ON	MORE EMPHASIS ON
Activities that demonstrate and verify science content	Activities that investigate and analyze science questions
Investigations confined to one class period	Investigations over extended periods of time
Process skills out of context	Process skills in context
Individual process skills such as observation or inference	Using multiple process skills—manipulation, cognitive, procedural
Getting an answer	Using evidence and strategies for developing or revising an explanation
Science as exploration and experiment	Science as argument and explanation
Providing answers to questions about science content	Communicating science explanations
Individuals and groups of students analyzing and synthesizing data without defending a conclusion	Groups of students often analyzing and synthesizing data after defending conclusions
Doing few investigations in order to leave time to cover large amounts of content	Doing more investigations in order to develop understanding, ability, values of inquiry and knowledge of science content
Concluding inquiries with the result of the experiment	Applying the results of experiments to scientific arguments and explanations

Management of materials and equipment

Management of ideas and information

Private communication of student ideas and conclusions to teacher

Public communication of student ideas and work to classmates

The *National Science Education Standards* envision change throughout the system. The **program standards** encompass the following changes in emphases:

LESS EMPHASIS ON	MORE EMPHASIS ON
Developing science programs at different grade levels independently of one another	Coordinating the development of the K–12 science program across grade levels
Using assessments unrelated to curriculum and teaching	Aligning curriculum, teaching, and assessment
Maintaining current resource allocations for books	Allocating resources necessary for hands-on inquiry teaching aligned with the *Standards*
Textbook- and lecture-driven curriculum	Curriculum that supports the *Standards*, and includes a variety of components, such as laboratories emphasizing inquiry and field trips
Broad coverage of unconnected factual information	Curriculum that includes natural phenomena and science-related social issues that students encounter in everyday life
Treating science as a subject isolated from other school subjects	Connecting science to other school subjects, such as mathematics and social studies
Science learning opportunities that favor one group of students	Providing challenging opportunities for all students to learn science
Limiting hiring decisions to the administration	Involving successful teachers of science in the hiring process
Maintaining the isolation of teachers	Treating teachers as professionals whose work requires opportunities for continual learning and networking
Supporting competition	Promoting collegiality among teachers as a team to improve the school
Teachers as followers	Teachers as decision makers

The emphasis charts for **system standards** are organized around shifting the emphases at three levels of organization within the education system—district, state, and federal. The three levels of the system selected for these charts are only representative of the many components of the science education system that need to change to promote the vision of science education described in the *National Science Education Standards*.

FEDERAL SYSTEM

LESS EMPHASIS ON	MORE EMPHASIS ON
Financial support for developing new curriculum materials not aligned with the *Standards*	Financial support for developing new curriculum materials aligned with the *Standards*
Support by federal agencies for professional development activities that affect only a few teachers	Support for professional development activities that are aligned with the *Standards* and promote systemwide changes
Agencies working independently on various components of science education	Coordination among agencies responsible for science education
Support for activities and programs that are unrelated to *Standards*-based reform	Support for activities and programs that successfully implement the *Standards* at state and district levels
Federal efforts that are independent of state and local levels	Coordination of reform efforts at federal, state, and local levels
Short-term projects	Long-term commitment of resources to improving science education

STATE SYSTEM

LESS EMPHASIS ON	MORE EMPHASIS ON
Independent initiatives to reform components of science education	Partnerships and coordination of reform efforts
Funds for workshops and programs having little connection to the *Standards*	Funds to improve curriculum and instruction based on the *Standards*
Frameworks, textbooks, and materials based on activities only marginally related to the *Standards*	Frameworks, textbooks, and materials adoption criteria aligned with national and state standards
Assessments aligned with the traditional content of science	Assessments aligned with the *Standards* and the expanded education view of science content

Current approaches to teacher education	University/college reform of teacher education to include science-specific pedagogy aligned with the *Standards*
Teacher certification based on formal, historically based requirements	Teacher certification that is based on understanding and abilities in science and science teaching

DISTRICT SYSTEM

LESS EMPHASIS ON	MORE EMPHASIS ON
Technical, short-term, inservice workshops	Ongoing professional development to support teachers
Policies unrelated to *Standards*-based reform	Policies designed to support changes called for in the *Standards*
Purchase of textbooks based on traditional topics	Purchase or adoption of curriculum aligned with the *Standards* and on a conceptual approach to science teaching, including support for hands-on science materials
Standardized tests and assessments unrelated to *Standards*-based program and practices	Assessments aligned with the *Standards*
Administration determining what will be involved in improving science education	Teacher leadership in improvement of science education
Authority at upper levels of educational system	Authority for decisions at level of implementation
School board ignorance of science education program	School board support of improvements aligned with the *Standards*
Local union contracts that ignore changes in curriculum, instruction, and assessment	Local union contracts that support improvements indicated by the *Standards*

Contributors List

Harold Asturias is co-author of "FAMILY MATH and Science Education: A Natural Attraction." He is the director of the Center for Mathematics Excellence and Equity at the Lawrence Hall of Science at Berkeley, California.

Rick Bonney is author of "Citizen Science at the Cornell Lab of Ornithology." He is director of program development and evaluation at the Cornell Lab of Ornithology in Ithaca, New York.

Jessica Camp is co-author of "Forecast—Cloudy With a Chance of Educational Reform: A New Weather & Water Partnership Offers Some Relief From the Drought." She is a project coordinator in the Center for Cooperation in Research and Education (CORE) at the Ocean Institute located in Dana Point, California.

Elaine Ceule is co-author of "Science With Attitude: An Informal Science Education Experience." She is the administrative assistant for attractions and science education at Union Station Kansas City at Kansas City, Missouri.

Grace Davila Coates is co-author of "FAMILY MATH and Science Education: A Natural Attraction." She is director of FAMILY MATH at the Lawrence Hall of Science in Berkeley, California.

Rick Crosslin is co-author of "Curious Scientific Investigators Solve Museum Mysteries." He is the science liaison at The Children's Museum of Indianapolis and an elementary teacher at Metropolitan School District of Wayne Township, Indianapolis, Indiana.

Jean Deeds is co-author of "Curious Scientific Investigators Solve Museum Mysteries." She is the school services assistant at The Children's Museum of Indianapolis, Indianapolis, Indiana.

Betty A. Dunckel is author of "Inquiry Is Taking Flight Through Project Butterfly WINGS." She is the center director and associate scientist for the Center for Informal Science Education at the Florida Museum of Natural History in Gainesville, Florida and PI/PD for the NSF-funded Project Butterfly WINGS.

Bonnie T. Ervin is co-author of "Splash, Flash, Crank, Slide, Alive! Interactive Standards-based Science Experiences for Grades PreK–2 at Discovery Center." She is the curriculum coordinator at the Discovery Center at Murfree Spring in Tennessee.

Preeti Gupta is author of "Science Career Ladder at the NY Hall of Science: Youth Facilitators as Agents of Inquiry." She is vice-president for education, New York Hall of Science, Queens, New York. She oversees all aspects of the Science Career Ladder program and won the Roy L. Schafer Leading Edge Award for Experienced Leadership in the Field in 2005 from the Association of Science Technology Centers for the Science Career Ladder.

Harry Helling is co-author of "Forecast—Cloudy With a Chance of Educational Reform A New Weather & Water Partnership Offers Some Relief From the Drought." He is the executive vice president of education and program development and director of the Center for Cooperation in Research and Education (CORE) at the Ocean Institute in Dana Point, California.

Dean Jernigan is co-author of "Science With Attitude: An Informal Science Education Experience." He is director of Science City Summer at Union Station Kansas City in Kansas City, Missouri.

Nikole K. Kadel is co-author of "Inquiry is Taking Flight Through Project Butterfly WINGS." She is Project Butterfly WINGS coordinator, Center for Informal Science Education, Florida Museum of Natural History, University of Florida, Gainesville, Florida.

Jacqueline Kasschau is co-author of "Forecast—Cloudy With a Chance of Educational Reform A New Weather & Water Partnership Offers Some Relief From the Drought." She is a project coordinator in the Center for Cooperation in Research and Education (CORE) at the Ocean Institute located in Dana Point, California.

Melissa Laughlin is co-author of "Forecast—Cloudy With a Chance of Educational Reform: A New Weather & Water Partnership Offers Some Relief From the Drought." She was a project coordinator in the Center for Cooperation in Research and Education (CORE) at the Ocean Institute located in Dana Point, California.

Nancy Linde is author of "A Burger, a Beer… and a Side of Science." She is a freelance writer and documentary filmmaker at WBGH Educational Foundation in Cambridge, Massachusetts.

Jennifer Long is co-author of "Forecast—Cloudy With a Chance of Educational Reform: A New Weather & Water Partnership Offers Some Relief From the Drought." She is a program director in the Center for Cooperation in Research and Education (CORE) at the Ocean Institute located in Dana Point, California.

Susan Magdziarz is co-author of "Forecast—Cloudy With a Chance of Education Reform: A New Weather & Water Partnership Offers Some Relief From the Drought." She is a project coordinator in the Center for Cooperation in Research and Education (CORE) at the Ocean Institute located in Dana Point, California.

Kathy C. Malone is co-author of "Inquiry is Taking Flight Through Project Butterfly WINGS." She is Project Butterfly WINGS coordinator, Center for Informal Science Education, Florida Museum of Natural History, University of Florida, Gainesville, Florida.

Elizabeth K. Metz is co-author of "A Sea of Possibilities: Inspiring Scientific Thinking in Teachers and Students Through the Charismatic Research Organisms at Mote Marine Laboratory." Her area of expertise is informal science education through interactive videoconferencing. She is director of the Center for Distance Learning at Mote Marine Laboratory and Aquarium in Sarasota, Florida.

Dana McMillan is co-author of "Science with Attitude: An Informal Science Education Experience." She is the child development specialist at Union Station Kansas City in Kansas City, Missouri.

Elizabeth Mulkerrin is co-author of "Omaha's Henry Doorly Zoo Academy: Where Science Education Comes to Life!" She is the education curator at the Omaha's Henry Doorly Zoo in Omaha, Nebraska.

Mary C. Nash is author of "'MITS' You Each Summer." She is program director of MITS, Inc., the Museum Institute for Teaching Science in Boston, MA.

David H. Niebuhr is co-author of "A Sea of Possibilities: Inspiring Scientific Thinking in Teachers and Students Through the Charismatic Research Organisms at Mote Marine Laboratory." His areas of expertise include informal and formal education, preservice teacher training, program development and analysis. He is the vice president of the education division at Mote Marine Laboratory and Aquarium in Sarasota, Florida.

Carol A. Parssinen is author of "Youth Leadership at The Franklin Institute: What Happened When the Grant Ran Out." She is the senior vice president, Center for Innovation in Science Learning, which conducts science learning research, program development, and educational services for The Franklin Institute in Philadelphia, Pennsylvania.

Katherine Patterson-Paronto is co-author of "Science With Attitude: An Informal Science Education Experience." She is the program manager at Union Station Kansas City in Kansas City, Missouri.

Stephen M. Pompea is co-author of "Knowledge and Wonder: Engagements With Light and Color in the Hands-On Optics Project." He is the manager of science education scientist at the National Optical Astronomy Observatory in Tucson, Arizona.

Kim Cleary Sadler is co-author of "Splash, Flash, Crank, Slide, Alive! Interactive Standards-Based Science Experiences for Grades PreK–2 at Discovery Center." She is an assistant professor of biology at Middle Tennessee State University, Murfreesboro, Tennessee and co-director for the Center for Cedar Glade Studies.

Dennis Schatz is author of "Can An Informal Science Institution Really Play the Key Role in K–12 Science Education Reform?" He is the vice president for education at the Pacific Science Center and co-director of Washington State LASER (Leadership and Assistance for Science Education Reform) in Seattle, Washington.

Michele Schilten is co-author of "Curious Scientific Investigators Solve Museum Mysteries." She is the educational programs manager at The Children's Museum of Indianapolis, Indianapolis, Indiana.

Eric Siegel is co-author of "Science Career Ladder at the NY Hall of Science: Youth Facilitators as Agents of Inquiry." He is Executive Vice President for Programs and Planning, New York Hall of Science. He oversees all programs, exhibitions, and planning for the NY Hall of Science, Queens, New York.

Jen Snively is co-author of "The Body of Evidence: COSI's *In Depth: Autopsy* Videoconference Program." She is senior director for community and outreach programs at COSI Columbus in Columbus, Ohio.

Robert T. Sparks is co-author of "Knowledge and Wonder: Engagements With Light and Color in the Hands-On Optics Project." He is a science education specialist at NOAO in Tucson, Arizona, as well as having taught high school physics in Wisconsin, Florida, and the Virgin Islands.

Emily V. Wade is co-author of "'MITS' You Each Summer." She is president of MITS, Inc., the Museum Institute for Teaching Science in Boston, MA.

Esther D. Wahlberg is author of "Grands Are Grand: A Cross-Generational Learning Experience at the North Museum of Natural History & Science." Her focus at the museum is the development of informal science programming related to early childhood. She is a Pennsylvania certified elementary school teacher, currently the education assistant at the North Museum of Natural History & Science in Lancaster, Pennsylvania.

Constance E. Walker is co-author of "Knowledge and Wonder: Engagements With Light and Color in the Hands-On Optics Project." She was trained as an astronomer; by trade she is also a senior science education specialist at the National Optical Astronomy Observatory in Tucson, Arizona.

James M. Wharton is co-author of "A Sea of Possibilities: Inspiring Scientific Thinking in Teachers and Students Through the Charismatic Research Organisms at Mote Marine Laboratory." His areas of expertise include informal science education program development.

He is director of the Center for School and Public Programs at Mote Marine Laboratory & Aquarium in Sarasota, Florida.

Gail Wheatley is co-author of "The Body of Evidence: COSI's *In Depth: Autopsy* Videoconference Program." She has 22 years experience in informal science education in a variety of museums and nature centers. She is Director of Electronic Education (videoconference programs) at COSI Columbus in Columbus, Ohio.

Elizabeth Wood is co-author of "Curious Scientific Investigators Solve Museum Mysteries." She is an assistant professor of teacher education and museum studies at Indiana University-Purdue University Indianapolis and the public scholar of museums, families and learning at The Children's Museum of Indianapolis, Indianapolis, Indiana.

Index

Page numbers in **boldface** type refer to figures. A following "t" indicates a table.